MODERN BUSINESS FINANCING

MODERN BUSINESS FINANCING
A Guide to Innovative Strategies and Techniques

Robert Douglas Colman

Prentice-Hall, Inc.   Englewood Cliffs, NJ

Prentice-Hall International, Inc., *London*
Prentice-Hall of Australia, Pty. Ltd., *Sydney*
Prentice-Hall Canada, Inc., *Toronto*
Prentice-Hall of India Private Ltd., *New Delhi*
Prentice-Hall of Japan, Inc., *Tokyo*
Prentice-Hall of Southeast Asia Pte. Ltd., *Singapore*
Whitehall Books, Ltd., Wellington, *New Zealand*
Editora Prentice-Hall do Brasil Ltda., *Rio de Janeiro*
Prentice-Hall Hispanoamericana, S.A., *Mexico*

© 1986 *by*

Prentice-Hall, Inc.

Englewood Cliffs, NJ

Library of Congress Cataloging-in-Publication Data

Colman, Robert Douglas.
  Modern business financing.

  Includes index.
  1. Business enterprises—Finance—Handbooks, manuals,
etc. 2. Corporations—Finance—Handbooks, manuals, etc.
I. Title.
HG4027.3.C64 1986   658.1'5   85-20490

ISBN 0-13-589060-8

Printed in the United States of America

This book is dedicated to
Jane, Eric, and Brad

What This Guide Will Do for You

MODERN BUSINESS FINANCING: A Guide to Innovative Strategies and Techniques is designed to help you in your search for the cheapest source and optimal form of capital. This comprehensive *Guide*, through an examination of innovative financing techniques and methods that have been developed in recent years, presents a framework for evaluating varied sources of capital and effectively accessing some of the less common ones.

In addition to providing a structure for evaluating a wide range of financing techniques, here are some of the practical ways *MODERN BUSINESS FINANCING: A Guide to Innovative Strategies and Techniques* can help you:

- *It shows you how to measure the profitability of your financing decision.* This *Guide* provides a framework for risk-benefit analysis and shows you how to weigh the immediate cost of financing against your company's long-term objectives regarding capital structure and financial reporting.

- *It helps you in the thinking, preparation, and negotiation process involved in raising capital.* Throughout this *Guide*, detailed examples lead you step-by-step through the financing process. In-depth analysis is given from multiple points of view: the company, the shareholders, the management, the lenders, and the auditors.

- *It offers a detailed analysis of tax consequences of various financing techniques*, and shows how the minimization of taxes is a key determinant of financial structuring. Joint ventures, limited partnerships, and trusts are all tax driven. A special chapter is devoted to tax-inspired financings.

- *It analyzes the various techniques by which financings can enhance the company's financial reporting posture.* The accounting aspects of numerous financings are considered, along with the building blocks of off-balance sheet financing.

- *It compares sources of capital.* Whether your company is large or small, public or private, this *Guide* provides the tools for evaluating these sources. It suggests methods by which risks of raising capital can be minimized or shifted to third parties.

- *It contrasts debt and equity financing* and examines various instruments that have features of both debt and equity—such as convertible debt, preferred stock, and warrants.

- *It helps develop hedges against inflation* or erratic interest rates by examining ways companies have accomplished this objective in recent years.

- *It systematically develops the building blocks of finance* so that fund raising can be undertaken deliberately and methodically.

Highlighted in this *Guide* is the notion that finance is an ever-changing and dynamic process. Finance is evolutionary in the sense that novel financing techniques are created in response to compelling business pressures, and these techniques gradually become more intricate and sophisticated over time.

This *Guide* is presented in a manner that shows you how to anticipate future refinements of existing financing methods. For example, you can trace the financing process step-by-step in the layers of complexity added to the basic concept of stock ownership plans in Chapters 5 and 6. Although the tax-exempt status of stock bonus plans existed as early as 1921, the appropriate economic environment for their use as financing vehicles did not occur for nearly 50 years. Stock ownership plans with broadly-based employee ownership (ESOPs) were first used in the 1950s, while the idea of using these plans as funding and leveraging mechanisms did not take hold until the 1970s.

Not only are financing techniques evolutionary, but they are also cyclical. Financing trends come and go and come again. It is a mistake to discard a financing technique from one's repertoire because of a sudden change in the capital markets. In finance you can learn from the past, because there's a good chance that, given enough time, financial conditions will repeat themselves. Techniques that are long forgotten or out of vogue since last year or the last decade might suggest a solution to your company's financial needs in the mid to late 1980s.

U.S. Steel is an example of a company that has effectively applied the concept of cyclicality by taking advantage of favorable developments in the financial markets as they occur. It has positioned itself to optimize its financing over time. Banks made loans with ceilings on interest rates twice in the 1970s, and both times U.S. Steel took the opportunity to borrow. It has also managed to successfully time the offering of its convertible debentures to coincide with the bottom of the interest rate cycle and near the peak of the company's stock price.

This *Guide* explores the practical, though often unintended consequences of difficult financial decisions. With the help of numerous detailed examples of actual corporate financings, you can follow the reasoning process by which others have chosen a financing alternative.

Additionally, illustrations throughout show both visually and with step-by-step checklists how financing techniques were accomplished.

Although there are detailed references to the Internal Revenue Code and to various accounting pronouncements, this *Guide* is not meant to be an accounting or legal text. It maintains a financial orientation while allowing for the fact that financial decision making invariably includes a legal and accounting dimension. In recent years the raising of capital has become an interdisciplinary endeavor, involving teams of professionals. Although tax and accounting constraints often divert the initial intent, the business objective remains the determining factor.

WHO CAN BENEFIT BY USING THIS GUIDE

This *Guide* has been structured to meet the needs of large, mid-sized, and small corporations that have occasion to raise money. It can also be of value to financial intermediaries and lending institutions—the providers of capital—by underscoring the subtle implications of various financing alternatives for the users of capital. Its joint consideration of rationale, procedure, and method make it a valuable learning tool as well as a handy reference. Specifically:

- *Financial officers* will benefit by increasing their repertoire of financial methods and techniques.
- *Treasurers and controllers* will find guidance in the planning and implementation of fund raising.
- *Staff accountants* should gain insight into the business and financial context of numerous accounting and financial reporting issues.
- *Financial managers* can observe the reasoning process of others engaged in the raising and managing of capital.
- *Entrepreneurs and owners of business* can develop a focus and understand the essential ingredients in financial structuring and decision making.
- *Corporate development managers* should be able to refine their analysis of corporate financing and corporate structure.

- *Strategic planners* will find that there are numerous unconventional and creative alternatives available to them regarding capital sources and capital structure.

- *High-level personnel* are likely to develop a broader awareness of the complexities of the financing decision and the analytical tools required to contribute to such decisions.

- *Financial intermediaries and lenders* should realize a greater appreciation of the objectives and constraints of the users of capital and a perspective for the design of improved financial instruments.

- *Those involved with acquisitions* can develop a framework for the analysis of the various sources of capital.

How to Use this Guide

MODERN BUSINESS FINANCING: A Guide to Innovative Strategies and Techniques has been carefully organized to be as easy to use as possible. Related chapters should be read in pairs or groupings. This is particularly true of the first four chapters, all of which discuss off-balance sheet financing. It is suggested that these chapters be read in sequence.

Chapters 5 and 6, which deal with stock ownership plans, are also related and should be read together. Chapters 7 and 8, which deal with unconventional debt, and Chapters 9 and 10, which cover hybrid securities, should likewise be treated as pairs. These pairs of chapters, as well as the remaining Chapters 11, 12, and 13, can be read in any order.

Robert Douglas Colman

About the Author

Robert Douglas Colman is the founder and President of Oxford Energy, Inc., an energy development and investment company located in New York. Prior to 1984, Mr. Colman was Vice President of Corporate Finance at Bankers Trust Company and Vice President of BT Capital Corp., the venture capital affiliate of Bankers Trust Company. Before joining Bankers Trust Company in 1977, Mr. Colman spent two years as a practicing attorney in New York. From 1970 to 1975 Mr. Colman was employed on the corporate staff of Western Electric Company in the areas of finance and plant design and construction. He received a Juris Doctor from Fordham Law School, an M.B.A. in finance from New York University Graduate School of Business Administration, and a B.S. in Physics from Union College. He is a member of the New York Bar and is the editor and contributing author of *The Handbook of Mergers, Acquisitions and Buyouts,* published by Prentice-Hall, Inc.

Contents

chapter 1

Unloading the Balance Sheet Through Equity Accounting and Joint Ventures

This chapter examines the motivations behind off-balance sheet financing. It then develops several fundamental concepts, including the use of equity accounting and the joint venture format.

Corporations engage in a broad range of financing techniques that allow them to enhance their financial reporting posture, insulate themselves from the business risk of certain transactions or investments, or circumvent restrictive debt covenants.

The structures employed include joint ventures, limited partnerships, leases, and grantor trusts. These approaches are considered in Chapters 1 through 4.

1.1 OFF-BALANCE SHEET FINANCING DEFINED

"Off-balance sheet financing" refers to a variety of financing methods or techniques that allow a company to use its corporate credit as partial backing for a financing, without having to record the full impact of the obligation in its financial statements. The company's obligation to back the financing may be buried in a footnote, explicitly or by implication, and the obligation or liability may be quantified or unquantified. The liability of the company may be treated in the footnotes as a contingent obligation, whereas in fact the contingency is not so remote as to be improbable.[1] The company's exposure may be treated as a long-term obligation, whereas the obligation is imminent and therefore is more accurately treated as a short-term obligation.

Despite footnote disclosure of many of these types of obligations, a comprehensive assurance is never offered by the company's management to the user of the financial statement that all potential liabilities have been fully and accurately disclosed. The following language is typical of what might appear in the Contingencies footnote of a corporation's Annual Report:

> There were contingent liabilities at year end consisting of notes and other commitments arising in the ordinary course of business. The financial risk relating to contingent liabilities is not considered material.

Although there has been significant effort (and some progress) by the Financial Accounting Standards Board and similar organizations, accountants and users of financial statements are still a long way from unanimity on the foundations of generally accepted accounting principles (GAAP). Accounting concepts of liability are ill-defined in many areas and are inadequate to deal with novel and sophisticated

---

[1]If both probable and measurable, it must appear as a reported liability.

financing structures. Accounting is not an exact science and there are no immutable laws. The objective of accounting as generally agreed upon is that financial reports should provide for the user to make reasoned judgments concerning the probable future economic performance of the company. This, however, requires a lot of soft data that is not readily available.

Part of the problem of inadequate disclosure derives from the fact that the concept of accounting liability has been based more on legal rather than economic considerations. That is, if the off-balance sheet financing has not resulted in direct debt for the company in the legal sense, then the company's management has frequently felt justified and has often been able to convince the auditors that the financing should not appear in the company's financial statements. The accounting profession has been more concerned in recent years with the economic underpinnings of transactions. Particularly in larger projects, the economic impact of a financing in which the company has a secondary or indirect liability may be so significant that auditors are resisting the pressures of management to avoid disclosure in the financial statements.

1.2 REASONS FOR OFF-BALANCE SHEET FINANCING

The inexactness of accounting rules coupled with the complexity of a broad range of transactions often places management in what may almost be considered a negotiating position with the auditors. There are a number of reasons that motivate management to encourage the auditors to "mask" certain liabilities.

1.2.1 Shedding Business Risk

In every prudent business transaction there is an attempt on the part of the company's management to shed business risk. In the process of shedding actual business risk, a liability is often removed from the balance sheet or the footnotes. There is nothing "improper" about this underlying motivation or its consequences.

However, the natural tendency on the part of management to reduce business or financial risk frequently gets misdirected so that there develops an emphasis on the form of the transaction rather than on the substance of it. When business risk cannot be adequately shed, the appearance of shedding business risk may often become the goal. This is accomplished when liabilities are removed from the balance sheet.

The company that is most sensitive about removing debt from its balance sheet and improving the quality of its financial reporting posture is frequently operating on the margin of a new credit rating. It is thus extremely concerned about weakening its debt-to-equity ratio or current ratio. As a sub-issue under the question of credit standing is the effect on the cost of borrowing. In general, lenders and rating agencies have tended to look on off-balance sheet obligations more favorably than direct debt, frequently ignoring obligations entirely unless they have amounted to more than 5 percent of the company's assets.

1.2.2 Circumventing Debt Covenants

Another motivation of management in considering off-balance sheet financing may be the attempt to circumvent covenants under lending arrangements. Drafters of covenants in loan agreements have begun to catch up with off-balance sheet financing techniques, especially in such areas as leasing, by requiring certain off-balance sheet obligations to be considered the equivalent of debt. However, there remains a variety of techniques that allow for financings to fall entirely outside the debt restrictions in loan indentures.

1.2.3 Internal Pressures on Management

Aside from considerations external to the company (i.e., maintaining credit standing and the circumventing of debt covenants), there are frequently internal pressures on management that encourage it to engage in off-balance sheet financing. These include internal corporate planning yardsticks as to debt levels within which a financial officer may be constrained.

1.2.4 Accounting Treatment of Devices Used to Keep Transactions Off the Balance Sheet

To the extent that a company's credit stands behind a particular financing, it will impact the company's future borrowing capacity. If the transaction can be structured to limit (not eliminate) the lender's recourse to the company, it will free up the company's balance sheet to provide additional borrowing capacity for future expansion. One method of utilizing a company's credit indirectly to stand behind a financing is the completion agreement.

The Completion Agreement. In a completion agreement a project sponsor agrees to supply sufficient additional equity above a project's initial capitalization for that project to be completed. This alleviates a major concern on the part of the lenders, but it does not act as a full guarantee of the project debt. Thus, completion agreements allow project sponsors to take part in many projects with limited exposure in each one. Because the completion agreement is off the balance sheet (although it will appear in the footnotes if it is material), it is often discounted by the user of the financial statement or it may even be missed entirely. This type of agreement has frequently been masked in the footnotes as a result of some flexibility in the prescribed footnote treatment. If the company has had many projects backed by completion agreements as part of the normal course of its doing business, then there is a good likelihood that the company has avoided reporting them at all.

Even when reported, the language may be unclear as to the nature or amount of the obligation. The following footnote shows a good disclosure of this type of arrangement. It discusses a majority-owned subsidiary ("LS").[2]

> The Company has guaranteed the obligations of LS under the terms of three loan agreements which can provide up to $100 million of funds. The Company has further agreed to cause LS to complete its construction obligation within three years.

Contingency Guarantees and Long-Term Purchase Commitments. The more novel and complex the structure of a project, the greater the flexibility in its accounting treatment. Large and complicated off-balance sheet transactions have often been structured around contingency guarantees and long-term purchase commitments. Financial Accounting Standards Board Statement No. 5, *Accounting for Contingencies*, which was released in 1975, has controlled many transactions utilizing these devices. The statement required that a corporation accrue an estimated loss from a contingency if the event that would confirm the loss were probable, that is, were likely to occur and were estimable. In addition, the statement required that if the loss were not probable but had a reasonable likelihood of occurring, the nature of the contingency and an estimate of the possible loss or range of loss had to be disclosed in the footnotes. If such an estimate could not be made, it further suggested that this should also be stated in the financial statements.

However, it was felt by 1981 that many transactions were not adequately covered by FASB No. 5, and two pronouncements were issued that attempted to address a variety of situations for which there was inadequate disclosure. FASB Interpretation No. 34, *Disclosure of Indirect Guarantees of Indebtedness of Others* (subtitled "An Interpretation of FASB Statement No. 5"), purported to clarify the earlier statement regarding its treatment of indirect guarantees. It extended the requirements of disclosure of "guarantees of others" to include "indirect guarantees" (i.e., agreements requiring the reporting company to transfer funds to another entity, such as agreements to advance funds if that

---

[2]This is a fictitious name.

entity's income, coverage of fixed charges, or working capital fell below a fixed minimum).

The second significant pronouncement in 1981 was the Statement of Financial Accounting Standards No. 47, *Disclosure of Long-Term Obligations*. It required that unconditional purchase obligations[3] associated with financing arrangements, such as take-or-pay contracts, should be disclosed and quantified. The statement pointed out the similarities between these types of arrangements and borrowings or lease obligations.[4]

Despite the requirements that have been promulgated by the FASB, it still requires a good deal of ingenuity to extract the true nature of many liabilities from a company's financial statements. The following language appears in the footnotes of Western Union's Annual Report. It shows a contingent commitment by the company, along with its partners, to complete a project within certain prescribed costs:

> Western Union, through a subsidiary, has a 50 percent interest in a partnership known as Space Communications Company ("Spacecom"). The other partners are subsidiaries of Continental Telephone Corporation and Fairchild Industries, Inc.
>
> Spacecom is engaged in the manufacture of a communications satellite system . . . . Operating and maintenance costs (currently estimated to range from $8 to $12 million annually) and overrun construction costs, if any, are to be borne by Spacecom. Negotiations are pending on NASA-directed changes which will substantially increase the cost of the system above currently estimated basic construction and launch costs of approximately $680 million. Although NASA has provided for provisional funding of these costs, the ultimate responsibility for a portion of such costs has not yet been determined.
>
> Western Union, Fairchild and Continental have guaranteed, in accordance with their respective subsidiaries' proportionate ownership interests in Spacecom, the payment by Spacecom of certain performance penalties under the NASA service agreement (which would not exceed $30 million in the aggregate, part of which may be recoverable from subcontractors) and any overrun construction costs paid by borrowings from the Federal Financing Bank. To date, Western Union has not been called on to make any payments under this commitment and none is anticipated in 1982.

Although the preceding language discloses a potential liability, the extent and likelihood of its occurrence can not be discerned with any certainty.

---

[3]An example of an unconditional purchase obligation is the last sentence of the preceding footnote. Take-or-pay contracts are dealt with at length in §1.5.

[4]Leases are the most familiar of the indirect liabilities and have been in use for quite a while. Although there is a formal evaluating procedure, a lease can still be used as the basis for an off-balance sheet financing. See page 37.

1.3 THE BUILDING BLOCKS OF OFF-BALANCE SHEET FINANCING

1.3.1 Off-Balance Sheet Financing vs. Project Financing

A number of techniques that have proved themselves in the area of project financing can be adopted to other off-balance sheet financings. At the onset we should distinguish between off-balance financing and project financing because there is a good deal of overlap.

Project Financing. Project financings have generally involved large, capital intensive projects such as mining and natural resource projects or power facilities, requiring huge sums of money that drain the financial capacity of even the largest corporation.

A loose definition of a project financing is the financing of a capital investment that is segregated from the project sponsor's other assets and obligations. The general credit of the project is usually not a significant factor to the lender. The credit support for the borrowings of the project carries limited recourse to the sponsor, relying more generally upon the business and economic context of the project, which includes commitments from the sponsor and third parties in the form of management, the supply of raw materials, and the purchase of output. There may be partial guarantees from the sponsors, but these do not cover all the risks. The lender to the project looks principally to the cash flows and earnings of the project as the source of funds for repayment and to the assets of the project as collateral for the loan.

Off-Balance Sheet Financing and Project Financing Distinguished. Off-balance sheet financing may take the form of a project financing. However, the term "off-balance sheet" financing also refers to techniques and structures that are not in the nature of project financings. The term applies to transactions of all sizes and to a variety of techniques—such as the financing of receivables and inventory, the use of captive leasing or insurance subsidiaries, the use of limited partnership or grantor trusts—that have nothing to do with project financing.

Project financings and off-balance sheet financings can best be distinguished by their differing objectives. The objective of project finance is not to conceal a liability of the project sponsor from a lender, rating agency, or shareholder (although this may be a consequence of the transaction structure). Rather, the purpose of project financing is generally to segregate the business or credit risk of the project.

A parallel between project financing and off-balance sheet financing is the risk/reward equation. If the economics of the venture (whether an off-balance sheet financing or project financing) are strong, it will be easier for the sponsor to shed some of the risk at the expense of another participant in the venture—such as the lender. The lender may not require as strong a commitment from the sponsors or other parties to make sure that the venture is on a strong footing. A project financing is largely an exercise in the analysis of the opportunities for reducing or laying off the risks. It will become apparent that the shedding of risk is a key factor in the ability to remove a liability from the balance sheet.

1.4 USING THE JOINT VENTURE STRUCTURE TO REDUCE BUSINESS RISK

A common structure for project financings has been the joint venture. A joint venture does not have a precise legal definition. It generally signifies an organization formed for some temporary or limited purpose involving collaboration by the participants. Even this designation is not always valid since joint ventures have engaged in continuing businesses with numerous transactions over prolonged periods of time. It is not necessary for the joint venture to adopt one of the more continuing legal relationships, such as a partnership or corporation, although this is frequently the case.

Joint Venture Disclosure: An Example. An example of footnote disclosure of several joint ventures appears in the following Annual Report:

Joint Venture Affiliates:

The Company has interests in five joint ventures operated by the Company, where the Company has less than a 50 percent interest. At year end, combined assets and liabilities of these joint ventures were $420,750,000 and $350,225,000 respectively. At year end, XYZ Company had total assets of $35,500,000 and liabilities of $17,000,000.

A business reason for the joint venture may be that a company wishes to expand into a new area of business but lacks some necessary skills or resources to do so. It seeks to obtain these requirements from another corporation, not only in the form of capital investment but also in the form of facilities or technology.

The joint venture structure, by allowing for multiple participants, meets the objectives of enlarging the amount of debt capacity of the project, as well as limiting a particular company's exposure to the project risk. The second objective parallels an implicit goal of off-balance sheet financing—to reduce business risk, or at least the appearance of business risk.

The business risks of a project financing are of several types. There are risks of: (1) start-up cost overruns due to delays during the start-up period, inflation effects, or inadequate design and engineering; (2) excessive operating costs due to labor or production problems, price hikes, or volatile market conditions; (3) inadequate or uneconomical raw material supply; (4) market risk for the output of the project.

Caution: High-Risk Projects Are Not Good Candidates. It is critical that risk be shifted away from the project sponsor in a project financing in order for the attendant debt to be off-balance sheet. Thus projects that have extremely high business risk are not good candidates for off-balance sheet financing. In those projects where there are intangibles and the risks are difficult to quantify, the lender or insurer is less inclined to bear business risk. More general guarantees, which show up as direct liabilities on the sponsor's balance sheet, will be required of the project sponsors.

To state the financial objectives of the joint venture structure in a slightly different form, a company participating in the project financing seeks to obtain leverage while minimizing the negative impact on its balance sheet. Furthermore, the company does not wish to have those liabilities incurred by the project reflected on its balance sheet. If possible, the company would like to avoid the appearance of the liabilities in its footnotes as well. The latter objective may be met if the debt incurred by the project is nonrecourse or has limited recourse to the company.

It should be emphasized that it is quite rare for a project financing to raise debt purely on its own merits on a stand-alone basis, without the sponsor company providing some sort of credit support. This may only amount to limited guarantees as to project completion, or—as has been mentioned earlier—a commitment for sufficient infusion of equity to make up capital shortfalls due to cost overruns. Lenders generally require that the project have specific completion tests that must be met before the project loans become nonrecourse to the sponsors.

Another type of indirect credit support in a project financing is cost sharing, where sponsors are committed to provide their pro-rata share of all costs including debt-service payments and working capital maintenance clauses.

1.5 USING TAKE-OR-PAY CONTRACTS TO PROVIDE INDIRECT CREDIT SUPPORT

A variety of financing arrangements has evolved in project financings that provide the indirect credit of the sponsor as support for the project. There is invariably an attempt to minimize risks associated with the disposition of the output of the project. The sponsor attempts to negotiate with the customers to absorb greater price risks in return for an assured future supply. If demand and supply conditions for the eventual output are favorable, the sponsor might obtain floor prices or price-escalation clauses. These enable the sponsor to shift the consequences of price uncertainties to the ultimate customer. However, if the market for a commodity is expected to be unfavorable, the sponsor may have to offer the customer price concessions in order to obtain a long-term purchase commitment.

One of the most notable credit-support arrangements in the form of a long-term purchase commitment is the take-or-pay contract. These are frequently used by utilities for the purchase of coal or natural gas.

Footnote Disclosure: An Example. ABC Corporation's[5] Annual Report shows a larger purchase commitment, and in greater detail:

> ABC's production facility has long term raw material supply contracts that commit ABC to annual future purchases at volumes that are less than anticipated annual requirements. Such purchases last year approximated $700 million. ABC is also committed to share in the costs to be incurred by its raw material joint ventures.

1.5.1 Two Types of Take-or-Pay Commitments

There are two types of "take-or-pay" commitments by the customer; one is conditional and one is unconditional.

Conditional. In the conditional take-or-pay, more commonly known as the "take-and-pay," the potential purchaser of the output commits to purchase such output only if tendered (i.e., delivered) by the project. If the output is not tendered, then there is no requirement to pay. In these situations, a portion of the business risk is not shifted to the purchaser but remains with the project. However, as will be shown in Case 1.2, the take-and-pay can be structured so that some degree of pricing risk is incurred by the purchaser.

Unconditional. The other type of purchase arrangement, which is unconditional in nature, is the true take-or-pay. Here, the purchaser commits to purchase a certain amount of output per year at an ascertainable price, regardless of whether the output is actually delivered. This has the effect of shifting the project risk to the ultimate purchaser and in substance is a guarantee. Frequently the purchase price is pegged to the debt-servicing requirements and operating costs of the project. When the take-or-pay is combined with the joint venture structure, the sponsor obtains the benefits of one-line equity accounting[6] while making the guarantee unquantifiable in the footnotes.

---

[5]This is a fictitious name.
[6]Equity accounting is first discussed on page 13.

Take-or-Pay/Joint Venture Disclosure: An Example. The following is an example of disclosure of a take-or-pay agreement from the 1981 Annual Report of Interlake, Inc., coupled with a commitment to share in the operating costs of two joint ventures. It is not possible to determine precisely how much Interlake will be required to pay:

> *Commitments and Contingencies*: With respect to the Company's interest in two mining joint ventures, the Company is required to take its ownership proportion of production for which it is committed to pay its proportionate share of operating costs of these projects, either directly or as a part of the product. Such costs include, as a minimum and regardless of the quantity of ore received, animal interest and principal payments on the debt of these projects of approximately $4,000,000 through 1983, and lesser amounts thereafter.

1.5.2 Accounting Treatment of Take-or-Pay Contracts

Statement of Financial Accounting Standards No. 47, *Disclosure of Long-Term Obligations*, attempts to address the problem of take-or-pay contracts. It requires that unconditional purchase obligations associated with financing arrangements should be disclosed and quantified, and that future cash payments of a company should be disclosed in a manner similar to disclosures of capital lease obligations.

The question then becomes "What is an unconditional purchase obligation?" FASB No. 47 indicates that this means the obligation is noncancelable, with a remaining life in excess of one year, and negotiated as part of the financing arrangement for the facility. If these conditions are met then the nature and term of the obligation must be disclosed, as well as the amount of the fixed and determinable portion of the obligation, the nature of any variable components, and the amounts already purchased under the obligations. The unconditional purchase obligations may be omitted only if the aggregate commitment for all such obligations not disclosed is immaterial.

Take-or-Pay Commitments as a Separate Footnote Classification. A company's take-or-pay commitments, if significant, may have a separate classification in the footnotes as opposed to being carried under Contingencies. The following example is typical of what might appear in the Annual Report of a natural resource company:

> *Take-or-Pay Obligations*: Under provisions of various coal supply contracts with coal producers, the Company is required to take or pay for minimum volumes. These commitments are included in Payments for Coal Supply and were $75,000,000 at year end. Future obligations may be substantially greater than those incurred historically.

1.6 JOINT VENTURES AND EQUITY ACCOUNTING

Joint ventures have proliferated for a variety of reasons, but particularly for the rising costs and high risks of new facilities. There is a natural desire to share these risks with other participants. When a decision is made by a participant to enter into a joint venture based upon business considerations, the next areas of concern are the legal and tax consequences and the accounting treatment of the investment.

A joint venture may be organized as a corporation, a partnership, or as a grouping of interests in which each joint venturer owns an undivided interest in each joint venture asset and is liable for its share of each joint venture liability. A simple illustration of a corporate joint venture involves two participants who form a corporation in which neither owns more than 50 percent of the common equity. It is thinly capitalized—that is, there is a small investment in the equity, with the majority of the financing in the form of debt. The debt may be non-recourse to the equity investors, or it may be partially or completely guaranteed by them.

Accounting Principles Board Opinion No. 18[7] would apply so far as a corporate joint venture is concerned. The joint venturers would account for their investments in the joint venture using the equity method. Thus no portion of the debt incurred by the venture would appear on the balance sheet of the venturers. The guarantees (if the debt is recourse) may appear in the footnotes as contingent liabilities and they may or may not be quantifiable.

Mead Corporation: An Example of Thorough Reporting. Mead Corporation provides an example of thorough reporting by a company using equity accounting for joint ventures in its consolidated statement. In 1981, it carried $333.2 million in "Investments in and Advances to Jointly Owned Companies." From the footnotes it is possible to extract much of the relevant information regarding the joint ventures:

> *Jointly Owned Companies—Description and Operations*: The company's principal domestic jointly owned investments are Georgia Kraft Company and Brunswick Pulp & Paper Company, each 50 percent owned. Georgia Kraft manufactures coated bottle carrier stock and uncoated kraft linerboard, and Brunswick manufactures bleached kraft pulp and board. These companies, which also produce lumber, supply Mead with raw materials used in its packaging, container or paper operations.
>
> The company's principal Canadian investments are Northwood Forest Industries Ltd. and British Columbia Forest Products

---

[7]*The Equity Method of Accounting for Investments in Common Stock.*

Ltd. Mead owns 50 percent of Northwood and 28 percent of BCFP. Both manufacture bleached softwood kraft pulp, lumber, plywood and waferboard. BCFP also manufactures paper and newsprint and has significant investments in three other forest products companies.

Financial Reporting: Mead's investments in jointly owned companies are stated at cost plus equity in undistributed net earnings, which approximate the portion of shareholders' equity applicable of Mead's investment. The composition of Mead's total investments in these companies is:

December 31 (all dollar amounts in millions)	1981	1980
Investments, at cost	$ 60.7	$ 60.9
Equity in undistributed net earnings	271.9	269.8
Total investments	332.6	330.7
Advances	.6	.9
Total investments in and advances to jointly owned companies	$332.2	$331.6

Pulp and paperboard produced by Georgia Kraft, Brunswick and Northwood (other than Northwood market pulp) are part of Mead's raw material supply system. Therefore, the pretax earnings relative to such products of these vertically integrated affiliates are recorded as an offset to Mead's cost of products sold. All pretax earnings from BCFP, other minor affiliates and the sawmill and market pulp earnings of Northwood are reported as equity in earnings of jointly owned companies. Applicable taxes on these earnings, as provided by these companies, are included in the provision for income taxes. Summary operating data of the combined jointly owned companies, presented in relation to Mead's reporting for these companies, is:

Year ended December 31 (All dollar amounts in millions)	1981	1980
Revenues	$1,676.1	$1,612.5
Costs and expenses	1,488.8	1,389.5
Interest expense	92.0	57.3
Income taxes	34.8	50.9
Net earnings	$ 60.5	$ 114.8
Sales to Mead included above	$ 386.2	$ 328.9
Mead's share of net earnings	$ 29.4	$ 44.7
Reported in Mead's statements of earnings as:		
Cost of products sold reduction	$ 42.1	$ 40.9
Equity in earnings before taxes of jointly owned companies	4.9	24.7

	1981	1980
Earnings before income taxes	47.0	65.6
Income taxes	17.6	20.9
As above	$ 29.4	$ 44.7
Net earnings remitted as dividends	$ 3.9	$ 3.4

Summary data on financial condition of the combined jointly owned companies, presented in relation to Mead's reporting for these companies, is:

December 31

(All dollar amounts in millions)	1981	1980
Current assets	$ 568.3	$ 520.4
Less current liabilities	343.4	315.1
Working capital	224.9	205.3
Investments and other assets	158.0	125.4
Property, plant and equipment, at cost less accumulated depreciation of $728.0 in 1981 and $693.1 in 1980	1,386.3	1,099.9
Timber sources, at cost less timber depletion	249.7	227.5
Less:		
Long-term debt due through 2010	1,023.8	681.5
Deferred taxes and other items	203.3	195.4
Shareholder's equity	$ 791.8	$ 781.2
Mead's share of equity	$ 332.6	$ 330.7

Under an agreement with Northwood, Mead is entitled to purchase the pulp it requires. Mead has agreements with Georgia Kraft (until 2010) and Brunswick (until 2003) which obligate Mead to purchase 50 percent of their output. The price to each parent for output purchased is determined by formulas specified in the agreements. These formulas allocate production and operating costs and other charges. For Brunswick, the formula additionally provides a per diem amount of $15,000. For Georgia Kraft, the formula additionally provides an annual 12 percent return on stockholders' equity as of the end of the preceding calendar year. Furthermore, the payments must provide adequate funds to meet all obligations and to pay current installments of funded indebtedness. Under these agreements, Mead purchased pulp and board amounting to 1,171,000 tons ($350 million), 1,114,000 tons ($296 million) and 1,045,000 tons ($241 million) for the years ended December 31, 1981, 1980 and 1979, respectively.

Note that it is impossible to determine from the information provided the capital structure of any individual joint venture. In addition, there are purchase commitments mentioned in the last paragraph of the footnote. However, these are not quantified as to future expected payments.

The use of the equity method is also required under APB No. 18 to account for investments in corporate joint ventures in which the investor's ownership of voting stock gives the investor significant influence over the venture. As a rule of thumb, an investment where there is lack of significant control is carried on the investor's books at cost and the investor recognizes income when it receives dividends. An investment that includes 20 percent or more of the voting stock creates a presumption that the investor has the ability to exercise significant influence, with the opposite presumption created if ownership is less than 20 percent.

There are ambiguities in the accounting literature as to noncorporate joint ventures that have resulted in diversity of practice. APB No. 18 does not address accounting for investments in partnerships and other unincorporated joint ventures. *Accounting Interpretation No. 2* of Opinion No. 18, *Investments in Partnerships and Ventures* is often cited as a reference that suggests the equity method for most of these joint venture arrangements.

chapter 2

Examples of Major Off-Balance Sheet Financings

In the prior chapter we developed a general framework and examined some of the fundamental building blocks of off-balance sheet financing. In this chapter we will apply these principals in the detailed examination of several major off-balance sheet financings.

The first example involves the financing of a major chemical plant using a joint venture format. The second situation was employed in removing certain nonproductive coal properties from the sponsor's balance sheet. Two further examples, provided in summary form, include the use of the nonmonetary production payment loan and the timber harvesting venture.

2.1 A CAREFUL LOOK AT TWO MAJOR OFF-BALANCE SHEET FINANCINGS

CASE 2.1 FINANCING A NEW PLANT USING THE JOINT VENTURE STRUCTURE

One recent off-balance sheet transaction involved a major chemical concern ("the Company"), which desired to construct a large facility. The Company required the output of the new plant but wished to keep this asset and its attendant liabilities off its balance sheet. Approximately $330 million in financing was required for the construction of the plant, and this was provided by the following sources:

1. $85 million in bank-revolving credits. These had an eight and one-half year term.
2. $160 million in secured notes from institutional lenders with fifteen year maturities (average life of approximately 10 years).
3. Convertible preferred stock of $68 million (convertible seven years after completion of the facility).
4. Common stock of $17 million.

How it worked. The Company created a joint venture in corporate form with an engineering construction company (the "Partner"), each owning 50 percent of the common stock. The joint venture was to construct and own the plant, with a significant portion of the output to be purchased by the Company under a long-term Product Purchase and Sale Agreement. The agreement required the Company to purchase a stipulated minimum quantity of output at the higher of market price or a formula price. (The formula price was calculated to cover scheduled principal and interest payments, as well as other cash-flow needs).

In the event that production problems resulted in a shortfall in the output of the plant, the Company would pay the formula price. However, such payment (or payments) would be in the nature of an advance payment against future delivery of product. If the shortfall in production was not made up by the facility within six months from the date of default under the Product Purchase and Sale Agreement through excess production, the Company would receive a refund of its advance payment and it would not be required to make any further payments under the Product Purchase and Sale Agreement.

The Product Purchase and Sale Agreement is the crux of the transaction from a credit point of view. It is not a guarantee by the Company but only assures the lenders against the first dollars of potential loss by making up any cash-flow shortfall by the joint venture on a temporary basis. Once the six-month period has ended, the lenders are once again at risk. Business or production risk is not the burden of the Company beyond the six-month period. Thus there is a true sharing of risk between the Company and other parties (here the lenders as well as the Partner) so that the rationale for off-balance sheet treatment seems to be a justifiable one.

Why it worked. This transaction structure can only be used when certain favorable business conditions exist. The reason it works here is because of the underlying nature of the production risk and the overall business context. The technology was a proven one, and the plant was constructed with two identical processes in tandem. The chances of both parallel production systems going down at the same time were very slight. In addition, both partners were major creditworthy companies that had vested interests in the success of the plant. The company had other outstanding loans with the same lenders who participated in the project. These lenders could exert severe pressure upon the Company if necessary to commit additional resources to the project. Thus the lenders felt that the business risk to which they were exposed was greatly mitigated. Nevertheless, from a purely legal standpoint, their risk was a real one.

The project structure is summarized in Exhibit 2.1.

Steps in Financing a Chemical Facility

1. Chemical Company and engineering firm (Partner) contribute a total of $17 million to corporate joint venture.
2. Chemical Company contributes $68 million in exchange for convertible preferred stock.
3. Banks lend $85 million and institutions lend $160 million.
4. Chemical Company enters into Product Purchase and Sale Agreement with the project.
5. Project repays loans to banks and institutions.
6. At the end of seven years, preferred stock is converted into common, giving the sponsor majority ownership of the facility.

EXHIBIT 2.1 Off-Balance Sheet Financing of Chemical Plant

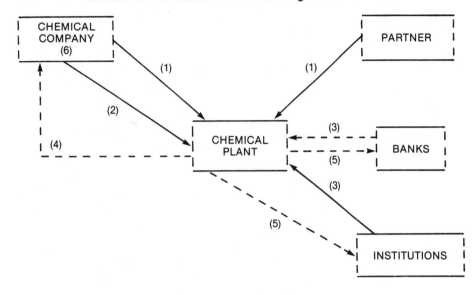

How convertible preferred stock allowed the Company to control risk/ reward. One factor that deserves special emphasis is the function of convertible preferred stock. This security allows the Company to control the risk/reward equation at various stages of the project. Before conversion of the preferred, the Company does not have majority ownership. The joint ownership structure initially allows the Company to shed sufficient business risk so that it can account for the project on an off-balance sheet basis. At a later date the convertible preferred stock allows the Company to increase its ownership position significantly. Assuming that the plant is completed and operates according to plan, the Company would convert its shares, boosting its common holdings to a majority position. It can thus maximize its return after the construction period (which is the period of highest risk), and presumably at the point in time when the plant is near peak capacity.

When the preferred is converted to common the Company would have to consolidate for accounting purposes, but at this point it would not matter to the Company: The assets would have become earning assets. It would have accomplished its goal of maintaining off-balance sheet for seven years, a project with limited return.

Also to be considered is the risk/return ratio of the Partner in the venture, the engineering construction company. It will be giving up its 50 percent ownership position for a minority position at a time when the plant is beginning to generate its maximum return. Although the Partner has the incentive of receiving a large construction contract, it ends up with substantial equity (resulting from an initial investment of $8.5 million in the common) in a facility over which it has no control.

Caution. In order to protect the minority investor, a mechanism is usually created that allows it to sell its shares to the project or other partner at a certain period in time. Caution must be exercised so that such a device does not undermine the desired accounting treatment. The concerns of the minority equity holder and the various methods of alleviating these concerns are considered at length in the following case.

CASE 2.2 REMOVING UNPRODUCTIVE COAL PROPERTIES FROM THE BALANCE SHEET

The general concern in the 1970s about the supply of oil resulted in a flurry of activity among energy resource companies and utilities to develop alternate sources of energy. It appeared for a time that the various regulatory commissions would mandate the use of coal as opposed to oil and gas. In addition, it appeared that there would be a large demand for the export of coal to Europe and the Far East in the 1980s. Thus quite a number of companies purchased coal reserves or partially developed coal operations with the expectation of developing them in the near future.

The mandate that was expected to force conversion from oil to coal did not occur; the demand for coal has lagged and the coal market is softer than expected. Many of the companies who had the apparent foresight to raise debt and purchase and develop significant coal properties were stuck with these properties on their balance sheet (along with the attendant debt), with little economic incentive to develop the properties and no market for their output.

As long as the market for coal remains soft there is a significant incentive to remove these properties from the balance sheet. There are several ways that this can be accomplished, the easiest being the *outright sale to a third party*. The problem with this solution is that if and when the coal market improves, the company will have given up the ability to capitalize on a strengthening of the demand for coal.

One alternative to an outright sale by companies that wish to divest themselves of assets that do not meet their minimum return-on-assets criteria is a *tax-free spinoff to shareholders*[1] of the properties. This is accomplished under §355 of the Internal Revenue Code. A special subsidiary is created to hold the nonproductive or low-earning assets. The shares of stock of the subsidiary, which are held by the parent, are distributed to the parent company's existing shareholders on a pro-

---

[1] Spinoffs are an attractive solution to regulatory pressure on certain utilities that have underutilized or overly expensive coal-production facilities. In certain jurisdictions where utilities purchase coal from their own subsidiary at above market, they are prohibited from recouping the total cost in their rate base. By spinning off the facility or property (i.e., putting it at arms length) the price paid can be passed on to the consumer.

rata basis. The shareholders end up with stock in two companies that together have the same assets as the original company. It would appear that the shareholders are no better or worse off than they were before the spinoff, but the parent company has freed itself from the burden of the unwanted assets.

To the extent that the spun-off properties appreciate at some time in the future, this upside potential still remains within the economic family (i.e., the original shareholders of the parent corporation). If the parent company wants to obtain the beneficial use of these assets, it may be able to work out a sweetheart arrangement with the new company. This arrangement should be structured as early as possible. There is a risk that sufficient time will have elapsed so that there is a significant divergence in the ownership of the two companies and future negotiations become adversarial rather than friendly. Optimally, some type of long-term purchase arrangement or management contract would be entered into between the two companies simultaneously with the spinoff.

2.1.1 Using a Joint Venture to Move a Coal Operation Off-Balance Sheet

Here is another method that might be used by a diversified resource company that desires to remove an existing coal operation from its balance sheet. It will be assumed that the Company has two constraints: (1) It requires that the financing associated with the new structure to be nonrecourse, and (2) The Company wants to remain in control over the property so that it can be in a position to benefit from its operations and the appreciation of its assets over the long run.

Aside from the fact that the market for the output of the properties is soft, the acquisition and initial development has been funded with floating rate bank debt. The debt service has become excessive with the surge in interest rates. Thus there are compelling reasons to remove the assets and attendant debt from the balance sheet, as well as to refinance the floating rate debt.

How it works. The first step in the creation of the off-balance sheet financing structure is for the Company to create a joint venture in the form of a corporation that would purchase the properties from the Company. Fifty percent of the common equity of this new corporation would be owned by the Company, and 50 percent would be held by a third party coventuror.[2] The latter would be either an institutional lender or an independent third party. The common equity would be a small percentage of the total capital, say 10 percent to 15 percent. There would also be a layer of convertible preferred stock (or con-

---

[2]See page 13 for a discussion of the types of coventurors in projects such as this one.

vertible debt) held by the company in sufficient amounts so that upon conversion the company would hold substantially all (80 to 90 percent) of the common equity of the joint venture. The joint venture would allow the company to carry its investment as a single line equity account on the asset side of the balance sheet. The company would manage the joint venture for which it would receive a management fee.

The venture would then raise senior debt on a stand alone, non-recourse basis against take-and-pay supply contracts and the funds raised would be paid to the Company in the purchase of the coal properties. The funds could then be applied to the repayment of the bank debt incurred in the original financing of the properties.

The amount of nonrecourse financing that can be raised is constrained by the venture's cash flow. Using a three year historic average and assuming a very modest increase over the life of the project, the following joint venture structure might be feasible:

1. $10 million in common equity, $5 million held by the Company and $5 million by a lender/investor.
2. $15 million in convertible preferred stock held by the Company and convertible only after repayment of the senior debt.
3. $75 million in senior debt provided by an institutional lender with a term of ten years.

At the end of ten years, when the senior debt would be fully repaid, the Company would exercise its conversion privilege and its ownership position would increase from 50 percent to at least 80 percent (and as high as 90 percent, depending upon the economics). At conversion, the lender/investor would be able to "put" its common shares back to the Company at fair market value, or be able to dispose of its shares through a buy-sell agreement.

How the owner benefits. Thus the owner of the unproductive coal properties achieves the following objectives:

- Moves the coal assets into a joint venture and off its balance sheet
- Enjoys a portion of the income (after debt service) during the life of the venture through the management fee and a return on the preferred stock
- Receives half of the residual value with the right to purchase the remainder at fair market value
- Refinances a substantial portion of its borrowings of floating rate debt on a fixed rate basis
- Replaces a direct debt obligation with a nonrecourse financing

The following diagram summarizes the transaction structure.

EXHIBIT 2.2 Off-Balance Sheet Financing of Coal Properties

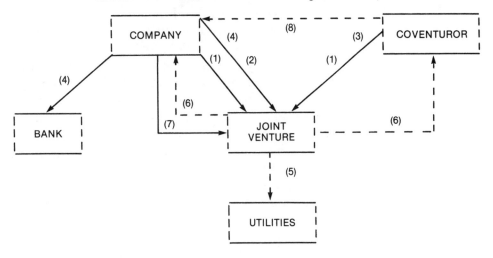

Steps in Financing of Coal Properties

1. Company and coventuror each contribute $5 million in common equity to the Joint Venture.
2. Company contributes $15 million in the form of convertible preferred stock.
3. Coventuror provides $75 million in senior debt.
4. Joint Venture purchases coal properties from the Company and the Company uses the proceeds to repay the bank debt.
5. Joint Venture sells output to utilities under take-and-pay contracts (some of which have been assigned by the company).
6. Joint Venture repays senior debt and pays preferred dividend.
7. Company converts preferred to common stock.
8. Coventuror sells its common shares to the Company at fair market value.

2.1.2 Interim Alternatives to Consider When the Time Isn't Right for Off-Balance Sheet Financing

Whenever off-balance sheet financing is being considered, the timing and position of the financial markets may work against the feasibility of the project. High interest rates, or the lack of availability of funds that allow for repayment on a long-term basis, may make the transaction uneconomical. The tactical objective would then be to create an interim financing structure that would allow the company to move into the off-balance sheet financing at the moment it becomes propitious to do so.

Interim loan. In the situation of the coal properties, depressed coal markets would make it difficult for the Joint Venture to service a reasonable amount of debt on a stand-alone basis. However, by using the Company's direct credit, a fixed rate private placement for an interim period might be obtained. Although not off-balance sheet, the interim loan could convert the floating rate bank debt to longer term fixed rate financing (5 to 7 years). Thus the Company could realize at least one of its financial objectives.

Two features could be offered as inducements for the fixed rate lender. The first might be an equity kicker in the form of an interest in the Company's coal reserves (say 3 to 5 percent). In addition, the lender may have the right of "roll over." That is, at the end of five years or sooner (assuming that the venture has reached an acceptable level of profitability), the lender would roll over its term loan into its equity and debt interests in the Joint Venture. In the process the lender would be shifting from the Company's credit to a loan against the Joint Venture on a stand-alone basis. As an inducement, the lender would be able to increase its equity position from roughly 3–5 percent to 15–20 percent. The lender would then be participating with the Company in the joint venture structure previously described.

Take-and-pay contract. Aside from the interim financing approach proposed above, there is a further modification that would allow the Joint Venture to currently raise financing on a stand-alone basis despite its inability to currently service the long-term debt. The Joint Venture could enter into a take-and-pay contract with the Company during the interim period, whereby the Company would purchase coal from the Venture at a floor price sufficient to allow the Venture to amortize its debt.[3] Because the floor price would be above market, the Company would realize a loss upon resale of the coal.

The economics of this alternative would not differ significantly from the circumstances existing between the Company and its coal subsidiary prior to the creation of the Joint Venture. It had been putting more cash into the coal operations for debt servicing purposes than it is taking out. With this new structure, however, the debt would be moved off-balance sheet,[4] but its repayment would still essentially remain the responsibility of the Company.

---

[3] This structure in certain ways parallels the Purchase Contract discussed earlier. See page 10.

[4] It would however, be a disclosure item. It is not an unconditional guarantee and business risk is not assumed by the Company.

2.1.3 Technical Issues to Consider When Structuring Off-Balance Sheet Financing

The preceding structure has been outlined in a cursory fashion. However, there are a number of technical considerations that would normally be addressed in structuring an off-balance sheet financing. These can be broken down into four basic areas: financing alternatives, tax planning, accounting impact, and strategic considerations.

Financing alternatives: three ways to attract institutional lenders. From a financial point of view, there are two groups of investors who would have a particular interest in the financing of coal reserves or coal mine development. These are coal management mining companies, and coal purchasers including overseas utilities or trading companies either in Europe or the Far East (Japan or Taiwan). These two groups are specific to coal so they will not be discussed in depth.

A third group, which is of more general interest, is comprised of institutional lenders in the United States. The equity position[5] offered to the institutional lender is what gives the transaction structure its appeal. In this situation there are three ways in which an institution might consider an equity type position coupled with a loan:

1. The loan would be priced at or near market with a royalty on production or a net profits interest to the lender. There would be no direct equity investment by the lender.
2. The loan would be priced below market and the lender would make a direct equity investment. A large current cash return on equity would be required, with limited expectation of future return based on residual value.
3. The loan would be priced below market and the lender would make a direct equity investment. However, substantial expected residual value would be necessary in lieu of a current cash return on equity.

If it were necessary to utilize the interim financing structure, this would further limit the number of institutional lenders who would consider the transaction. One institution that recently considered this transaction structure viewed the equity kicker as an inducement to enter the deal, but offered no rate savings. Another institution proposed a slight concession in rate in exchange for a more substantial equity position. It further required that the transition from the interim

---

[5]See discussion of equity positions in real estate lending on page 39.

financing to the off-balance sheet joint venture structure be tied to the performance of the Joint Venture and the coal industry during the next five years.

Tax planning. The second area of concern involves taxes. In Case 1.2 there are a number of complicated and critical tax issues including (1) the availability of capital gains or loss treatment at the time of sale of assets to the Venture; (2) the deductibility of debt interest should convertible debt be used in place of the preferred stock; (3) tax treatment upon conversion of the convertible securities; (4) tax treatment of the "put" of the common shares to the Company; (5) the impact upon the Company of using the take-and-pay contract when the purchase price is above market.

Recommendation. There are differing opinions as to the desirability of tax rulings in these transactions. To the extent that there is a substantial amount of potential tax liability involved, it is suggested that all efforts be made to obtain a ruling. At the very least, an opinion letter should be obtained from tax counsel. The following discussion shows the extent and complexity of the tax issues involved, without attempting to resolve them definitively.

There are significant tax consequences at the initial point of sale of the assets to the Venture. If the assets are sold at or near their tax basis, the impact of any capital gain or loss upon the Company would be minimized. Also to be considered are ITC and depreciation recapture. There is also the possibility that the transaction between the Company and the Joint Venture may not be deemed "arms length." This could undermine the valuation of the assets as well as the Company's ability to book a true "sale." In the actual transaction upon which this case is based, the assets had only been purchased a year earlier by the Company. Thus there was a recent comparable transaction with a third party that could be used to substantiate the sale price to the Joint Venture.

If the interim financing structure is employed, the sale of the assets to the Joint Venture could be delayed up to five years. Thus there would be a widening gap between the Company's tax basis and "fair market value," resulting in a larger tax impact. This would require greater care by the Company in its tax planning. In addition, the initial purchase of the coal properties by the Company from a third party would be further removed in time, undermining its validity as a true measure of purchase price.

Another tax issue has to do with the type of convertible security employed in the transaction structure. To the extent that there are pretax earnings in the Joint Venture, convertible subordinated debt would be preferable to convertible preferred stock because of the deductibility of interest payments. There is the possibility that the Internal

Revenue Service would refute the deductibility of interest payments, treating them instead as dividends. The IRS would argue that the security is really an equity security. In order to counter this argument care should be taken to reduce or eliminate its equity features by properly structuring and valuing the instrument in terms of conversion premium and coupon.

The conversion of the preferred stock or debt instrument to common would be a nontaxable event to the Company and to the Joint Venture. Exercise of the put on the common stock by the Partner would be a nontaxable event to the Company, but there would be capital gains consequences to the Partner.

One further consideration in the tax area results from the use of the take-and-pay arrangement between the Joint Venture and the Company. If the coal is purchased by the Company at a price above market, then resale by the Company at market will result in ordinary losses for the Company. These losses would result in tax savings to the Company by virtue of the reduction to pretax income. Assuming that the Joint Venture and the Company are both in the 50 percent tax bracket, the tax savings to the Company would be roughly equal to the tax liability (i.e., marginal increase in taxes) incurred by the Joint Venture as a result of its increased revenues from the take-and-pay. Although the total tax liability to the combined entities would not be increased, dislocations in cash flow and reported earnings for the individual entities would result.

Accounting considerations. The third technical area involves a number of accounting considerations. As it has been structured, the Joint Venture would not be consolidated with the Company for accounting purposes until such time as the Company converts its preferred or debt security position. Equity accounting rules would apply. The addition of a take-and-pay contract from the Company would not change the accounting treatment, although there might be footnote treatment of this arrangement. At inception, the Company would merely book a sale of the assets to the Joint Venture.[6]

Caution. A significant accounting issue arises with the use of the preferred stock. Care must be given to avoid tainting the preferred stock and having it treated as common, which could result in consolidation. Thus the preferred should have a market rate of return.

A take-and-pay contract at a fixed price (as opposed to fair market value) requires the immediate recognition for accounting purposes of the expected loss by the Company over the life of the contract. There are a number of imponderables involved in making such an estimation,

---

[6]Alternatively, part of the assets might be contributed to the Joint Venture as an equity contribution in lieu of cash.

and it is for this reason that the take-and-pay arrangement would appear to be the least attractive interim alternative to the Company given its off-balance sheet financing objectives. A take-and-pay contract at market does not incur a balance sheet liability, and disclosure in the footnotes would not be quantifiable.

Operational and strategic considerations. The final major area of concern involves operational and strategic considerations. Aside from an engineering report of reserves that would always be required, other issues would include the structuring of management contracts to run the Joint Venture after the transaction, modification of existing leasing, royalty and contract mining arrangements, negotiation of long-term purchase contracts with utilities and development of a methodology for making capital expenditures for new processing plants.

The purpose here in this prolonged discussion of coal financing is to show in detail the potential pitfalls of an actual situation, as well as the depth and variety of expertise—legal, accounting, and financial—required to overcome various problem areas.

2.2 USING NONMONETARY PRODUCTION PAYMENTS TO FINANCE OIL, GAS, AND MINERAL PROPERTIES OFF-BALANCE SHEET

A method frequently used to finance producing oil and gas or other mineral properties is the production based loan. There are several types of production based loans, some of which do not appear as debt on the balance sheet if properly structured.

2.2.1 Using a Production Proceeds Loan

One fairly typical structure was utilized in 1982 by a company that desired to purchase certain producing properties. The company required that the borrowings be on a nonguaranteed or stand-alone basis. It created a special purpose, wholly owned subsidiary that borrowed $120,000,000 under a "proceeds production loan" and purchased the properties from an unrelated third party.

Under the proceeds production loan there was a covenant that required development cost funding by the parent company as might be required to bring the fields to an optimal production based upon two factors: the ratio of debt to cash flow and the size and quality of the reserves relative to development cost. In addition, the loan was supported by a series of fifteen year take-and-pay contracts for a total of nearly 80 percent of the output of the properties. Payment under these contracts were assigned to the lenders, who would offset a predetermined quantity of cash on a monthly basis to service the debt.

2.2.2 The Production Payment Loan Provides Greater Repayment Flexibility and Is Nonrecourse to the Borrower

Although this structure allows the parent company to shed much of the risk associated with the project, the liability of the subsidiary for the debt would appear in the consolidated financial statements. There is, however, a method whereby the company actually transfers the mineral rights outside the economic family in favor of the lenders. The result is that the debt will not appear as such on the balance sheet. This method is called the "production payment loan."

In a production payment loan, the lender has actually purchased a specified share of future mineral production (or cash proceeds thereof) from a designated portion of a mine, which serves as collateral for the loan. This takes the form of a legal interest in real property. The operating subsidiary (i.e., the seller of the production payment) is required to deliver to the lender a specified quantity of minerals (or cash) out of future production until principal and interest has been repaid. Thus the production payment loan provides greater repayment flexibility and is nonrecourse to the ultimate borrower.

Accounting treatment. Financial Accounting Standards Board Opinion No. 19 requires that oil and gas production payments payable in cash be reported as ordinary debt, but those payable in kind can be classified on the balance sheet as a "deferred revenue" item. They are also variously shown on the balance sheet as "mineral production payment liability," "deferred credit," or "proceeds from the sale of future production."

Because the nonmonetary production payment loan is not classified as debt, it may avoid restrictive covenants in loan and indenture agreements and may be treated more liberally by the rating agencies. For example, the mineral producing subsidiary may carry an asset called "leasehold" of $20,000,000 and a "liability for production payment" of $9,000,000. Rather than consolidate the asset and the liability with the parent, the net equity of $11,000,000 in the leasehold is all that would appear on the parent's balance sheet.

2.3 TIMBER HARVESTING VENTURE FOR FINANCING TIMBER PROPERTIES OFF-BALANCE SHEET

One structure has been developed specifically for the off-balance sheet financing of timber properties. It emphasizes the extent to which the desired accounting treatment depends upon the real transference of economic benefits and risks, particularly the risk of market price fluctuations.

How it works. A quantity of timber, without the underlying land, is sold by the owner ("Timber Company") to a newly created, thinly capitalized special purpose entity ("Shell Company") at fair market value. Shell Company is owned by an unrelated third party whose identity will be discussed shortly. Timber Company, who is in the timber harvesting business, enters into a cutting contract with Shell Company, under which it will harvest a specified amount of timber for Shell Company on an annual basis. This contract would be structured as an operating rather than a financial liability for Timber Company, and would cover its operating expenses.

Actual timber harvesting would commence one year after full ownership of the timber by Shell Company to assure capital gains tax treatment[7] upon sale of the timber. The annual cut would run between 7.5 percent and 10 percent of the total physical timber yield.

Timber Company would agree to make certain payments to Shell Company if a minimum annual specified timber harvest has *not* been achieved. Timber Company would disclose its aggregate commitment in the footnotes to its financial statements.[8] This would lessen (but would not completely eliminate) the business risk that would remain in Shell Company.

Timber Company would purchase the harvested timber from Shell Company each year on a take-and-pay basis. It would pay cash at a minimum base price sufficient to allow amortization of the debt incurred by Shell Company in the purchase of the properties. In addition, Timber Company would have to pay an increment above the base price tied to (1) the consumer price index of some other inflation index, and (2) real price appreciation in the market price of timber.

The increment would be shared by Timber Company and Shell Company on some basis—let's say 20 percent to Timber Company and 80 percent to Shell Company. Shell Company would receive cash for its portion, whereas Timber Company would merely be credited with an allocation that would accumulate each year and be received at the end of the contract period. Thus Timber Company's portion of the appreciation would be completely deferred.

Of particular importance to Shell Company is the appreciation of the uncut timber during the ten- to twelve-year period. The history of the particular property would suggest that, absent casualties, a physical growth factor of 2 to 5 percent per year could be expected. This growth would be realized by Shell Company upon termination of the venture through the exercise of a purchase option by Timber Company.

---

[7]Under §631a of the Internal Revenue Code. This discussion should be referenced when reading Chapter 11, "Tax-Inspired Financing."

[8]Timber Company could take the position that this obligation occurred in its normal course of doing business and was therefore an operating and not a financial liability.

Shifting the business risk. In order for the purchase option to avoid undermining the off-balance sheet nature of the transaction from Timber Company's standpoint, it must be nonmandatory and market-price related. Thus business risk is being shifted in a significant way to Shell Company. Comfort for Shell Company with respect to the exercise of the option would be derived from the overall business context (i.e., a detailed examination of the specific stumpage and fiber needs of Timber Company in the specific geographic market represented). Analysis should reveal that the shortfall to Timber Company upon nonexercise of the purchase option would not be in its best interest.

The actual amount of timber that would be subject to the purchase option would be comprised of (1) the quantity that had not been harvested under the annual cutting management, plus (2) an amount representing the physical growth factor, less (3) the amount representing Timber Company's subordinated interest in the yearly increments above the base price. Assuming the cutting contract would run for a period of ten to twelve years, and based on an annual physical cut of 7.5 percent beginning after the first year, approximately 17 to 32 percent of the initial timber quantity would remain upon termination. Assuming a 3 percent per year growth factor, the aggregate terminal quantity of the timber should be in a range between 44 and 50 percent of the initial amount.

chapter 3

How to Use Leases and Receivables in Off-Balance Sheet Financing

Leases remain the best known and most widely used off-balance sheet technique. A lease may be used by itself to remove a particular piece of equipment or real estate from the balance sheet, or it can be utilized in conjunction with many of the off-balance sheet structures that have already been considered. Despite FASB Statement No. 13, which provides comprehensive guidance for accounting for leases, many of the objectives of off-balance sheet financing can still be achieved using a lease. In addition to leases, this chapter examines the important exceptions to the consolidation rules that allow nonconsolidation of subsidiaries. The final section discusses a special off-balance sheet vehicle for the financing of receivables.

3.1 USING LEASES IN OFF-BALANCE SHEET FINANCING

One of the considerations in the evolving accounting treatment of leases has been the concept that certain types of leases have qualities similar to secured debt. This has resulted in the lease being capitalized on both sides of the balance sheet. FASB Statement No. 13 makes it more difficult to structure leases on an off-balance sheet basis, but it remains possible to structure a lease agreement so that it does not meet any of the criteria that would require its capitalization. Long-term leases that pass substantially all the risks and rewards of ownership of the leased property to the lessee continue to be accounted for as operating leases. In the operating lease, lease payments are accounted for rental expenses, as compared to the sales finance lease, which is accounted for as an outright sale.

3.1.1 Tax vs. Accounting Treatment of Leases

A distinction should be drawn between the treatment of leases for tax purposes and the treatment of leases for accounting purposes. The Internal Revenue Code has distinguished between "true leases" and conditional sales-type leases.[1] In true leases the tax benefits derived from the ownership of the leased property, such as depreciation, have accrued to the benefit of the lessor. The lessee has been able to deduct the full lease payment, and the investment tax credit ("ITC") could be claimed by either party.

Tax requirements for true leases and conditional sales leases. In order to qualify as a true lease under IRS guidelines, the fair market value of the leased property at the end of the lease term had to have an

---

[1]Recent changes under the Code have created "Safe harbor leases." See the discussion in Chapter 11.

expected value equal to or greater than 20 percent of the original cost of the leased property. In addition, the remaining useful life of the property had to be equal to or greater than 20 percent of the estimated original useful life of the property. Two further criteria required that the lessee could not have a bargain purchase option, and that the at-risk investment of the lessor at all times had to be equal to or greater than 20 percent of the cost of the leased property.

If the preceding criteria were not met, then the lessor could be deemed to have *legal* title to the property, but the lessee was the owner for *tax purposes*. Thus the lessee could claim the depreciation deduction and ITC, but could only deduct the interest portion of the rental payments for tax purposes.

Accounting requirements for capital and operating leases. For accounting purposes, as opposed to the tax definition, leases are distinguished as either capital leases or operating leases. The operating lease is off-balance sheet and the capital lease is not. A lease is accounted for as a capital lease if it meets any one of the following criteria:

- the lease term is equal to or greater than 75 percent of the estimated economic life of the property
- the net present value of the rental payments less any ITC retained by the lessor and other minimum required payments under the lease are equal to or greater that 90 percent of the fair market value of the leased property
- there is a bargain purchase option
- the lease otherwise transfers ownership of the property to the lessee by the end of the lease term.

The net present value of the unpaid lease rentals of a capital lease are reported as an asset and corresponding liability on the balance sheet, whereas at worst the future rental payments of an operating lease may appear in the footnotes. It should be pointed out that the requirements for qualifying as a true lease for tax purposes have been easier to meet than the financial accounting requirements for operating leases. Nearly all operating leases have been true leases.

3.1.2 Structuring Leases as Operating Leases to Qualify as Off-Balance Sheet Financing

Case 3.1, which follows, shows the significance of qualifying leases as operating leases in order to preserve the off-balance sheet nature of a financing. By incorporating several of the concepts previously discussed regarding joint ventures and equity accounting, it allows the sponsoring company (lessee) to treat leases as operating leases while retaining 50 percent of the long-term economic benefits of the property. Thus the structure circumvents the constraint that the lease not transfer ownership to the lessee by the end of the lease term.

CASE 3.1 HOW ONE COMPANY COMBINED OPERATING LEASES WITH A JOINT VENTURE TO AVOID AN EQUITY OFFERING AND RETAIN LONG-TERM ECONOMIC BENEFITS

Prodco[2] was a public company that desired to finance the development of its store locations on an off-balance sheet basis. The off-balance sheet financing was needed by Prodco in order to postpone its need for an equity issue, which otherwise would have been needed to maintain its debt-to-equity ratio. Thirty million dollars in debt financing was needed to purchase additional properties, the addition of which would have reduced Prodco's debt-to-equity ratio from 1.75x to 1.08x. If this amount of debt were raised on a conventional basis, as opposed to off-balance sheet, Prodco would have needed an equity offering. An equity offering was not viable at the time.

A further requirement was imposed by Prodco on the financing structure. Prodco desired to share in the long-term appreciation of properties. Although the company did not require total ownership, it sought at least a 50 percent position at the end of the lease term.

3.1.3 How the Leasing Joint Venture Was Structured and Operated

A joint venture structure was devised to accomplish the off-balance sheet financing, and three separate ventures were created using this structure. Each venture was structured as a partnership in which Prodco and an unrelated third party ("the Partner") each invested $500,000 in exchange for a 50 percent partnership interest in the joint venture. The remaining capital of each joint venture consisted of approximately $9,000,000 supplied in the form of mortgage debt by the Partner. Thus a total of $30 million was raised in three separate entities.

For purposes of simplicity only one of the joint ventures will be discussed in detail. All three of them functioned in essentially the same manner.

Real estate, including land and buildings, was purchased by the joint venture from Prodco. Some of the locations were completed stores while others required further development. The completed facilities were to be leased back to Prodco on an operating lease basis.

The $9,000,000 of long-term debt was the obligation of the joint venture and was nonrecourse to Prodco. It was secured by the land and buildings and an assignment of the leases with Prodco.

The term of the debt was 20 years with repayment on a level pay

---

[2]This is a fictitious name.

basis, whereas the leases were for terms of 15 years with two non-obligatory five-year renewal options. This mismatching of debt term and security was critical in obtaining the operating lease status of the leases. As further backup for the leases, Prodco guaranteed the lease payments for the initial lease term of 15 years. The lease payments were calculated to adequately cover the amortization of the notes for 15 years.

The lender had an optional "call" provision on the debt at the end of 15 years. This provision gave the lender a lever that it could utilize in the event that Prodco did not renew its leases at the end of 15 years.

The assets of the joint venture consisted of ten units, six of which had been recently opened and were currently being operated by Prodco. Four of the units were under development and had not yet been completed. The completed units were sold to the joint venture at historic costs and additional units were to be sold as completed. The proceeds of the $9,000,000 were to be taken down as the units were purchased by the joint venture, with equity contributions to be made by Prodco and the Partner on a pro-rata basis.

Prodco and the Partner, by virtue of their 50 percent ownership in the joint venture, were to share equally in the returns from the venture (with the exception of interest and principal repayments on the loan that flowed exclusively to the Partner). The returns consisted of the following three elements: (1) the distribution of the venture's net cash flow, which could include overages on sales of individual units, (2) tax consequences[3], and (3) gains from the sale of the properties during or at the end of the lease.

The overages were built into the lease payments from Prodco to the venture. The portion attributable to the Partner, although to be paid as received by the venture, was to be deducted from the Partner's allocation of the proceeds upon sale or liquidation.

A diagram showing the steps in the creation and operation of the venture appears in Exhibit 3.1.

Steps in the Creation and Use of the Joint Venture

1. Prodco invests $500,000. Partner invests $500,000 and lends $9,000,000 to the venture.
2. The venture purchases existing sites and has new buildings constructed for $10,000,000.

---

[3]The tax shelter benefits represented the smallest component of the overall return to the Partner.

EXHIBIT 3.1 The Use of a Leasing Joint Venture

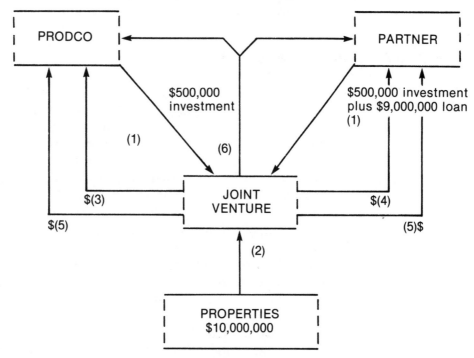

3. Prodco leases land and buildings from the venture.
4. The loan of $9,000,000 is repaid by the venture.
5. During the lease term, Prodco and the Partner share equally in the net cash flows and tax shelter benefits of the venture.
6. During or at the end of the lease term, the properties are sold and profits are divided equally by Prodco and the Partner.

Prodco entered into a management contract with the venture under which it would be required to meet certain performance standards, with the right of cancellation being retained by the venture. Prodco was to select, develop, and sell the sites as well as manage the day-to-day operations of the venture, such as rent collection and distribution of excess cash.

It was expected that the majority of the properties would be sold at the end of the lease term. However, the possibility existed that certain properties might not be performing satisfactorily. Prodco, as manager of the venture, was given the right to remove those properties from the venture through sale or exchange if their appreciation or sales volume fell below minimum annual levels. The removal of all other properties suggested by Prodco would require the consent of the Partner. The cash received from the sale of properties had to be applied pro rata to the reduction of the outstanding debt.

3.1.4 Cash-Flow Impact of the Joint Venture

The following exhibit shows the cash-flow impact of the joint venture upon Prodco and the Partner. A 50 percent marginal tax bracket had been assumed at the time of this analysis with a 28 percent capital gains rate applied to the estimated gain on disposal of the properties. The projected cash flows further assumed that Prodco's operating lease commitment was exercised for only one of the two five-year renewal periods. The benefits to the partnership from the percentage overage of sales to be paid by the lessee (Prodco) have not been considered.

Of approximately $10,000,000 of initial capital, roughly 44 percent was to be used to purchase buildings and 56 percent to purchase land. Approximately 25 percent of the building's original cost was depreciated over eight years and the remaining portion over twenty years, both on a straight-line basis. Notwithstanding the fact that at least one new property was to be included in the venture, the cash flows have assumed that all properties included were existing properties. New properties acquired by the venture would have resulted in investment tax credits on a portion of the building costs.

The cash flows were based on a 13 percent constant on the leases, without the benefit of 2 percent sales overages, and a 12.5 percent coupon associated with the mortgage debt. The overage was to consist of a 2 percent sales surcharge applied on an individual unit basis to that portion of the revenues that were in excess of $1,250,000 but less than $1,750,000.

The land was assumed to appreciate at 20 percent per year and the buildings were expected to be sold at one-half of original cost.

3.2 PUTTING THE CONSOLIDATION RULE TO WORK IN OFF-BALANCE SHEET FINANCING

Thus far the discussion of off-balance sheet financing has focused on a number of concepts derived from project finance. To the extent that a project sponsor has had less then 50 percent "ownership" of a project, as for example in Case 2.1A, the rules of equity accounting apply. However, once the sponsor has gone over 50 percent ownership, equity accounting is no longer operative and the rules governing consolidation apply.

TABLE 3.1 Return on Investment for Joint Venture Partnership ($000)

	1981	1982	1983	1984	1985	1986	1987	1988	1989	1990	1991	1992	1993	1994	1995	1996	1997	1998	1999	2000
INCOME STATEMENT OF JOINT VENTURE																				
Lease Revenues	1300	1300	1300	1300	1300	1300	1300	1300	1300	1300	1300	1300	1300	1300	1300	1300	1300	1300	1300	1300
Less: Interest	1121	1107	1090	1072	1051	1027	1001	971	937	898	855	806	751	689	619	540	450	349	235	106
Depreciation	382	382	382	382	382	382	382	382	174	174	174	174	174	174	174	174	174	174	174	174
PRETAX INCOME (LOSS)	(203)	(189)	(172)	(154)	(133)	(109)	(83)	(53)	189	228	271	320	375	437	507	586	676	777	891	1020
CASH FLOW OF JOINT VENTURE																				
Lease Revenues	1300	1300	1300	1300	1300	1300	1300	1300	1300	1300	1300	1300	1300	1300	1300	1300	1300	1300	1300	1300
Less: Interest	1121	1107	1090	1072	1051	1027	1001	971	937	898	855	806	751	689	619	540	450	349	235	106
Principal Payments	112	126	143	161	182	206	232	262	296	335	378	427	482	544	614	694	783	884	998	1127
NET CASH FLOW	67	67	67	67	67	67	67	67	67	67	67	67	67	67	67	67	67	67	67	67
CASH FLOW TO PARTNER[1]																				
Interest Income (taxed at 50%)	561	554	545	536	525	514	500	486	469	449	427	403	375	345	310	270	225	175	118	33
Principal	112	126	143	161	182	206	232	262	296	335	378	427	482	544	614	694	783	884	998	1127
Share of JV's net cash flow	33	33	33	33	33	33	33	33	33	33	33	33	33	33	33	33	33	33	33	33
Share of JV's tax shelter (exposure)	51	48	43	39	34	28	21	14	(48)	(57)	(68)	(80)	(94)	(110)	(127)	(147)	(169)	(194)	(223)	(255)
NET CASH FLOW	757	761	764	769	774	781	786	795	750	760	770	783	796	812	830	850	872	898	926	938
INVESTMENT	(9500)																			
NET UPON SALE OF PROPERTIES[2]																				

At a compounded annual appreciation rate of 8% = 9,083
12% = 17,062
16% = 32,771
20% = 62,984

Notes:
1. The net cash flow to the Partner consists of (a) The interest payment taxed at 50%, (b) the principal payment, (c) the Partner's share of the joint venture's net cash flow, and (d) the Partner's share of the after tax (at the Partner's assumed marginal tax rate of 50%) cash effect of the joint venture's tax shelter impact.
2. Net upon sale of properties consists of the Partner's 50% share of the proceeds of the asset sales.

43

3.2.1 Four Areas Excluded From Consolidation Requirements

Although a company generally must consolidate a subsidiary if it has voting ownership of more than 50 percent, certain subsidiaries are regularly excluded from this requirement on the basis that they are in an unrelated business. Such subsidiaries may conduct business in the areas of finance, insurance, leasing, and real estate. If a company's activities reach a significant size in any of these areas—financing of sales to customers, obtaining insurance coverage, developing and leasing real estate, or maintaining a fleet of cars or trucks—it becomes attractive from both an operational and accounting standpoint to set up a captive subsidiary rather than administer the activity directly.

Typically, a statement is made in the footnotes to the financial statements along the following lines:

> *Consolidated*: The consolidated financial statements include those of the company and its wholly owned and majority subsidiaries other than its wholly owned captive insurance company. The Company accounts for its investments in unconsolidated companies, including the captive insurance company, on an equity basis.[4]

This statement, combined with an examination of the balance sheet, indicates that the investment in the subsidiary does not appear to be substantial. Out of total assets of $701,799,000, investments in the unconsolidated companies amount to $20,341,000. However, there is no indication as to the leverage in the subsidiary and this cannot be determined from the Annual Report.

The American Institute of Certified Public Accountants' (AICPA) Accounting Research Bulletin No. 51, *Consolidated Financial Statements*, specifically exempts insurance and banking subsidiaries of a manufacturing concern from the consolidation requirement, as well as finance subsidiaries (which will be discussed subsequently). The rationale of the Bulletin is that the activities of the subsidiary are essentially different from those of the parent. Thus the argument is made that consolidation would not result in a more meaningful presentation of the combined activities of the two entities. On the contrary, consolidation would cause a distortion of the parent's operating results.[5]

One-line consolidation. When a subsidiary is not consolidated, Accounting Principles Board Opinion No. 18,[6] which has already been discussed in conjunction with joint ventures in Chapter 1, required that the parent account for its investment by the equity method. Thus in the case of an unconsolidated subsidiary, the parent's balance sheet would include one line item or account representing its percentage

---

[4] 1981 Annual Report Harsco Corporation.
[5] The SEC has ARB 51 under review and may require consolidation in the near future.
[6] *The Equity Method of Accounting for Investments in Common Stock*, See page 13.

ownership of the equity, which would then be periodically adjusted to reflect net income or loss of the subsidiary on a pro-rata basis. This is commonly referred to as a one-line consolidation.

3.2.2 Problems Posed by Nonconsolidation

The consolidation rules are criticized for providing too much flexibility in allowing nonconsolidation. Thus companies in the same industry follow different consolidation policies, which often makes direct comparison of their financial statements quite misleading. Those companies that do not consolidate are required to provide summary information about their unconsolidated subsidiaries in the footnotes. If unconsolidated subsidiaries meet certain size tests, then complete separate financial statements of the subsidiary are required in certain filings with the Securities and Exchange Commission.

Nonconsolidation is also criticized for masking the liabilities (and less frequently, the assets) of the parent. This set of rules has helped to encourage growth in the number of captive finance subsidiaries. It is a frequent practice for roughly equal amounts of receivables and associated debt (secured by those receivables) to be transferred to the unconsolidated captive finance subsidiary. As a consequence the current assets and their attendant liabilities are eliminated from the consolidated balance sheet. The parent company, by virtue of its ownership of the subsidiary (which is usually 100 percent) effectively controls the receivables. In addition, the parent may provide guarantees of the subsidiary's debt obligations.

Example: company with a finance subsidiary. In contrast to the previous example of the unconsolidated insurance subsidiary, the following is an example of a company with a substantial finance subsidiary:

> *"Consolidation"* Except for its wholly owned subsidiary, ABC Finance Company ("ABC Finance"), all subsidiary companies are consolidated. The investments in ABC Finance 50 percent-owned subsidiaries are treated using the equity method.

The footnote would then provide a condensed balance sheet and income statement. Although debt oligations might be roughly 95 percent of total capital in the subsidiaries, debt might only be 40 percent of capital in the parent company. Thus the lack of consolidation would have a significant impact on the Company's apparent financial strength. On a consolidated basis debt would have been nearly 45 percent of total capital.

Credit support. The remainder of the footnote would disclose the additional liability by the parent company to stand behind contracts in default that were financed by ABC Finance. In order to understand the language of the footnote, it should be pointed out that ABC Company, a wholly owned subsidiary of the Company and consolidated with the parent, is a manufacturer of equipment. The critical language follows:

ABC Finance is solely engaged in financing the sale of ABC Company equipment and ABC Company guarantees contracts that become in default.

The impact of the commitment suggested by such language was that the parent company, through ABC Company, was guaranteeing a certain interest coverage ratio on the debt of ABC Finance. Although ABC Finance's debt did not appear in the consolidated balance sheet, the credit of the parent company stood fully behind it.

This is not at all unusual in the case of finance subsidiaries. The credit support often takes the form of an operating agreement between the parent company and its finance subsidiary in which the holders of the long-term debt of the subsidiary also take part. The parent company may commit to compensate the finance subsidiary with fees sufficient to cover interest expense and amortization of debt. Also frequently required by long-term lenders to the finance subsidiary are restrictions upon the maintenence of net worth, creation of additional debt, payment of dividends, and acquisition of capital stock. These obligations and restrictions ultimately fall upon the parent company.

It will be shown in Section 3.3 that there are other ways to finance receivables off-balance sheet. Unlike the typical unconsolidated finance subsidiary approach, more innovative types of off-balance sheet techniques for the financing of receivables actually allow the company to shed a good deal of the business risk to an unrelated third party.

3.2.3 Realizing Operational and Tax Benefits From a Captive Leasing Company

A third form of captive arrangement involves leasing companies. There are a number of reasons to set up a captive leasing company, both operational and from a tax-planning standpoint.

Operational benefits. An example of an operational motivation for the creation of a captive leasing company is provided by the following situation: A company that was producing a particular product distributed this product through a series of independent national distributors. As opposed to merely aiding the distributors through contributions to advertising, which is frequently the case, the company wished to aid the distributor truck fleet financially and operationally.

It set up a captive leasing company that provided the vehicles for the distributors. The company was able to negotiate favorable discounts and warranties for large-scale purchases of trucks. It also benefited from other economies of scale such as maintenance, the purchase of gas and tires, the selling of used trucks to realize residual values at better than wholesale, and the obtaining of insurance coverage.

As is frequently the case, the parent company entered into a maintenance contract with its leasing subsidiary similar to the arrangements previously discussed for the financing of receivables by a captive finance company. Under this arrangement, the parent was required to maintain certain interest coverage ratios of the subsidiary and to provide it backup of the handling of bad debts.

Tax benefits. Another motivation for the creation of a leasing subsidiary is based on tax planning. When the leasing arrangement is motivated by tax considerations, the parent company usually has no desire to get into the leasing business from an operational or strategic standpoint. The leasing subsidiary will purchase and retain ownership of equipment that it leases to a third party. It will retain the tax benefits and it will attempt to significantly reduce business risk by limiting its leases to known lessees of high-quality credit standing.

The return on the investment by the leasing subsidiary in the equipment consists of revenues from lease rental plus depreciation and investment tax credits.[7] Although the leasing subsidiary is not consolidated for financial reporting purposes, it is consolidated for tax purposes.[8] The tax benefits of the subsidiary can therefore be applied against the taxable income of the parent.

Example: An International Corporation. The following corporation provides an example of a leasing subsidiary as revealed in its footnotes:

Basis of Consolidation: The consolidated financial statements include the accounts of all significant subsidiaries, except XYZ Leasing Corporation, a finance company, which is accounted for on the equity basis. Intercompany balances and transactions are eliminated.

A detailed footnote would then show the condensed balance sheet and income statement of XYZ Leasing Corporation. The equity in XYZ Leasing Corporation would be carried on the parent's balance sheet at say $20.0 million, whereas XYZ's balance sheet might show liabilities of $25.0 million against total capital of $45.0 million.

3.2.4 Real Estate Subsidiaries

The final area of discussion under the general topic of consolidation involves real estate related subsidiaries. There is a broad spectrum of activities involving real estate that, because of the consolidation rules, do not appear on the balance sheet of the parent company.

An Example. The following is typical language of a real estate mortgage subsidiary:

Principles of Consolidation. The consolidated financial statements include all wholly owned subsidiaries except J&J Mortgage Com-

---

[7]Unless it is a "conditional sales" type lease, where tax benefits are passed on to the lessee.
[8]The same holds true for finance subsidiaries.

pany.[9] Investments in affiliates, which consist of ABC Inc. (a 50 percent joint venture) and J&J Mortgage Company (100 percent owned, included in Other Realty Assets) are stated at cost plus equity in undistributed earnings. Separate financial statements are not included because they are not significant.

Example: A development company. Another example shows the investment of a major corporation in its unconsolidated XYZ Development Company,[10] a wholly owned real estate developer. Using the equity method, XYZ was carried at $210 million. XYZ operated a number of real estate developments independently and also entered into joint ventures with third party developers. Detailed Statements of Income and Financial Position of XYZ were given in the Annual Report. A condensed balance sheet follows:

Condensed Balance Sheet, XYZ Development Company ($000)

	At Fiscal Year End 1984 XYZ	At Fiscal Year End Joint Ventures
Assets		
Real Property	400,000	450,000
Investment in Joint Ventures	10,000	—
Total Assets	410,000	450,000
Liabilities	200,000	270,000
Joint Venture Capital		
XYZ	—	(8,000)
Others	—	(12,000)
Shareholders' Equity	210,000	—

Thus there were over $850 million in real estate assets involving the parent or XYZ credit to varying degrees that were not consolidated in the parent company's balance sheet. It cannot be determined from the Annual Report the extent to which XYZ was contingently liable for cost overruns or other exposure in these real estate projects.

Before leaving the subject of consolidation, one final example underlines the amount of flexibility in the accounting treatment of subsidiaries. The following fictitious company consists of three wholly owned, independently operated subsidiaries serving three different

[9]This is a fictitious name.
[10]This is a fictitious name.

industries: (1) heavy equipment, (2) food distribution and (3) truck servicing. Despite the diversity of its business, its annual report carries the following language:

> *Consolidation.* The consolidated financial statements do not include the accounts of the Company's wholly owned drug chain subsidiary which is not consolidated because of the nature of its operations, and is accounted for by the equity method.

A literal application of the consolidation rules allowed the parent to avoid consolidation of its drug chain operation. Thus the accounting rules governing consolidation continue to create opportunities for off balance sheet financing.

3.3 HOW TO FINANCE RECEIVABLES OFF-BALANCE SHEET

Creation of a captive finance subsidiary is not the most common method of financing receivables. The most widespread method is to turn the receivables directly over to a bank or commercial finance company.

3.3.1 Nonrecourse Receivables Financing

If the sale of the receivables to the financing entity is "with recourse," it is in substance a secured borrowing. That is, the purchaser of the receivables has recourse to the seller as if the seller were really borrowing against the receivables. The transaction is treated as a liability by most accountants on the seller's books.[11]

The objective of a seller of receivables seeking off-balance sheet financing would be to treat the sale of the receivables as a true sale, with a reduction in receivables and a similar reduction in liabilities through the application of the proceeds of the sale. This can be accomplished if the transaction occurs "without recourse." In a sale of receivables without recourse, those receivables that remain uncollected are not the responsibility of the seller. The collection risk is borne by the buyer/lender, who has no recourse to the seller.

There is, however, an additional cost to the seller in the sale of receivables without recourse, resulting from the increased exposure of the lender. When receivables are sold nonrecourse there is a greater discount to allow for bad debts than if the sale were with recourse. Billions of dollars of receivables are financed each year using both of these methods.

---

[11]Pronouncement No. 77 of the FASB in December, 1983, suggests that recourse is not the controlling factor, but a weighing of the elements of risk, ownership, and residuals.

3.3.2 How to Remove Receivables From the Balance Sheet, Shed the Business Risk, and Reduce the Discount

A new method has evolved that allows a corporation to remove receivables from its balance sheet, while at the same time completely shedding the business risk (i.e., they are nonrecourse to the seller). Most importantly, it provides a vehicle for reducing the discount that must be offered by the seller of receivables when such a sale is nonrecourse.

Under this new method the vehicle that holds the receivables for the sponsoring corporation may be either a trust[12] or a corporation. In the example that follows, the corporate structure is utilized.

CASE 3.2 HOW MADCO[13] HANDLED RECEIVABLES FINANCING

Madco wished to remove certain accounts receivable from its balance sheet. It established a special purpose corporation (Receivco). Madco and Receivco entered into a contract whereby Receivco was to purchase certain specified accounts receivable from Madco on a regular basis during the next five years. The purchases by Receivco were to be made at a discount from the invoiced amounts of the receivables. The discount was calculated in such a manner that it would be sufficient to cover Receivco's borrowing costs, administrative and other expenses over the life of the receivables.

Madco's receivables had a clearly demonstrable and stable collection record. (*Important*: It is a requirement that any company considering this receivables financing structure should be able to clearly demonstrate its credit loss history.) The collection record allowed Receivco to obtain financing for the purchases of receivables from Madco in the form of five-year notes.

In order for Receivco to obtain the highest possible credit standing on its notes, thereby minimizing its interest costs, an insurance company[14] provided insurance against aggregate first losses for uncollected receivables. The percentage of loss required to trigger the insurance was substantially higher than the loss history associated with the particular receivables. The ratio of insurable loss to historical loss was four-to-one. That is, the insurance company was willing to guarantee all losses up to 8 percent of the amount of receivables outstanding, whereas the historical loss percentage was actually as low as 2 percent.

---

[12]See the discussion of trusts in Chapter 4.
[13]This is a fictitious name.
[14]A letter of credit could have been used in place of the insurance policy.

The transaction is summarized in the following exhibit.

EXHIBIT 3.2 Off-Balance Sheet Accounts Receivable Financing

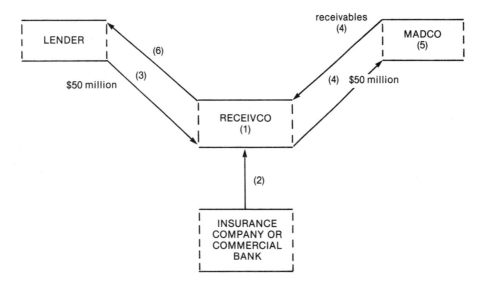

Steps in Receivables Financing

1. Receivco is created, either as a corporation or trust owned by an unrelated third party.
2. Insurance company issues policy or commercial bank issues letter of credit to cover uncollected receivables.
3. Lender loans Receivco $50 million against the security of the receivables and the insurance policy.
4. Receivco uses the $50 million to purchase receivables from Madco without recourse.
5. Madco handles the collection of the receivables under a management contract with Receivco.
6. Receivco services the debt as receivables are collected.

From an accounting standpoint, Madco expected to treat the discount upon sale of the receivables as a loss on the sale of assets, which was to be expensed on its income statement. Madco would treat the discount as an interest expense for tax purposes.

Alternative borrowing arrangement. It should be pointed out that this structure can be readily adapted to a floating rate type borrowing arrangement for Receivco. Receivco, instead of borrowing with five year notes, might issue commercial paper backed by Letters of Credit from a major commercial bank.

Receivco would be functioning in a manner similar to an independent finance company or factoring company, but at what would appear to be a substantially lower cost to Madco. There would be no equity requirement on the part of Madco to support Receivco's debt as there would be if Madco were to issue debt through a captive finance subsidiary.

Although this is a relatively new financing structure for receivables, its use promises to grow among companies whose receivables have good collection records.

chapter 4

How to Use Limited Partnerships and Trusts for Greater Flexibility in Tax Planning

There are two off-balance sheet financing structures that allow for a great deal of flexibility in the area of tax planning: limited partnerships and trusts. In the discussion that follows the limited partnership is first distinguished from a general partnership. Then the limited partnership is examined from two different perspectives: that of the general partner and that of the limited partner. Both construction trusts and grantor trusts are discussed in the later portion of the chapter.

4.1 PARTNERSHIPS AND LIMITED PARTNERSHIPS COMPARED

When a joint venture is constituted as a general partnership with several general partners, each general partner has unlimited liability for the obligations of the partnership. A *limited* partnership is a partnership formed by two or more entities having as members one or more general partners and one or more limited partners. The primary purpose of a limited partnership is to allow one or more participants in a venture to invest a limited amount in the partnership without incurring the unlimited liability of the general partner.

4.1.1 Characteristics of a Partnership

It is more practical to consider the characteristics of a partnership rather than attempt to define it precisely. This is because partnerships are created and governed by state law and state law definitions of partnerships are generally inadequate from a business standpoint. Partnerships are broadly defined as *associations of two or more persons to carry on as co-owners of a business for profit,* or *a contractual relationship existing between two or more persons who join together to carry on a trade or business, each contributing money, property, labor, or skill, and all with the expectation of sharing in the profits and losses of the business.*

Liability. In a partnership all the partners are liable jointly and severally for all the debts[1] and obligations of the partnership, including liabilities resulting from a breach of trust or wrongful acts of the partners acting in the ordinary course of business of the partnership or with the authority of its copartners. Each partner has a right to be repaid its contributions to the partnership, whether by way of capital or advances to the partnership, and to share equally[2] in the profits and surplus remaining after all liabilities, including those to the partners,

---

[1]Unless the debt is specifically nonrecourse.
[2]The share or profits and losses is fixed by the partnership agreement.

are satisfied. Each partner must contribute toward the losses according to its share in the profits.

Management. All partners in the partnership begin by having equal rights in the management and conduct of the partnership business. However, it is customary to make one of the partners the "managing" partner, whose responsibilities are specified in a management contract. Matters arising that are not specifically delegated to the managing partner may be decided by a majority of the partners.

4.1.2 Characteristics of a Limited Partnership

Typically, the state statutes that govern the formation and operation of limited partnerships have language similar to this: "A limited partner shall not become liable as a general partner unless, in addition to the exercise of his rights and powers as a limited partner, he takes part in the control of the business." Therefore a limited partner must be content to be an inactive or passive partner.[3] The limited partner can, however, exercise voting rights specified in the certificate of limited partnership affecting the basic structure of the partnership, including the following matters or others of a similar nature: (1) election or removal of general partners, (2) termination of the partnership, (3) amendment of the partnership agreement, and (4) sale of all or substantially all of the assets of the partnership.

Limited partner's rights and responsibilities. A limited partner generally has the same rights as a general partner to inspect and copy the partnership books and have access to all information affecting the partnership. Where there are several limited partners there may be an agreement that one or more of the limited partners shall have a priority over other limited partners as to the return of their contributions, and as to their compensation by way of income. In the absence of a formal agreement, all the limited partners stand upon equal footing.

The limited partner is not entitled to receive any part of its capital contribution until all liabilities of the partnership (except liabilities to the general and limited partners) have been paid and the consent of other members is obtained. A limited partner can have the partnership dissolved if it rightfully but unsuccessfully demands the return of its capital contribution, or if the liabilities of the partnership have not been paid and the partnership property is insufficient for their payment. Upon dissolution of a limited partnership, the creditors have the first priority claim to the assets, with the limited partners then

---

[3]It should be noted that one entity may be both a general and a limited partner, being treated as a general partner except in respect of its contribution as against the other partners.

coming ahead of the general partner both in respect to profits and return of capital contributions.

Loans. It should also be noted that a limited partner may make a bona fide loan to the partnership, over and above its capital contribution. The use of loans by limited partners to cover cost overruns is discussed in Case 4.2.

4.2 HOW A PARTNERSHIP IS TAXED

Unlike a corporation, a partnership is not a separate taxable entity and is not subject to federal income tax. Rather, each partner is subject to income tax only in its individual or separate capacity. The partnership serves merely as a conduit through which each partner takes its distributive share of the partnership's capital gains and losses, ordinary income and loss (including interest and depreciation deductions), and tax credits regardless of whether there are actual distributions to the partner. The distributive shares are determined by the partnership agreement.

For federal income tax purposes, the Internal Revenue Code gives a much broader definition than under state law.[4] It defines a partnership as a syndicate, group, pool, joint venture, or other unincorporated organization through or by means of which any business, financial operation, or venture is carried on, and that is not classified as a corporation, trust, or estate. An individual, estate, trust, corporation, or another partnership can each be a partner in the same partnership.

A limited partnership can provide the pass-through tax advantages of the partnership form while limiting the limited partners' liability to their original investments. It accomplishes this through the use of nonrecourse financing, which allows the limited partners to deduct losses in excess of their original investment.

In nonrecourse financing, the project acquires assets with loan proceeds and these serve as security for the loan. The liability, however, is not assumed (i.e., it is "nonrecourse") to any of the partners. As a result, all the limited and general partners are considered as sharing the nonrecourse liabilities (for tax purposes) in the same proportion as they share partnership profits. Because a partner's tax basis in its partnership interest is increased by its share of liabilities, a limited partner can deduct losses in excess of its actual investment in the partnership because of the additional tax basis created by the nonrecourse debt.

---

[4]Several state law definitions appear on page 55.

4.2.1 How the General Partner Can Avoid the Problem of Unlimited Liability

Although the limited partnership form restricts the liability of the limited partners, the general partner retains its unlimited liability just as it would in a normal partnership. However, the general partner can avoid the unlimited liability problem by being constituted as a corporation. There are a number of constraints imposed upon the general partner if it is a corporation. These include a limit on the amount of ownership of the general partner by the limited partners, and a net worth requirement for the general partner of at least 10 percent of the capital contributions of the partnership.

4.3 USING LIMITED PARTNERSHIPS IN REAL ESTATE, OIL AND GAS, AND NEW PRODUCT FINANCING

Limited partnerships have proliferated in recent years primarily to meet the needs of certain classes of investors who have wanted to limit their liability or exposure in a project, yet maximize the tax benefits flowing to them. The corporate form limits liability but it does not allow the flow through of tax benefits except in very small projects. The limited partnership form has been used extensively in tax-sheltered investment programs in oil drilling ventures and real estate, as well as new product marketing.

4.3.1 When a Company Acts as General Partner

An Example. An example of a company using this off-balance sheet financing technique in the real estate area is embodied in the following language in its footnotes:

> The Company has formed a limited partnership that will own a number of properties to be managed by a wholly owned subsidiary of the Company. The Company will serve as general partner, and will contribute its interest in certain work to date. Upon closing of the sale of the limited partnership interests, the company will be reimbursed for its investment. The Company has agreed to advance up to $50.0 million to cover short falls in partnership debt service and construction cost overruns.

Note that the company, as general partner in the limited partnership, is committing to advance a total of $50.0 million to cover debt service and cost overruns. This is on top of its capital investment in the properties of at least $140 million.

A limited partnership for oil and gas drilling. The following provides an example of the use of the limited partnership structure for oil and gas drilling ventures. A parent company's balance sheet would carry accounts receivable and notes receivable from affiliated partnerships as separate asset line items, as well as a mineral properties account. These accounts must be interpreted in conjunction with the following language in the footnotes:

"Partnership Interests"

The Company has interests in various private oil and gas limited partnerships, and recognizes revenue when the wells have been successfully completed. Its share of the assets and liabilities is included in Mineral Properties in the consolidated balance sheet.

The footnotes would indicate that there are further liabilities on the part of the Company as General Partner. These are of two types: a contingent liability for the debt of the partnership and an operational liability in the form of "turn-key contracts," which require the general partner to complete the projects within certain time and cost constraints. The contingent liability for debt is typically covered by the following language:

The Company, as general partner to various limited partnerships, has contingent liability for debts of those partnerships. The Company is the guarantor for a loan agreement extended to one such partnership by a major bank in the amount of $5,000,000.

The language regarding the operational exposure of the Company would be as follows:

The Company typically enters into turnkey drilling contracts with its affiliated partnerships and recognizes income and expense on these contracts when a well is completed using the completed contract method.

4.3.2 Why Companies May Opt for Limited Partnership Status

Thus far the focus has been upon the use of the limited partnership structure from the standpoint of the company that is willing to act as General Partner. This structure cannot be used when there is no one prepared to assume the risks of a general partner because the state statutes (which define and create limited partnerships) require at least one general partner in every limited partnership. However, a company may wish to assume the role of limited partner in a partnership for a number of reasons.

A company may seek limited partner status rather than act as general partner because it is unfamiliar with the operational risks in the project and does not want a management role. It may prefer to remain a passive investor with limited exposure. The primary attractiveness of such a position, where control is relinquished to the managing partner, is usually the tax benefits that flow to the limited partner.

4.4 ECONOMIC ANALYSIS FROM THE GENERAL PARTNER'S PERSPECTIVE

The situation frequently arises where a public corporation wishes to enter into a new business that is of significant size relative to the overall business of the original company. The new business requires a substantial initial investment and there is a lead time of three to five years before the investment in the new business begins to pay off. In the meantime, funds must be obtained and allocated to the new business. The borrowing costs of the needed funds and other carrying costs of the new business result in an adverse impact on the sponsor company's earnings per share.

It is often very difficult for management to plan on a long-range basis because of the need to consider the short-run impact on earnings per share and other highly visible measures of performance. Despite overriding strategic considerations, management may be forced to make the "wrong" decision. The following case, which is modelled after an actual situation that occurred in 1981, highlights the dilemma of management in being responsive to short-term measures of performance. The off-balance sheet financing mechanism is chosen over an alternative structure in order to meet short-run objectives at the expense of overall economic return.

CASE 4.1 COLAMED AS GENERAL PARTNER

A public company that shall be referred to as "Colamed, Inc."[5] wished to expand into a new line of business. It was considering the creation of a subsidiary for this new line of business, the investment decision for which was to be based upon an economic horizon of seven years. The expected impact of the wholly owned subsidiary (which would be consolidated) on Colamed's overall performance for financial reporting purposes can be analyzed with the aid of the following three tables: (1) Table 4.1 shows Colamed's projected performance over the seven year period, (2) Table 4.2 shows the projected performance of the new "Zolar" subsidiary over the seven year period, and (3) Table 4.3 shows the projected consolidated performance of the two entities.

Colamed's projected performance. Table 4.1 begins with a base year, 1981. Interest expense was assumed to be at a rate of 20 percent in 1981 and 18 percent per annum thereafter. The tax rate was 46 percent of pretax income less investment tax credits, and depreciation was five year straight line on applicable assets. It had further been assumed that the average debt outstanding in any year was that year's beginning level of debt outstanding plus that year's ending level of debt outstanding divided by two.

---

[5]This is a fictitious name.

TABLE 4.1 Colamed Proforma Income Statements (Parent Company) ($ millions except EPS)

	Base Year 1980	1981	1982	1983	1984	1985	1986	1987
Sales	172.2	209.3	230.8	267.5	310.1	359.7	417.4	484.6
Operating Profit	44.0	51.2	59.5	69.2	80.6	93.3	109.3	127.4
Interest Expense	6.0	6.7	6.0	5.5	4.9	4.4	3.7	3.3
Other Income	2.0	2.0	2.0	2.0	2.0	2.0	2.0	2.0
Profit Before Tax	45.0	51.5	65.5	75.7	87.7	101.5	117.6	136.1
Tax at 46%	20.7	23.7	30.1	34.8	40.3	46.7	54.1	62.6
Net Income	24.3	27.8	35.4	40.9	47.4	54.8	63.5	73.5
EPS (10, 136, 250 shares)	2.40	2.74	3.49	4.04	4.68	5.41	6.26	7.25

TABLE 4.2 Zolar Company Proforma Income Statements (Subsidiary) ($ millions)

	1981	1982	1983	1984	1985	1986	1987
Sales	2.3	4.6	30.1	64.8	69.5	77.2	77.5
Operating Profit	(4.4)	1.0	9.6	16.7	17.7	19.8	19.9
Interest Expense	1.5	4.7	8.3	9.5	8.2	6.8	5.3
Depreciation	2.8	8.0	13.2	13.2	13.5	10.8	5.7
Profit Before Tax	(8.6)	(11.7)	(12.0)	(6.0)	(4.0)	(2.2)	8.9
Tax at 46%	—	—	—	—	—	1.0[1]	4.1[1]
Add ITC[2]	1.6	2.8	2.9	.1	.1	.1	.1
Net Income	(8.6)	(11.7)	(12.0)	(6.0)	(4.0)	1.3	4.9

[1]Net operating loss carryforwards have been ignored since losses of the subsidiary would be utilized by the consolidated group.
[2]This ITC cannot be used by the subsidiary except in 1986 and 1987, but would be utilized upon consolidation—see Table 4.3.

Zolar's projected performance. Colamed capitalized its new Zolar subsidiary by investing $7.4 million in Zolar in 1981 in the form of equity, with the subsidiary borrowing an additional $14.8 million (which included interest on the debt). In 1982 Colamed planned to invest $11.1 million in Zolar with Zolar borrowing an additional $22.1 million, and in 1983 Colamed expected to make an investment of $9.5 million with the subsidiary borrowing an additional $18.9 million. Construction was to be completed in 1983, with debt repayment to begin in the following year. The following table shows the results of the Zolar subsidiary.

Projected consolidated performance. What cannot be discerned from Table 4.1 and Table 4.2 is the cost of the equity that Colamed would have to borrow for its investment in the Zolar subsidiary. This is accounted for in the following table under the line item "Equity Borrowing Costs." The consolidated income statement of Colamed and Zolar would look like this:

TABLE 4.3 Condensed Consolidated Proforma Income Statements (Colamed and Subsidiary) ($ millions)

	1981	1982	1983	1984	1985	1986	1987
Profit Before Tax (Parent)	51.5	65.5	75.7	87.7	101.5	117.6	136.1
Profit Before Tax (Subsidiary)	(8.6)	(11.7)	(12.0)	(6.0)	(4.0)	2.2	8.9
"Equity" Borrowing Costs	.7	2.3	4.2	5.0	5.0	5.0	5.0
Profit Before Tax (Consolidated)	42.1	51.5	59.6	76.7	92.5	114.8	140.0
Net Income (Consolidated)	24.3	30.6	35.1	41.5	50.0	59.7	75.5
EPS (Consolidated)	2.40	3.02	3.46	4.09	4.93	5.89	7.47
% Change in EPS from Colamed Nonconsolidated	(12.4)	(13.5)	(14.4)	(13.0)	(8.9)	(5.9)	.3

Before the creation of its Zolar subsidiary, Colamed was projecting the kind of steady earnings growth (in Table 4.1) that would have been quite attractive to a public shareholder. However, despite the fact in this actual example that there were long-run strategic considerations and financial justifications for creating the new subsidiary, Colamed as a public company was inhibited in doing so. This was because the projected impact of Zolar on Colamed's earnings per share *in the short run* were devastating when the new subsidiary was consolidated with the parent company.

The negative impact on Colamed's balance sheet was equally apparent in the early years, as is shown in the following two tables.

TABLE 4.4 Colamed Proforma Condensed Balance Sheet (Before Acquisition) ($ millions)

	Base Year 1980	1981	1982	1983	1984	1985	1986	1987
Long Term Debt	81.2	74.4	66.9	61.0	55.0	48.9	41.6	37.8
Equity Before Adjustments	114.6	132.3	152.9	179.9	210.2	245.3	285.9	332.9
Plus: Net Profit	24.3	27.8	35.4	40.9	47.4	54.8	63.5	73.5
Less: Dividends	6.5	7.3	8.3	10.6	12.3	14.2	16.4	19.1
Year-End Equity	132.4	152.9	179.9	210.2	245.3	285.9	332.9	387.4
Selected Ratios:								
LTD/Equity	.62	.49	.37	.29	.22	.17	.12	.10
Times Interest Earned	8.5x	8.7x	11.9x	14.8x	18.9x	24.1x	32.8x	42.2x

TABLE 4.5 Colamed Proforma Condensed Consolidated Balance Sheet—(Consolidated with Zolar) ($ millions)

	1981	1982	1983	1984	1985	1986	1987
Long Term Debt	96.6	122.2	144.7	132.7	118.6	110.0	90.8
Equity Before Adjustments	132.4	149.4	172.7	198.6	229.6	267.1	314.2
Plus: Net Profit	24.3	30.6	35.1	41.5	50.0	62.1	75.7
Less: Dividends	7.3	7.3	9.2	10.5	12.5	15.0	18.6
Year End Equity	149.4	172.7	198.6	229.6	267.1	314.2	371.3
Selected Ratios:							
LTD/Equity	.65	.71	.73	.50	.44	.33	.24
Times Interest Earned	5.7x	5.0x	4.3x	5.0x	6.3x	8.4x	11.3x

The effect of the new Zolar subsidiary, when consolidated with Colamed, is shown in Table 4.5.

In 1981 in the Consolidated Balance Sheet there is a difference of $22.2 million in long-term debt, which consists of $14.8 million borrowed at the subsidiary level and $7.4 million at the parent level, which was then invested in the subsidiary as equity. In 1982 an additional $22.1 million was to be borrowed by Zolar and $11.1 million "equity" at the parent level. In 1983 an additional $18.9 million was to be borrowed by the subsidiary and $9.5 million "equity" at the parent level. Thus a total of $27.9 million would have been invested by Colamed in Zolar in the first three years along with $55.8 million of borrowings by Zolar. No further outside sources of capital were to be required by Zolar after 1983, at which time it was to begin repaying its debt.

4.4.1 How Colamed Employed a Limited Partnership Structure to Avoid an Adverse Short-Term Financial Impact

Zolar might well have been an attractive investment for Colamed if Colamed were a private company. As a publicly reporting company, Colamed was not able to pursue the Zolar investment as a wholly owned subsidiary because of the adverse short-run impact on its financial statements. The alternative that it ultimately implemented involved the structuring of Zolar as a limited partnership in which Colamed was the general partner.

As a limited partnership, "Zolar Associates" had a similar capital structure to Zolar, Inc.—that is, the same amount of debt was to be taken down at the same time (at the same interest rates),[6] with the remainder of the "equity" capital supplied by several limited partners.

---

[6]This assumption is probably not valid. On a stand-alone basis, the cost of financing for Zolar Associates would almost certainly have been higher.

The projected operating statement of Zolar Associates was identical to that of Zolar Inc. (Table 4.2).

Colamed could have put "equity" into Zolar Associates, either through the purchase of a limited partnership interest or through a nominal investment as General Partner. In either case equity accounting rules would apply. The equity investment would be carried on Colamed's books at cost but there would be no consolidation. Thus from a public reporting standpoint, the limited partnership vehicle was more attractive to Colamed. Its liabilities were off-balance sheet to Colamed.

The following exhibit shows the structure and operation of Zolar Associates as a limited partnership.

EXHIBIT 4.1 Creation of Zolar Associates Limited Partnership

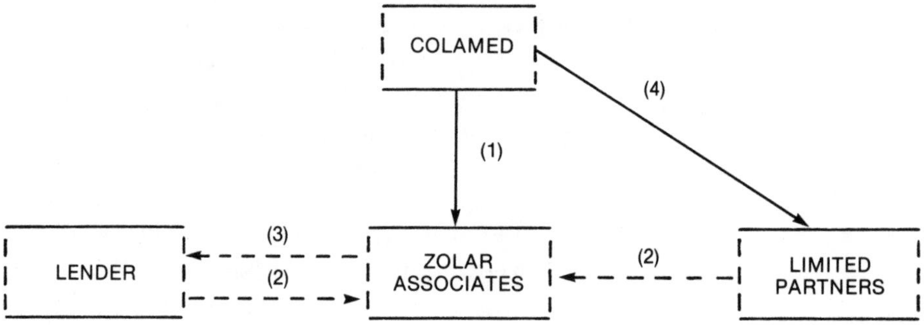

Steps in the Creation of Zolamed Associates

1. Colamed, as General Partner, creates Zolar and puts in a nominal investment.
2. Limited Partners invest equity in Zolar and lender provides financing to Zolar as follows:
   a. $7.4 million by Limited Partners and $14.8 million by Lender in 1981.
   b. $11.1 million by Limited Partners and $22.1 million by Lender in 1982.
   c. $9.5 million by Limited Partners and $18.9 million by Lender in 1983.
3. Repayment of bank debt begins in 1984.
4. Colamed buys out Limited Partners at a discount from fair market value and obtains 100 percent ownership of Zolar.

Impact of Zolar as a consolidated subsidiary. What about the relative merits to Colamed of the two structures from an economic point of view? This question will be approached through a discounted cash-flow analysis of the two alternatives. Table 4.6 shows the impact of Zolar as a consolidated subsidiary.

Included in Table 4.6 is a line item "Dividend to Parent" that is included in order to indicate that Zolar may have been able to dividend funds up to Colamed if permitted by the terms of its bank financing. These dividends would have been used by Colamed to reduce the borrowings it incurred in capitalizing Zolar.

Based upon market multiples of earnings and cash flow for the business in which Zolar was engaged, the projections indicated a terminal value for Zolar of $100 million at the end of 1987. Subtracting $26 million (i.e., the amount of debt remaining in Zolar in 1987) from the market value of $100 million leaves a net terminal value of $74 million.

TABLE 4.6 Net Present Value Analysis Impact of Zolar as Consolidated Subsidiary

Cash Flow of Zolar	1981	1982	1983	1984	1985	1986	1987
Profit Before Tax	(8.6)	(11.7)	(12.0)	(6.0)	(4.0)	2.2	8.8
Taxes at 46%	—	—	—	—	—	1.0	4.1
Net Income	(8.6)	(11.7)	(12.0)	(6.0)	(4.0)	1.3	4.9
Depreciation	2.8	8.0	13.2	13.2	13.5	10.8	5.7
Bank Debt Taken Down	14.8	22.1	18.9	(6.0)[1]	(8.0)	(8.4)	(8.4)
Equity Invested by Colamed	7.4	11.1	9.5	—	—	—	—
TOTAL SOURCES	16.4	29.5	29.6	1.2	1.5	2.7	2.2
Less: Capital Expenditures	16.2	29.4	29.5	1.0	1.2	1.0	1.0
Dividend to Colamed	—	—	—	—	—	1.4	.9
Beginning Working Capital of Zolar	0	.2	.3	.4	.6	.9	1.2
Ending Working Capital of Zolar	.2	.3	.4	.6	.9	1.2	1.5
Cash Flow of Colamed							
Investment in Zolar	(7.4)	(11.1)	(9.5)	—	—	—	—
Dividend to Parent	—	—	—	—	—	1.4	.9
Tax Shield from Zolar Loss (@46%)	4.0	5.4	5.5	2.8	1.8	0	0
Tax Shield from Unused ITC	1.6	2.8	2.9	.1	.1	0	0
Interest Expense Incurred by Colamed[2]	(.3)	(1.1)	(1.9)	(2.3)	(2.3)	(2.3)	(2.3)
NET CASH FLOW	(2.1)	(4.0)	(3.0)	.6	(.4)	1.9	(1.4)

[1]Debt Repayment begins in 1984.
[2]Net of Tax

The net present value to Colamed of its Zolar investment would appear as follows:

TABLE 4.7 Present Value of
Investment in Zolar Subsidiary

Discount Rate	Value in Millions
12%	$26.8
15%	$21.4
18%	$17.2

Impact of Colamed as general partner. The alternative of Colamed acting as General Partner in Zolar Associates would be analyzed in a similar manner. It was assumed that Colamed would not have to borrow funds for an equity investment in Zolar. Instead, the equity would be invested by the limited partners with debt borrowed directly by the partnership in the same proportions as if Zolar were a subsidiary of Colamed (i.e., a debt/equity ratio of 2 to 1). The following table shows the income statement and cash flow for the limited partnership.

TABLE 4.8 Income and Cash Flow Statement Zolar Associates Limited Partnership ($000)

Income Statement of Zolar	1981	1982	1983	1984	1985	1986	1987
Operating Profit	(4.4)	1.0	9.6	16.7	17.7	19.8	19.9
Interest Expense	1.5	4.7	8.3	9.5	8.2	6.8	5.3
Depreciation[1]	2.8	8.0	13.2	13.2	13.5	10.8	5.7
Income Before Taxes	(8.6)	(11.7)	(12.0)	(6.0)	(4.0)	2.2	8.9
Taxes[2]	—	—	—	—	—	—[4]	—[4]
Net Income	(8.6)	(11.7)	(12.0)	(6.0)	(4.0)	2.2	8.9
Cash Flow							
Cash Flow of Zolar[3]							
Net Income	(8.6)	(11.7)	(12.0)	(6.0)	(4.0)	2.2	8.9
Depreciation	2.8	8.0	13.2	13.2	13.5	10.8	5.7
Equity Invested by Partners	7.4	11.1	9.5	—	—	—	—
Bank Debt Taken Down	14.8	22.1	18.9	(6.0)	(8.0)	(8.4)	(8.4)
TOTAL SOURCES	16.4	29.5	29.6	1.2	1.5	2.7	2.2
Less: Capital Expenditures	16.2	29.4	29.5	1.0	1.2	1.0	1.0
Taxes of Limited Partners[4]	—	—	—	—	—	1.0	4.1

TABLE 4.8 (continued)

Income Statement of Zolar	1981	1982	1983	1984	1985	1986	1987
Distribution to General Partner	—	—	—	—	—	1.4	.9
Beginning Working Capital	.0	.2	.3	.4	.6	.9	1.2
Ending Working Capital	.2	.3	.4	.6	.9	1.2	1.5

[1]This analysis has ignored differences between book and tax depreciation.
[2]The partnership is not a tax-paying entity. Tax benefits and ITC are passed on to limited partners.
[3]This does not consider the cash consequences of the tax benefits flowing through to the limited partners.
[4]The partnership makes distributions to partners in those years in which they must pay taxes.

As part of its long-range strategic plan, Colamed required eventual ownership of Zolar. It would have had ownership of Zolar from the onset using the subsidiary approach. With the limited partnership it would have to purchase its ownership of Zolar from the limited partners at some discount from fair market value. Under the terms of the Limited Partnership Agreement, the General Partner would have the right to purchase Zolar at 70 percent of its terminal value, which had previously been assigned a value of $100 million at the end of seven years. Zolar would thus receive a windfall of 30 percent of the *net* terminal value or 30 percent x $76 million = $39 million.

The present value analysis of the limited partnership approach would show a nominal investment by Colamed (which is assumed to be zero) at the inception of the project, two cash distributions in 1986 and 1987, and a cash inflow of $39 million in 1987. A summary of this analysis appears in Table 4.9:

TABLE 4.9 Present Value Analysis of Investment in Zolar Associates

Discount Rate	Value in Millions
12%	$17.6
15%	$14.7
18%	$12.2

Thus the economic return to Colamed would be much greater if it structured its investment in Zolar as a wholly owned subsidiary. However, for public reporting purposes it was forced into the limited partnership structure. This course of action results in a significant loss in economic value to the shareholders in the long run.

4.5 THE LIMITED PARTNER'S PERSPECTIVE

As a limited partner participating in a limited partnership, a company's investment is typically found under "Other Assets" on the balance sheet, with a reference to the footnotes, which give greater detail if the investment is material. Language in the footnotes to cover a typical investment by a company as limited partner would be similar to the following:[7]

> During 1985 the company invested approximately $6,200,000 for the purchase of a limited partnership interest in Delplato Gas Drilling Associates. To date, the company has realized $3,945,000 of U.S. investment tax credits related to the project which were used to reduce the carrying value of its investment.

CASE 4.2 ENERGY PROJECT LIMITED PARTNERSHIP

4.5.1 How the Limited Partnership Was Structured

Several companies participated in a small energy project with a total capital cost of approximately $8 million. Construction was begun in 1982 and was to be completed in 1983. The project was structured as a limited partnership. The general partner, which controlled the project site, was a small consulting firm that put in a nominal investment. It managed the project, for which it received a management fee. In addition, the general partner received a carried interest of 10 percent of the value of the project after the third year of operation if certain earning goals were achieved.

There were two limited partners, each of whom committed to purchase its limited partnership interest upon completion of the project at a cost of $2 million. The remainder of the capitalization consisted of a $4 million, eight-year term loan.

The returns to the limited partners consisted of tax benefits and cash distributions. Interest during the construction period, estimated to be $966,000, could be passed on to the investors as incurred during the construction period—that is, even before the limited partners invested $2,000,000 each for the purchase of their limited partnership interest.[8]

Also available in the project was an energy tax credit (11 percent of qualifying investment) and an investment tax credit (10 percent of qualifying investment) totaling $998,000. Additionally, the investment

---

[7]This is a composite of several footnotes. "Delplato" is a fictitious name.

[8]At inception of the project the limited partners had to sign subscription agreements in which they committed to purchase their limited partnership interests. This established their tax ownership so that they could take deductions prior to completion.

in the plant could be depreciated over five years, resulting in $1,276,000 of tax depreciation during the first two years of operation of the facility.

When the significant early year tax benefits were combined with anticipated cash distributions, each limited partner's net investment of $2,000,000 was expected to be reduced to $380,000 by the end of the first year and zero by the end of the third year of operations (on a nondiscounted basis).

4.5.2 Two Factors That Reduced Business Risk

Two features significantly reduced the business risk associated with the project. Construction of the facility was undertaken by a major construction firm under a "turn-key" contract. In such an arrangement the contractor commits to deliver the plant according to specification at a fixed time and price. To the extent the contractor improved upon the price of constructing the project, the savings would be shared by the project and the contractor. Thus a mechanism was in place for reducing a major element of risk—cost overruns during construction.

Even in the event that cost overruns did occur, there was a commitment from the limited partners to cover such additional costs in the form of loans to the project. More frequently, the commitment to cover cost overruns is made by the general partner. However, in this project the general partner had limited resources so that this exposure was assumed by the limited partners.

EXHIBIT 4.2 Energy Project as Limited Partnership

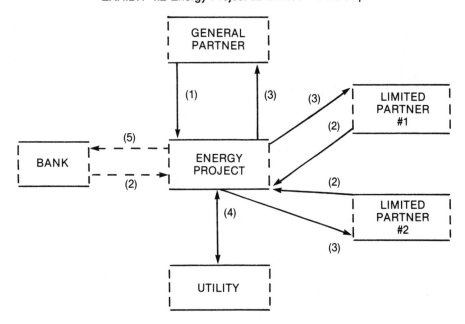

TABLE 4.10 A Limited Partnership Energy Project

Year	1982	1983	1984	1985	1986	1987	1988	1989	1990	1991	1992	1993	1994	1995	1996	1997	1998	1999	2000	2001	2002
One Limited Partner's Portion of the Project:																					
Income Statement																					
Revenues		433	770	770	770	770	770	770	770	531	511	589	562	687	820	812	846	923	990	1043	1091
Interest IMC		8	26	9	2	5	8	12	15	17	28	33	29	37	44	40	42	46	49	51	53
Expenses																					
O&M		33	54	57	61	66	70	75	80	86	92	98	105	113	120	129	138	148	158	169	181
Prop Taxes		22	39	39	39	39	39	39	39	27	26	29	28	34	41	41	42	46	49	52	55
Interest		213	320	320	284	231	178	124	71	18	0	0	0	0	0	0	0	0	0	0	0
Rent		6	9	17	26	33	38	43	48	55	17	10	25	27	51	82	91	94	105	114	121
Mgmt.		15	32	11	3	6	10	14	18	21	34	40	36	46	54	49	52	57	61	63	66
Dev Fee		0	0	0	0	5	22	30	38	51	73	87	77	98	116	106	111	122	131	136	142
Dept (Book)		80	120	120	120	120	120	120	120	120	120	120	120	120	120	120	120	120	120	120	120
LP PBT (Book)		71	223	215	239	275	301	336	370	170	177	236	200	286	361	324	334	381	414	439	460
LP Cash Flow Statement:																					
LP PBT (Book)		71	223	215	239	275	301	336	370	170	177	236	200	286	361	324	334	381	414	439	460
+ DEP (Book)		80	120	120	120	120	120	120	120	120	120	120	120	120	120	120	120	120	120	120	120
− Principal				222	333	333	333	333	333	111											
Net Cash Flow		152	344	113	26	62	88	124	157	180	298	356	320	406	481	445	454	502	535	559	580
Distribution		125	344	113	26	62	88	124	157	206	298	356	320	406	481	445	454	502	535	559	580
Taxable Income:																					
LP PBT (Book)		71	223	215	239	275	301	336	370	170	177	236	200	286	361	324	334	381	414	439	460
+ Dept (Book)		80	120	120	120	120	120	120	120	120	120	120	120	120	120	120	120	120	120	120	120
− DEP (Tax)		517	759	724	724	724															
− IDC	187	296																			
− Pre-Expense	18	50																			
− Entry Fee		40																			
LP PBT (Tax)	−205	−752	−415	−389	−365	−329	421	457	491	291	298	356	320	406	481	445	454	502	535	559	580
After-Tax Impact:																					
PBT (TX)$ −.50	102	386	207	194	182	164	210	228	245	145	149	178	160	203	240	222	227	251	267	279	290
+ Tax Credits		499																			
Cash Dist.		125	344	113	26	62	88	124	157	206	298	356	320	406	481	445	454	502	535	559	580
After-Tax Impact On Limited Partner	102	1010	551	307	208	226	298	352	401	351	447	534	480	609	721	667	681	853	802	838	870

Steps in Creations of Energy-Limited Partnership

1. General Partner oversees project construction under a turn-key contract.
2. Upon project completion, limited partners each invest $2 million and bank makes term loan of $4 million.
3. Partners receive tax benefits during construction, and tax benefits and cash distributions after project completion.
4. Utility purchases the output under take-and-pay contract.
5. Bank loan is repaid over eight years.

Long-term purchase commitment. Another aspect of the project that reduced the business risk was a long-term purchase commitment for the output. A nearby utility entered into a thirty year take-and-pay contract for the entire output of the project. During the first eight years of the project, the contract was at a fixed price per unit of output. After this eight-year period, the unit price was tied to market factors at a slight discount. The discount in later years allowed the utility to recoup its potential loss during the first eight years. The fixed price nature of the purchase contract was the primary factor that enabled the project to obtain eight-year term financing.

4.5.3 Cash-Flow Projections

Table 4.10, which follows, shows only twenty years of cash flows, although the project had an expected life of thirty years. The depreciation was thirty years straight line for book purposes, and the ACRS statutory percentage for five-year recovery was used. Management fees to the general partner were calculated at 10 percent of cash flow less interest income.

4.6 HOW TO USE TRUSTS IN OFF-BALANCE SHEET FINANCING

The remainder of this chapter discusses trusts as an off-balance sheet financing vehicle. It is a method by which either the tax benefits, or residual value, or operating control of a project can be retained by the sponsor without it requiring balance sheet disclosure.

There is no definition of the term "trust" in the Internal Revenue Code. Rather, it is a creation of state law. A trust typically involves three parties: the grantor, the trustee, and the beneficiary. However, it is possible to combine these so that the grantor may be the beneficiary or the trustee.

When the grantor also remains a direct or indirect beneficiary of the trust, it is considered a *grantor* trust. The result is that the trust income (or losses) will generally be taxable to the grantor. This may or may not be desirable depending upon the circumstances, as will become evident in the cases that follow. The likelihood of a trust being treated as a grantor trust becomes even greater under circumstances where one party is both a beneficiary (usually through a reversionary interest) and grantor and also has a significant measure of control over the management of the trust.

Case 4.3 shows the use of a construction trust. This device was popular for many years among the utilities. It was principally aimed at removing interest costs from the regulated entity's balance sheet during the construction period while still allowing consolidation by the grantor under the tax-consolidation rules. Thus the grantor/utility could deduct interest for tax purposes. The short-term borrowings that were raised to finance the construction were backed up by either an unconditional takeout guarantee of the sponsor or long-term lenders (which in turn were guaranteed by the sponsors.)

In order to curtail distortions in the reporting of large construction projects, the Securities and Exchange Commission issued Staff Accounting Bulletin No. 28, which required electric utilities to include in their balance sheet the assets and liabilities of construction period trusts. The following example involves the use of a construction trust by a nonutility.

CASE 4.3 THE USE OF A CONSTRUCTION TRUST

How the trust was structured. Tanko Corporation[9] wished to finance an office building. It established a Trust with an independent trustee and chose a University as the beneficiary. It was significant that the beneficiary was unrelated to the grantor of the Trust in order to assure nonconsolidation for accounting purposes.

It was also essential for the desired accounting treatment that there was an actual transference of the risks and economic benefits away from the sponsor. Tanko assigned its rights of ownership of the land and assets to the Trust, which directly assumed the obligation under the construction contract. Tanko entered into an arms-length management contract with the Trust, priced at fair market value with normal cancellation provisions for nonperformance, under which it would administer the Trust's affairs during the construction period.

The Trust then obtained irrevocable letters of credit from several major banks, which were guaranteed by Tanko. The letters of credit

---

[9]This is a fictitious name.

were used as a backup for the issuance of commercial paper by the Trust, with the proceeds applied to finance the construction.

Upon completion of the construction, Tanko had the right to: (1) purchase the building from the Trust at cost, or (2) arrange for a sale of the building to a third party, from which it would lease the facility.

Disclosure. Although this arrangement remained off the balance sheet of Tanko, it was a disclosure item in the footnotes as a contingent liability under FASB No. 34. Several factors were weighed by the auditors to determine whether there should have been disclosure and whether it was quantifiable. A materiality test was applied using 10 percent of net worth, but this was not considered a valid measure for a large construction project in the $200 million range.

Also of significance to the accountants was the expected impact of the project upon the grantor at the end of the construction period. If the banks supplying the letters of credit had required that Tanko purchase the building upon completion, then it clearly would have been a quantifiable disclosure item. However, since Tanko had the right to conduct a sale/leaseback and since there was a good likelihood that this would occur, this factor argued strongly against quantifying the contingent obligation in the footnote.

FASB No. 34 speaks of loss contingencies. In this example, the banks had a right to proceed against Tanko in the event that there was a draw down under the letter of credit. However, FASB No. 34 allowed for the fact that there could be a recovery against the loss (either through insurance or against the Trust's asset) and that such estimated amount could also be noted in the footnote.

CASE 4.4 USE OF A GRANTOR TRUST IN EQUIPMENT LEASING

An equipment manufacturer, Equico Corp.[10], supplied significant amounts of lease financing for the purchaser of its equipment. The rental stream from the leases was applied against borrowings incurred by Equico for the purchase of the equipment. Equico desired to remove the leased assets and the related debt from its balance sheet.

How the trust was structured. Equico created a grantor trust pursuant to a trust indenture, with Equico as the sole beneficial owner. The trust purchased existing equipment from Equico at roughtly $70 million, which was 20 percent over the net book value of $58 million. The sale price was comparable to Equico's normal distributor selling prices and was subject to its standard warranties and sales conditions.

The trust was able to obtain 100 percent financing (nonrecourse to Equico), which enabled it to cover the entire sales price. The loan

---

[10]This name is fictitious.

to the trust was secured by the equipment and the leases, the rental proceeds of which were assigned to the trust by Equico along with all other proceeds from disposition of the equipment (such as sales or insurance). The leases, which were daily, weekly, and monthly operating leases, were generating an annualized average of approximately $2 million per month of rental income.

Subsequent to the sale of the equipment to the trust, Equico was to administer the trust's leasing activities at fees pegged to a market rate (roughly .3 percent per month of the equipment value). The equipment value was expected to increase or decrease as the trust purchased and sold equipment. The fees to Equico would vary accordingly. Equico's administration activities were to include record keeping and the billing and collecting of rental proceeds of the leases, as well as remitting funds to the lender.

The transaction structure appears in the following diagram.

EXHIBIT 4.3 Off-Balance Sheet Financing With a Grantor Trust

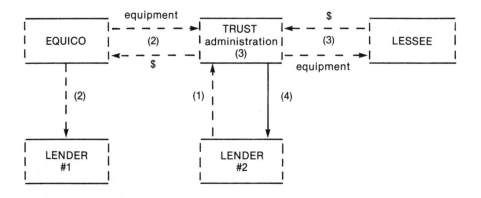

Steps in the Use of a Grantor Trust

1. The trust obtains nonrecourse financing (from Lender No. 2) using the equipment and leases as security.
2. The trust purchases the equipment from Equico. Equico uses the proceeds to repay existing debt (to Lender No. 1).
3. Equico administers the equipment leasing on behalf of the trust.
4. The proceeds of the leases are remitted to the lender to repay the outstanding debt.

Equico was not at risk in the transaction. It received full payment at the time of sale and the debt was nonrecourse to it. The trust was the only obligor on the debt. Equico had no debt on its books and no contingent liability in its footnotes. It did give its standard equipment warranties to the trust. However, there was no requirement in the administration contract that Equico give priority to the trust's equipment under its remarketing agreement.

The trust was to exist for a period of less than ten years, with Equico having the right to reacquire the property placed in the trust by substituting equipment of an equivalent value.

Tax treatment. Thus Equico recorded a clean sale for book accounting purposes[11] of the total amount of the sale to the trust less the net depreciated value of the equipment. However, there was no change in the manner in which Equico treated the equipment for tax-reporting purposes. That is, Equico continued to receive the investment tax credit based upon its costs in the equipment, and the deferral of taxes arising from accelerated depreciation of the equipment. However, the sale of equipment to the trust was not a sale for tax purposes. Rental payments to the trust were treated as income to Equico and interest payments to the lender were treated as a deduction for Equico for tax purposes.

---

[11]The sales to the trust were actually sales-type leases under paragraph 17 of FASB No. 13, Accounting For Leases.

chapter 5

How to Use Employee Stock Ownership Plans to Improve Cash Flow in Divestitures and When Transferring Ownership of Private Corporations

5.1 THE EVOLUTION OF EMPLOYEE STOCK OWNERSHIP PLANS

There has been a growing interest in stock as a form of compensation in recent years. Two outgrowths of this interest, particularly since the mid-1970s, have been Employee Stock Ownership Plans (ESOPs) and Tax Reduction Act Stock Ownership Plans (TRASOPs). The following two chapters deal with the various aspects of these two types of stock compensation plans, with the emphasis, especially in the case of ESOPs, on their use in solving a number of financial problems.

The ESOP Association of America estimates that there are between 2500 and 3000 ESOP companies in the United States today, whereas there were only a few hundred just one decade ago. Most ESOPs are in closely held firms and control an average of 10 to 40 percent of total company stock and only limited voting rights.[1] While most employee ownership plans provide workers with only a small interest in their company, an increasing number of companies have become majority owned by employees. The Senate Small Business Committee[2] estimates that at least 100 companies, ranging in size from under twenty employees to over 10,000, are now majority owned by employees.

5.1.1 Why ESOPs Are Gaining Popularity

This growth has come largely in response to two developments: the passage of major federal legislation to encourage employee ownership, coupled with an increased understanding of how employee ownership can be used to alleviate a variety of traditional business concerns. There has been an increasing tendency for employees to purchase plants that would otherwise close, for retiring owners to transfer their companies to their employees, for ongoing firms to grant a substantial ownership share to their workers, and for new worker-owned enterprises to get started.

5.1.2 The History Behind the ESOP

Before delving into a technical definition of ESOPs and the refinements of ESOPs as contrasted with other stock compensation schemes, it would be worthwhile to trace their recent evolution. Interest in ESOPs

---

[1]ESOPs require full voting rights in publicly held companies, but only limited voting rights in closely held firms.

[2]Congressional Record, Vol. 126, No. 168, December 2, 1980.

has resulted largely from incentives created by federal legislation for both employees and employers.

Legislative support. The Employee Retirement Income Security Act of 1974 (ERISA) created a new statutory definition of the Employee Stock Ownership Plan as a qualified[3] stock bonus plan designed to invest "primarily" in qualifying employer securities, conferring on the ESOP the unique ability to leverage by utilizing an employer's credit[4] without violating the prohibited transaction provisions of ERISA. The TRASOP was created by the Tax Reduction Act of 1975 as a type of stock ownership plan that can be funded by an additional 1 percent investment tax credit.

ESOPs and TRASOPs were given further definition and encouragement by the Tax Reform Act of 1976 and the Revenue Act of 1978. The Small Business Employee Ownership Act of 1980 gave the Small Business Administration the authority to guarantee loans to ESOPs.[5] The Economic Recovery Tax Act of 1981 broadened the application of TRASOPs by creating a new "payroll-based" tax credit beginning in 1983 for contributions to a tax credit ESOP.

Under current law, a company can get a credit for contributions to a TRASOP equal to 1 percent of qualified investments under the Investment Tax Credit (ITC), and 1½ percent if employees make an additional ½ percent contribution. This provision was attractive mainly to capital-intensive firms making large contributions under the ITC. The new law phased out this TRASOP in 1983, replacing it with a payroll based TRASOP. In 1983 and 1984, companies can get a credit equal to .5 percent of payroll for TRASOP contributions while in 1985, 1986, and 1987 the credit is equal to .75 percent. This credit, if unused in the current tax year, can be carried back three years or forward fifteen.

Current law allows companies a right of first refusal on stock employees are given when they leave the firm, but there is no guarantee that the employees will not sell to an outsider. A new provision allows companies, whose by-laws specify that all or substantially all of the company's stock must be owned by employees, to "cash-out" employees who leave the company at the fair market value of their stock.

The Economic Recovery Tax Act of 1981 also increased limits for employer contributions used to repay an ESOP stock acquisition loan, and allows contributions used to pay loan interest to be fully deductible.

---

[3]§401 (a) Internal Revenue Code. Qualification basically means that contributions to the plan are tax deductible, and comply with all requirements of ERISA. Benefits to employees are not taxed until the employee actually removes stock from the plan.

[4]It is permitted to have a bank extend credit to a plan without guarantees from the employer, though this is rarely the case.

[5]See Chapter 13, which deals at length with SBA financing. The SBA's ESOP loans are limited to $500,000 and may only be used to finance company expansion or give the ESOP a 50 percent controlling interest in the company.

Contributions used to pay loan principal will be fully deductible up to 25 percent of covered payroll and these contribution limitations will apply even if the employer makes contributions to another qualified employee plan. These more liberal limits apply, however, only if not more than one-third of the contributions go to officers, major shareholders, or employees making over $83,000 per year in 1981 dollars.

5.1.3 Two ESOP Transactions That Made History

Aside from legislative support, the ESOP received more notoriety in 1981 than in any other period in its history as a result of the battle for control of Continental Airlines. It was one of the largest attempted ESOP transactions ever, involving over 10,000 employees and $185 million worth of stock. The four unions involved agreed collectively to require future wage deductions on the part of their member participants to pay for their stock. This situation is considered in detail in Chapter 6.

Also in 1981 the Bay Bank of Commerce began operations in San Leandro, California. It was the first time that a bank had an ESOP as part of its initial capitalization. The ESOP acquired 10,000 shares of bank stock, utilizing a five-year loan from another bank. The largest 100 percent-owned ESOP Company in the country, Okinite Wire & Cable Co., made its first distribution to retired employees in 1981. The distribution came to approximately $1.5 million in the company's stock.

5.1.4 Be Aware of These Trade-offs

It should be kept in mind throughout this discussion that ESOPs, like most of the off-balance sheet financing techniques discussed previously, require certain trade-offs. This is exemplified by two of the most successful ESOPs, South Bend Lathe and E-Systems. At 100 percent-owned South Bend Lathe, in its first six months with an ESOP, it has been estimated that costs associated with poor workmanship dropped 70 percent. At E-Systems, since the ESOP was instituted in 1974, turnover declined 64 percent and absenteeism dropped 50 percent. However, South Bend Lathe suffered a costly and bitter strike in the fall of 1980,[6] while one of the most economically successful employee buyouts, the Vermont Asbestos Group, recently became conventionally controlled (although still largely employee owned) within a few years of the creation of the employee ownership plan.

A significant issue often arises in ESOP companies when the role

---

[6]Although 100 percent employee-owned, the employees did not having voting rights, which were controlled by management.

of employees as owners is sidestepped by management. Closely held ESOP firms generally do not provide for more voting rights than they are legally required to and few ESOP firms, whether publicly or closely held, allow for significant employee participation in management. Other criticisms include manipulation of plans by management for tax purposes or as a way to avoid or weaken unions, and difficulties in the valuation of stock held by the ESOP.

Despite these criticisms, the ESOP is a financial tool that is clearly established in both law and practice. Specific applications will now be explored.

5.2 HOW TO USE ESOPS AS A MEANS OF RAISING CAPITAL

CASE 5.1 ESOP ACQUISITION OF A NEW FACILITY BY A CLOSELY HELD CORPORATION

Assume that a company wishes to purchase some asset, such as a plant for $6 million, from which it expects a 33 percent pretax return. Under conventional debt financing, the company would simply borrow the $6 million, build the plant, and use its cash flow to repay the debt.

There are two alternatives to the conventional debt financing. One is an equity offering, which is usually impractical for the closely held company because there is no ready equity market and because there is a dilution effect and interference with control of the existing owners.

The advantages of an ESOP. The second alternative is the use of an ESOP. Although with the ESOP there is some dilution to existing owners, this is mitigated to some extent because the owners (as employees) participate in the ESOP. In addition, allocation and vesting takes place over a period of years and there is often a commonality of interest between participants in the plan and management. Lastly, the employees are a "known" entity, whereas an outside party who purchases newly issued shares is an unknown quantity that injects additional risk into the transaction.

How it works. With the introduction of the ESOP, the corporation does not borrow. Rather, the ESOP borrows the $6 million from the lender, with the corporation making guarantees to satisfy the lender that it will make payments to the ESOP in amounts sufficient to amortize the loan. The ESOP uses the loan proceeds to purchase newly issued shares of employer stock, thus transferring the funds to the corporation which are used to build the plant. The company makes annual contributions to the ESOP sufficient to repay the ESOP loan with essentially the same repayment schedule as under conventional debt financing.

The ESOP vs. conventional debt financing. The big difference from conventional debt financing is the deductibility of principal payments under the ESOP because the yearly ESOP contribution includes both interest and principal. Given a 50 percent tax rate, the company would have to earn an additional $12 million on a pretax basis to repay the principal amount of $6 million under a conventional loan. With the ESOP the same company would only have to earn an additional $6 million to repay the loan with pretax dollars.

EXHIBIT 5.1 Corporate Financing Using a Leveraged ESOP

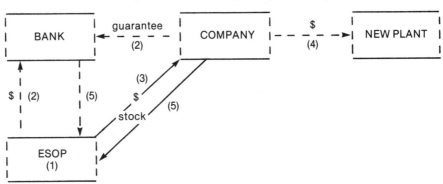

Steps in ESOP Financing of Plant

1. Company establishes an ESOP.
2. Bank loans ESOP $6 million in exchange for note plus Company guarantee.
3. ESOP purchases $6 million worth of stock from the company.
4. Company uses proceeds of stock sale to buy plant.
5. Company makes cash contributions to ESOP over time, which ESOP uses to repay loan.

The following table compares the ESOP, equity-offering, and debt-financing alternatives. It assumes that the plant makes a pretax return of 33 percent, making a contribution of $2,000,000.

Two drawbacks of an equity offering for closely held corporations. As the table indicates, the equity offering is the most attractive alternative from both an earnings and cash-flow standpoint. However, this is misleading in several respects. First, it is unlikely that there will be a ready equity market for the stock of a closely held corporation.[7] Secondly,

---

[7] If this were a public company, the use of an ESOP could not be justified as a capital-raising mechanism. There are more practical uses of an ESOP for a public company, which are addressed in the next chapter.

TABLE 5.1 Comparison of Financing Alternatives ($000)

	Before Financing	*ESOP Financing*	*Equity Offering*	*Conventional Borrowing*
Pretax income before financing	6,000	8,000	8,000	8,000
New interest expense (at 12%)	-0-	-0-	-0-	720
ESOP contribution	-0-	1,720	-0-	-0-
Adjusted Pretax income	6,000	6,280	8,000	7,280
Taxes (at 50%)	3,000	3,140	4,000	3,640
Net Income	3,000	3,140	4,000	3,640
Outstanding Shares	1,000,000	1,150,000	1,150,000	1,000,000
Earnings Per Share	$ 3.00	$ 2.73	$ 3.48	$ 3.64
Cash Flow:				
Income	3,000	3,140	4,000	3,640
Depreciation	1,000	1,600	1,600	1,600
Less: Principal	-0-	-0-	-0-	1,000
Dividends	500	600	600	500
Cash Flow	3,500	4,140	5,000	3,740

closely held corporations frequently pay nominal dividends or no dividends at all to their common stockholders. In our case there was an assumed payout ratio of 15 percent (i.e., $500,000 in dividends on $3,000,000 of net income) prior to the new financing. This payout ratio would probably have to be increased in order to induce an investor to purchase illiquid common stock in a closely held corporation. The payout would presumably be increased on all shares, not just those newly issued, thus infringing upon the cash flow under the equity offering. The issuing of shares to the ESOP would not require an increase in the dividend.

Thirdly, in a closely held company the existing owners, by virtue of their salaried management positions, would participate in the ESOP. This would limit the dilution effect of the ESOP as compared to the straight equity offering. Between 20 and 30 percent of the newly issued shares to the ESOP could ultimately go to the existing owners.

There is a second ESOP structure that might be utilized to lessen the adverse effects of the ESOP on earnings. This is outlined in the following modification of Example 1.

CASE 5.2 ESOP FINANCING ON A STAGGERED BASIS

How it works. The company wishes to purchase the plant for $6 million and borrows this amount directly. With the borrowing it simultaneously establishes an ESOP. As principal repayments are due on the loan each year, the Company makes a deductible cash contribution to the ESOP in the amount of the principal repayment. The ESOP uses the cash to purchase newly issued shares of the Company. The company has received the same amount of cash from the ESOP that it has contributed to the ESOP, which it then uses to repay the loan.

From a cash-flow standpoint, this is the same transaction as in Case 5.1. Each year the company receives a tax deduction equal to the amount of the principal repayment by virtue of the ESOP contribution, thus in effect repaying the loan with pretax dollars.

The key benefit. There is one important difference, however, in utilizing the ESOP in this manner. It lessens the dilution effect of the issuance of a large block of shares in the early years. Instead, shares are being issued over time, entirely under the control and within the discretion of management. If cash flow is sufficient to repay the loan and management chooses not to make an ESOP contribution in a particular year, it is free to do so.

Unlike Case 5.1, this is a nonleveraged ESOP. The loan is made to the Company and not to the ESOP. Even if the cash contributions using a nonleveraged ESOP are identical to those under the leveraged ESOP in Case 5.1, the dilution effect over time will still probably be less. In a company that is increasing in value each year, it will require fewer and fewer shares each year to shelter the principal repayments. For instance, in the leveraged ESOP 150,000 shares are issued immediately and the ESOP makes principal repayments of $1,000,000 per year for six years. In the nonleveraged ESOP, assuming the Company's value grows near 10 percent per year, the company might issue 25,000 shares the first year, 23,000 the second year, 21,000 the third, 18,000 the fourth, and only 15,000 the fifth and sixth years, for a total 117,000 shares.

Caution: be aware of this drawback. Although the nonleveraged structure appears to be more attractive, the problem that frequently occurs with it arises with the lender. In a leveraged ESOP transaction, the lender is assured that the Company is committed to repay the ESOP loan and that the cash flow will be improved significantly by virtue of the ESOP device. However, in the nonleveraged ESOP in the future there is no guarantee that the Company will utilize the ESOP to improve cash flow. The company can give assurances to the lender that it will utilize the ESOP to improve cash flow but it is under no obligation to do so. If the management finds the dilution effect of the newly issued shares unduly onerous, it can discontinue the ESOP contributions, even at the expense of improved cash flow. Thus the lender is at greater risk in making a loan to a Company utilizing a nonleveraged ESOP and may require that the transaction be structured as a leveraged ESOP.

EXHIBIT 5.2 Corporate Financing Using a Nonleveraged ESOP

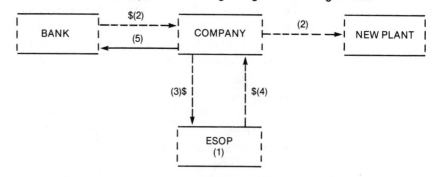

Steps in ESOP Tax Sheltering of Principal Repayments

1. Company establishes an ESOP.
2. Bank loans Company $6 million for plant. Company repays loan of $1 million per year, as follows.
3. Company contributes $1 million to ESOP each year.
4. ESOP pays $1 million to Company for $1 million of stock.
5. Company uses proceeds of stock sale to repay loan at $1 million per year.

5.3 HOW TO USE AN ESOP TO TRANSFER OWNERSHIP IN CLOSELY HELD CORPORATIONS

When an ESOP functions in this manner it is frequently referred to as providing an "in-house" market for the stock of closely held companies. There are two general ways in which the ownership of a closely held business may be transferred. The first involves a sale of shares over an extended time period where the ownership transition is a gradual one. The second involves the immediate transfer of a control block. The gradual transfer is easier to finance because less leverage is required and this situation will be examined first.

CASE 5.3 SALE OF AN OWNER'S STOCK TO AN ESOP

Refrigeration Company[8] was 100 percent owned by its owner/founder, Mr. Jones, who, as he neared retirement age, wished to transfer ownership and control of his company to management over the course of seven to ten years. However, management could not afford to pay the purchase price. In addition, the owner wanted to include

---

[8]This is a fictitious name.

other key employees who were not part of management. These employees could not raise any cash on their own. On the advice of tax counsel, the owner had already rejected the idea of having the Company redeem his shares over time because this would have resulted in ordinary income tax treatment of the redemption as a dividend. The Company was valued by the owner and by independent appraisal at roughly $10,000,000 and there were 800 nonunion employees with an annual payroll of $9,000,000.

How it works. The Company established an ESOP and the owner entered into a long term buy/sell agreement with the ESOP for the disposition of his shares. He realized his objectives in the following manner.

EXHIBIT 5.3 Transfer of Ownership Using an ESOP

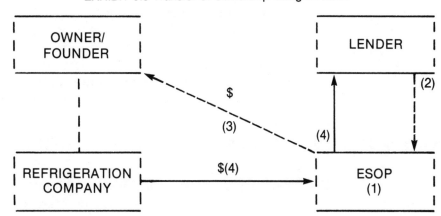

Steps in Transfer of Ownership Using an ESOP

1. Refrigeration Company establishes an ESOP.
2. A bank loans $3,000,000 to the ESOP in exchange for a five-year note, which is guaranteed by the Company.
3. The ESOP uses the loan proceeds to purchase stock from Jones.
4. The company makes annual cash contributions of $1,200,000 the first year ($750,000 principal and $450,000 interest) with constant principal each year thereafter for the next three years, and declining interest payments during the four-year term of the loan. The Company would receive a deduction for its annual contributions,[9] which would be applied by the ESOP for repayment of the loan.

---

[9]As a result of the Economic Recovery Tax Act of 1981, the deductible amount is limited to 25 percent of covered payroll for principal deductions and unlimited interest deductions.

5. After four years (unless the bank is willing to supply additional funds on a revolving credit basis as discussed below), Jones may sell additional shares to the ESOP with these steps repeated.

This example would involve several repetitions of the steps outlined above in order for Jones to sell his entire holdings. It required $3,000,000 of bank debt in order for Jones to maximize his initial receipt of cash. If bank debt were not obtainable, or if the Company did not desire to incur additional leverage, or if Jones did not require a large initial cash payment, Jones could have entered into a "staggered purchase" arrangement with the ESOP. This is to be distinguished from an installment sale. In an installment sale there would have been an immediate transfer of $3,000,000 worth of shares in exchange for some cash plus notes totalling $3,000,000. In a staggered purchase, there would have been a contract between Jones and the ESOP to sell $3,000,000 of shares over time at some agreed-upon price for a specified number of shares each year. In a staggered sale arrangement for the transfer of ownership of a company, just as in the staggered transaction illustrated in Case 5.2, there is no need for a "leveraged" ESOP.

5.4 TRADE-OFFS TO CONSIDER WHEN ESTABLISHING AN ESOP

There are a variety of technical problems that must be considered in establishing and utilizing the ESOP. Many of these will be touched on in subsequent sections. However, as a general concept it should be kept in mind that there is a certain balancing of interests that the practitioner must always consider in establishing a stock ownership plan for employees.

Financing vs. fiduciary responsibility. On the one hand there is a corporate finance objective (e.g., financing of new capital, transferring ownership in a closely held corporation, implementing a divestiture, going private, or resisting a takeover), while on the other side the Trustees of the ESOP must conduct themselves in the best interests of the participants of the Plan (i.e., meet general fiduciary standards of prudence as to propriety of investment and the price paid for it). The question of prudence was highlighted in 1981 with the attempted takeover of Grumman Corporation. The Trustees of the Grumman Pension Plan purchased a large block of Grumman Stock in a defensive effort to ward off the takeover. The Trustees were subjected to scrutiny by the Department of Labor for purchasing the stock merely for strategic reasons as opposed to a purchase as a prudent investment in the best interests of the participants of the Pension Plan.

Favored tax treatment vs. ESOP participation. Referring to the previous example of the transfer of stock by an owner/founder to an ESOP, one of the motivating factors was the desire to avoid ordinary income tax treatment that he would have received if he had merely redeemed his stock. Under Revenue Procedure 77-30 (1977), the Internal Revenue Service indicated that it would not issue a ruling that a sale to an ESOP would not be treated as a redemption unless certain guidelines were complied with. These guidelines required that the seller (Jones) and certain other related parties could not receive more than 20 percent of the plan benefits.[10] Typically, when an owner/founder such as Jones is cashing himself out of the Company, he will remain on the payroll either as an officer or consultant, thus falling within the IRS guidelines. In order to avoid this IRS limitation, Jones waived his rights to participation in the ESOP.

Cost of ESOP contributions. Whenever considering a transfer of ownership situation, the practical problem that has to be faced is whether the Company can afford a commitment to make ESOP contributions. In the case of Jones, the entire purchase price was not committed to at once so that the Company did not expose itself to an undue amount of leverage. This consideration is not as important when the ESOP is employed as a capital formation device—where the proceeds of a loan actually build capital. In the case of Jones, the loan proceeds were flowing out of the Company to the ESOP. However, because of the deductibility of the contributions, the funds were flowing out at roughly half the rate that they would if Jones' stock were being redeemed.

5.4.1 Avoiding Outside Financing

Another alternative for Jones would be to have the ESOP make an installment purchase of $3,000,000 of his stock without the use of outside financing. This could occur in the following manner. The ESOP is established and one year's contribution of $1,200,000 is contributed to the ESOP. The ESOP pays this cash to Jones as a down payment and issues its note to Jones for $1,800,000 in exchange for $3,000,000 of Jones' stock. Then as annual contributions are made, the ESOP uses this cash to pay off the note. Although Jones has not received as large a cash payment up front, he has received roughly the same amount over the duration of the loan, and the ESOP has avoided the need to obtain outside financing.

---

[10]The Economic Tax Recovery Act of 1981 appears to raise this limit to 33 percent in certain instances.

5.4.2 Documents Required to Form an ESOP and ESOT

There are two basic documents that are required to form the ESOP and its related Employee Stock Ownership Trust (ESOT): the Employee Stock Ownership Plan document and a Trust Agreement empowering the Trustee to purchase and distribute employer securities. These documents are not unique to ESOPs but are required for all qualified employee benefit plans. There are, however, two key provisions for leveraged ESOPs that are important enough to deserve inclusion here. The following are paraphrased samples from several Employee Stock Ownership Plan documents:

EXHIBIT 5.4 ESOP Loans and Release From Encumbrance

A. The Trustee may borrow money for purposes of the Trust including but not limited to borrowings to finance the Trust's purchase of Company Stock. In the event that any such borrowing is an exempt loan (i.e., it is made to the Plan by a disqualified person), as such term is defined in section 4975(e)(2) of the Code, or is guaranteed by such person either directly or by the use of such person's assets as collateral for the loan, the exempt loan must satisfy the following stated requirements, together with such other requirements as may be imposed by law:

1. It must be primarily for the benefit of Participants and their beneficiaries.

2. At the time the exempt loan is made, the interest rate for the loan and the price of the Company Stock to be acquired with the loan proceeds must not be such that Plan assets might be drained off.

3. The proceeds of the exempt loan must be used within a reasonable period of time after their being borrowed by the Plan only for any or all of the following purposes:

   a. to acquire Company Stock

   b. to repay such loan

   c. To repay a prior exempt loan

4. The terms of the loan must, at the same time as the loan is made, be at least as favorable to the Plan as the terms of a comparable loan resulting from arms-length negotiations between independent parties.

5. The exempt loan must be without recourse against the Plan, and the only assets of the Plan that may be given as collateral for the loan are Company Stock acquired with the proceeds of the loan and Company Stock that was used as collateral for a prior exempt loan repaid with the proceeds of the current exempt loan.

6. No person entitled to payment under the exempt loan shall have any right to assets of the Plan other than (a) collateral given for the loan, (b) contributions (other than Company Stock) that are made to the Plan to enable it to meet its obligations, and (c) earnings attributable to such collateral and the investment of such contributions.

7. Payments made by the Plan during a Plan Year with respect to an exempt loan must not exceed an amount equal to the sum of the contributions and earnings referred to in (6) received during or prior to the Plan Year less such payments in prior Plan Years, and all such contributions or earnings must be accounted for separately in the books of account of the Plan until the loan is repaid.

8. In the event of default upon an exempt loan, the value of the Plan assets transferred in satisfaction of the loan must not exceed the amount of the default and, if the lender is a disqualified person, the loan must provide for a transfer of plan assets upon default only to the extent of the failure of the Plan to meet the payment schedule of the loan.

9. The interest rate of an exempt loan must not be in excess of a reasonable rate of interest, as determined upon, among other things, the amount and duration of the loan, the security and guarantee involved, the credit standing of the Plan and the guarantor, and the interest rate for comparable loans.

B. Shares of Company Stock that are pledged as collateral for an exempt loan shall not be allocated to the Individual Accounts of Participants. The exempt loan must provide for the release from encumbrance of Company Stock used as collateral for the loan pursuant to either one of the following methods, as determined by the Committee or the Trustee, as the case may be, at the time the exempt loan is incurred:

1. For each Plan Year during the duration of the loan, the number of shares of Company Stock released must equal the number of encumbered shares held immediately before release for the current Plan Year multiplied by a fraction, the numerator of which is the amount of principal and interest paid for the Plan Year, and the denominator of which is the sum of the numerator plus the principal and interest to be paid for all future Plan Years over the remaining term of the loan, excluding possible extension or renewal periods, and if the interest rate is a variable rate, then the interest rate to be used in the denominator at any particular time shall be the interest rate in effect for the ten current Plan Year with respect to which the computation is being made, or

2. By using the same formula as in (1) above, except that interest payments shall be omitted from both the numerator and denominator of the fraction.

The method set forth in No. 2, Section A, may be used only if all of the following conditions are satisfied: (a) the exempt loan must provide for annual payments of principal and interest at a cumulative rate that is not less rapid at any time than level annual payments of such amounts for ten (10) years, (b) the amount of interest disregarded with respect to any payment shall not exceed that which would be determined to be interest under any standard loan amortization table, and (c) by reason of a renewal, extension or refinancing of the exempt loan, the sum of the expired duration of the exempt loan, the renewal period, the extension period and the duration of a new exempt loan does not exceed ten (10) years.

Before considering further the technical requirements of ESOPs, several varied applications are examined in Cases 5.4 through 5.7. The following example highlights some different problems in the sale of a company by an owner/founder.

CASE 5.4 SALE TO MANAGEMENT GROUP COUPLED WITH ESOP

The founder, Smith, desired to sell 100 percent of the ownership of the Company to an outside third party ("Barlow") and other members of management ("the Management Group") with the aid of an ESOP.

How it worked. It was decided that the sale would take place in steps, because of the high purchase price, over a period of between seven and ten years. Smith would expect to realize a minimum of $1,000,000 upon closing, $700,000 on the first anniversary date, and $700,000 on the second anniversary date. Smith would receive additional payments so that the total received by him would be $7.2 million. Smith required that all payments received by him would be accorded capital gains treatment and would avoid any imputed interest problem.

Further, Smith would remain with the Company in a consulting capacity, actively engaged in management, for at least the first three years of the buyout period. The Management Group, which included Barlow, would put up $300,000 from their own sources, a significant portion of which was borrowed funds, and would look to the cash flow of the Company to repay a portion of these loans.

The Company's W-2 covered payroll for the latest fiscal was roughly $3.2 million and this was expected to grow at least 5 percent per year during the next five years. Pretax income was $2 million for the current fiscal and this was conservatively projected to remain constant or rise slightly during the next five to seven years. The Management Group sought to obtain a majority position, or at the very least a controlling interest in the Company.

In keeping with the above constraints, the following transaction was consummated.

EXHIBIT 5.5 Purchase by Management Group Plus ESOP

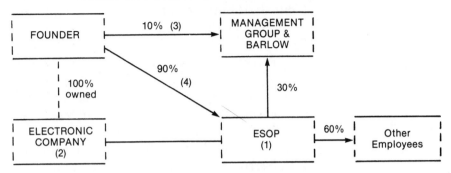

Steps in Purchase by Management Group plus ESOP

1. The Company created an ESOP authorized to accept deductible contributions up to 25 percent of payroll, with a provision also permitting contributions above this amount (which are nondeductible). The Founder would not participate in the ESOP.

2. The Founder entered into a management contract with the Company.

3. The Management initially purchased $300,000 worth of stock from the Founder.[11]

4. The Founder entered into a contract to sell the remaining shares to the ESOP over a seven- to ten-year period for:

   a. $700,000 at closing for an equivalent amount of stock

   b. $700,000[12] at the first anniversary date for an equivalent amount of stock

   c. $700,000[12] at the second anniversary date for an equivalent amount of stock,

   d. a minimum of $800,000 per annum thereafter.

A bank entered into a loan agreement with the Company whereby it extended a term loan of $700,000 on closing, $700,000 on the first anniversary date, and $700,000 on the second anniversary date. The loans at the first and second anniversary dates were subject to repayment of the earlier loans, as well as certain performance standards of the Company being met. In addition, the bank required a security

---

[11]Selling a large block to Management at a price substantially less than that offered to the ESOP may create a problem because it can undermine the "fair market valuation" required by the ESOP Trustees. Some discretion is allowed in an arms-length transaction.

[12]These were minimum amounts and could be increased depending upon performance of the Company.

interest in the Company's stocks and assets and a personal guarantee from the Founder. The commitment of the bank was couched as a minimum commitment and did not preclude its advancing further funds, allowing for a quicker buyout if projections were surpassed.

At the end of the three-year loan period, assuming performance had been strong and the new management had an established track record, the bank would consider advancing additional funding.

How the ESOP produced greater cash flow. Consider the impact of the ESOP on the Company (assuming a 50 percent combined tax bracket for federal and state taxes) as compared to a redemption by Smith with borrowing directly by the Company:

TABLE 5.2 Comparison of Redemption With ESOP Purchase

	Redemption Without ESOP	*Purchase by ESOP*
Pretax income	$2,000,000	$2,000,000
Interest on borrowed funds (@15%)	105,000	—
Contribution to ESOP		
Principal	—	700,000
Interest	—	105,000
Adjusted Pretax income	1,895,000	1,195,000
Taxes	947,500	597,500
After tax income	947,500	597,500
Cash Flow:		
Net Income	947,500	597,000
Plus: Increase in Bank Borrowings	700,000	700,000[1]
Less: Redemption of shares	(700,000)	—
Purchase of shares by ESOP		(700,000)[1]
Repayment of Bank Borrowings	(700,000)[2]	—
Net Cash Flow	$ 247,500	$ 597,500

[1]These are flows to the ESOP as an extension of the Company.
[2]This repayment was accounted for in the income statement item "Contribution to ESOP-Principal."

The larger cash flow using the ESOP is due to the tax savings on the $700,000 ESOP contribution. Although the contribution is a cash movement from the company to the ESOP, this cash is not lost since it is used to repay bank borrowings.

The difference of $350,000 in cash flow between the redemption and the ESOP purchase is in effect a tax subsidy to the employee shareholders.

Accounting treatment of the balance sheet. Also significant is the accounting treatment of the balance sheet. If the company agrees to make payments to the ESOP sufficient to service its debt, this is recorded on the books as a new liability and then deducted from shareholders' equity. The following table compares a $15 million ESOP buyout with a conventional leveraged buyout. The debt incurred by an ESOP appears as a liability just as the leverage in the conventional buyout would appear as long-term debt.

TABLE 5.3 Comparison of ESOP and Leveraged Buy Out

	Direct Leverage Without ESOP	Leverage Through ESOP
Current assets	8 million	8
Fixed assets	12	12
Total	20	20
Current Liabilities	5	5
Long term debt	15	–
ESOP liability	0	15
Shareholders Equity	0	0
Total	20	20

In the preceding example, the Company is bought for its book value, using 100 percent conventional or ESOP debt. The Company's obligation to contribute amounts sufficient to repay the ESOP's debt reduces net equity to zero. As the ESOP debt is repaid a "windfall" item appears and net equity increases by the amount of yearly principal repayment.

5.5 DIVESTITURE OF A SUBSIDIARY OR DIVISION USING AN ESOP

The ESOP-owned Okinite Cable & Wire Company, which was aluded to in Section 5.1, resulted from a divestiture. Okinite was Omega Alpha, Inc.'s only profitable subsidiary in 1974 when Omega Alpha filed for bankruptcy. Because of Okinite's history of profitability and its independent Board of Directors, the Bankruptcy Trustees recommended that Okinite be sold.

A number of companies took part in the bidding contest. One financial institution represented a foreign firm that saw the acquisition of Okinite as a means of breaking into the U.S. market. However, most of the acquisition offers included plans for the closing of Okinite's older New Jersey plants, with the attendant loss of a substantial number of jobs. As a result, Okinite's management turned to the ESOP as an alternate purchaser.

Okinite's management put together the highest bid for the property with the help of a $13 million U.S. Economic Development Administration Loan and $31 million of private financing. Since the acquisition by the ESOP, the company has had a stable performance with increasing profitability. It is owned by the 1900 participants in its ESOP.

Because of the sizeable amount of debt incurred in the purchase, Okinite's ESOP had an initial five year waiting period before any distributions of stock would be made to employees. Thus no additional cash would flow out of the Company as a result of its buying back shares from retiring employees.

CASE 5.5 DIVESTITURE OF X-COM CONSULTANTS, INC.

The following example shows how a Fortune 100 Company (ABC Company) divested one of its properties in 1978 utilizing an ESOP.

ABC Company wanted to divest itself of its subsidiary, X-Com Consultants, Inc., but could not find a buyer willing to pay its asking price of $12.00 per share. ABC decided to sell its interests to an ESOP that was to be created by X-Com.

There were approximately 305,000 shares of X-Com outstanding at the time. The decision to sell to the ESOP was complicated by the fact that ABC only owned 245,000 shares, with 25,000 owned by X-Com's Employee Stock Purchase Plan, which was a simple profit sharing plan empowered to purchase X-Com stock in small amounts. In addition, 35,000 shares of X-Com were broadly distributed among roughly 60 stockholders.

As a first step, X-Com's Stock Purchase Plan was converted to an ESOP. Then, with the simultaneous execution of the purchase agreement between ABC and the new ESOP, the Company made a tender offer to all record holders for the remaining 35,000 shares at $12.00 per share. The shares received by the Company through the tender offer were contributed to the ESOP. The ESOP ended up with 98 percent of the shares of X-Com.

EXHIBIT 5.6 Divestiture Using an ESOP

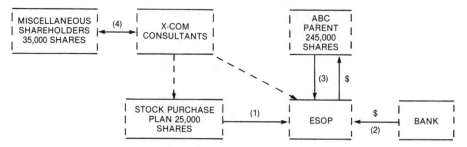

Steps in Divestiture Using an ESOP (Case 5.5)

1. X-Com converts Stock Purchase Plan to an ESOP, transferring its 25,000 shares to the ESOP.

2. ESOP borrows $2,940,000 from a bank for a term of seven years at prime plus 2 percent interest. There is a 15 percent cap on the interest rate. The loan is guaranteed by X-Com and the bank is given a security interest in substantially all of X-Com's assets and a pledge of substantially all the shares acquired by the ESOP. In addition, ABC guarantees the first 10 percent of the bank's possible loan loss for five years. X-Com is obligated under the loan agreement to make contributions to the ESOP sufficient to make principal and interest payments on the loan. X-Com is restricted from paying dividends over the seven-year term of the loan.

3. The ESOP uses the proceeds of the loan to purchase the 245,000 shares held by ABC at $12.00 per share.

4. Simultaneously with the purchase of the shares from ABC, X-Com uses its excess working capital of $420,000 to tender for the remaining outstanding shares.

It is instructive to examine the pro-forma balance sheet of the company before and after the transaction:

TABLE 5.4 Divestiture of X-Com Consultants, Inc. Comparative Balance Sheets Before and After Transaction

	Before Transaction	After Transaction
Assets		
Cash	$ 415,718	$ 187,802[1]
Receivables	5,060,381	5,060,381
Deferred Taxes	367,009	367,009
Prepaid Expenses	95,703	95,703
Total Current Assets	$5,938,811	$5,710,895
Fixed Assets (Net)	878,004	1,378,004
Other Assets	27,976	27,976
Total Assets	$6,844,791	$6,616,875
Liabilities		
Accounts Payable	806,303	806,303
Notes Payable to Parent Co.	227,916[1]	—
Taxes Payable	162,952	162,952
Accrued Expenses	1,847,356	1,847,356
Current ESOP Liability	—	645,890

TABLE 5.4 (continued)

	Before Transaction	*After Transaction*
Other Liabilities	654,854	654,854
Total Current Liabilities	3,699,381	3,673,140
ESOP Liability	—	2,294,110
Stockholders Equity		
Common % $1.00 Par Value	373,676	373,676
Capital in Excess of Par	1,948,547	1,948,547
Retained Earnings	1,348,792	1,348,792
ESOP Adjustment	—	2,940,000
Less Treasury Stock	525,605	525,605
Net Equity	3,145,410	205,410
Total Liabilities	$6,344,791	$6,616,875

[1]$227,916 in cash was used to repay a note to the Seller. The Seller absorbed the closing expenses.

The language in the ESOP document contained much of the standard language previously set forth under Exhibit 5.4. In addition it contained the following: "The Company obligates itself, in a manner reasonably satisfactory to the Trustee, to contribute to the Trust amounts sufficient to enable it to pay each installment of principal and interest on the loan before the date of such installment is due, even if no tax benefit results from such contribution."

Upon completion of the transaction, voting control of the Company shifted to the Administrative Committee of X-Com's ESOP, which was appointed by X-Com's Board of Directors. This Committee instructed the Trustee on how to vote the shares in the ESOP.

Because the divestiture using an ESOP is one of the most common types of ESOP transaction, several further variations of the basic transaction are included here.

CASE 5.6 PARTIAL DIVESTITURE TO AN ESOP

As in the case of the transfer of ownership of a closely held corporation, there is no reason why a management group or outside third party cannot join the ESOP as co-owners in the purchase of the division or subsidiary. An ESOP need not own 100 percent—it can own any percentage.

How it works. Let's say that a buyer can only come up with $8,000,000 in financing, whereas the purchase price is $10,000,000. As $1,000,000 is provided as equity by the buyer, $7,000,000 can be borrowed against the assets to be acquired. The buyer decides to implement an ESOP, the use of which will increase the cash flow sufficient to allow him to borrow a total of $9,000,000. The buyer wants to minimize the amount of ownership flowing to the ESOP, so that he will only utilize a loan to the ESOP to the extent necessary to make up his shortfall without the ESOP (i.e., $2,000,000). This is not surprising. It is unlikely that a buyer will put up a substantial amount of the purchase price for less than majority control. In fact, many ESOP transactions are not consummated because the buyer, who is putting up a significant amount of his own funds, feels that he is giving up too much to the ESOP. This transaction is summarized in the following Exhibit.

EXHIBIT 5.7 Asset Purchase of Parts Division Leveraged ESOP

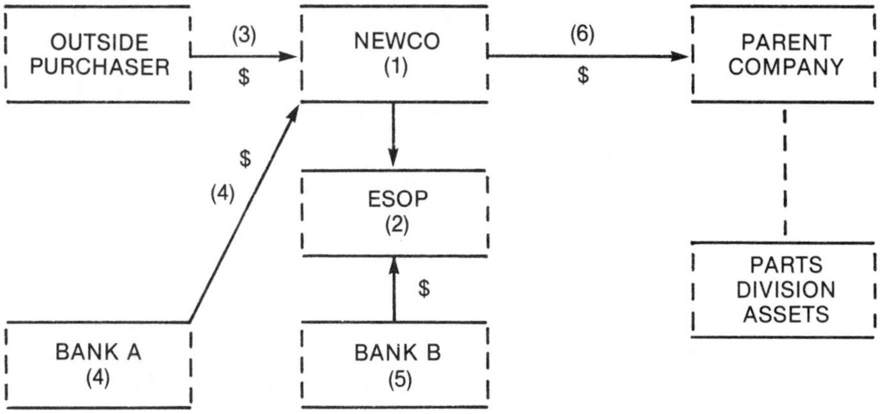

Steps in Purchase of Assets by ESOP and Outside Party

1. Outside purchaser organizes NewCo.
2. NewCo establishes ESOP.
3. Outside purchaser invests $1 million in NewCo in exchange for NewCo Stock.
4. Bank A lends $7 million to NewCo.
5. Bank B lends $2 million to ESOP, which pays the cash to NewCo in exchange for $2,000,000 worth of NewCo Stock.
6. NewCo pays the Parent Company $10,000,000 for the assets of the Parts Division.

Problem. The problem with the above structure is that the buyer has received only $1,000,000 worth of stock in NewCo, whereas the ESOP has received $2,000,000. Even assuming that the buyer has paid less for his shares than the ESOP, he has still given up a substantial control position to the ESOP, without the ESOP having put up anything in return. Of course, it is the improved cash flow resulting from the ESOP that allows the transaction to take place.

CASE 5.7 HOW A DIVESTITURE WITH A NONLEVERAGED ESOP SOFTENS THE DILUTION TO THE BUYER'S POSITION

There is a variation of the preceding transaction that softens the dilution to the buyer's ownership position. This can be done in the following manner.

The buyer invests $1,000,000 as before and Bank A lends $7,000,000. However, Bank B is induced to lend $2,000,000 directly to NewCo with the requirement that NewCo establish an ESOP, and contribute a minimum number of shares to the ESOP sufficient to tax shelter the principal repayments to Bank B. From a cash-flow standpoint, as far as Bank B is concerned this transaction is identical to Case 5.6.

How the buyer benefits. There is a significant difference as far as the buyer is concerned. The buyer begins with 100 percent ownership of NewCo because no shares have been issued to the ESOP. His ownership position will be diluted over time as newly issued shares are contributed to the ESOP. However, during this period the Company is presumably increasing in value. More of this increase in value will accrue to his shares than to the ESOP, and as the per-share value increases, less shares will have to be contributed to the ESOP to shelter the principal repayment.

The bank is critical. If a document can be drafted that will induce Bank B to take part in this transaction, as opposed to the structure in Case 5.6, it is preferable and much more equitable from the buyer's standpoint. The ESOP receives contributions of stock over time during which the value of NewCo stock will change. If the stock grows in value, the ESOP participants will receive less stock than they would have in an "up-front" purchase. It should also be pointed out that the ESOP participants will have less at risk in the early years if the stock subsequently declines in value.

EXHIBIT 5.8 Asset Purchase of Parts Division Nonleveraged ESOP

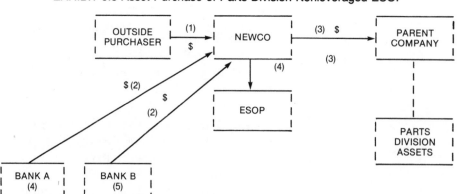

Steps in Nonleveraged ESOP Purchase

1. Outside Purchaser invests $1,000,000 in NewCo and receives 100 percent ownership position.
2. Bank A lends $7 million and Bank B lends $2 million to NewCo.
3. NewCo purchases the assets of Parts Division for $10,000,000.
4. NewCo issues new shares and contributes these to the ESOP over time and in an amount equal to the principal repayments on the loan to Bank B.

5.6 GENERAL GUIDELINES FOR IMPLEMENTING AN ESOP

We have now examined enough examples of ESOPs so that we can suggest a general approach toward their implementation. The following analysis would apply to the transfer of ownership of a closely held corporation or to the divestiture of a subsidiary or division of a company. It provides a structural framework for analyzing a potential ESOP situation and is fashioned after an actual analysis of an ESOP candidate.

The management of "DEF Stores" indicated that they were considering the selling of DEF or of merging it with another company. An ESOP was being considered on a very preliminary basis because (1) it could be adopted unilaterally by management and (2) the potential purchaser's awareness that an ESOP is a viable alternative gives management a fallback position and establishes the credibility of DEF's asking price. Both these considerations strengthened management's negotiating position with respect to a potential merger partner.

Step 1: Determining Whether an ESOP Was Feasible and Practical

To determine whether in fact an ESOP was feasible and practical for DEF, it was necessary to answer the following questions:

1. What were management's intentions regarding the future ownership of DEF?
2. What were the alternatives that would allow these intentions to be realized?
3. What were the advantages and disadvantages of each of these alternatives?
4. Should an ESOP prove to be the most attractive alternative,

what financial and operation problems would have arisen with its establishment?

5. What steps should DEF have taken to set up an ESOP?

Management's Intentions. It was the desire of management to pursue a course of action that would result in either the sale, at a fair price, of 100 percent of the ownership of DEF at a specified time, or a gradual transfer of 100 percent of the ownership over a reasonable period of time. Further, such a transfer was desired in a manner that offered the best chances for the long-run viability of DEF, providing employment for its personnel and continued service to its customers.

Alternative solutions. The alternatives that could have been pursued by DEF are as follows:

- Liquidation of the assets of DEF.
- Sale to or merger with another company, as soon as possible.
- Continued operation of the Company with the intention of selling it in the future.
- Establishment of an ESOP to which the Company's stock would be sold.

The relative merits of each solution are summarized below:

TABLE 5.5 ESOP Feasibility Analysis

Alternative	*Advantage*	*Disadvantage*
Liquidation of assets	Unilateral decision	Time consuming with uncertain values (sale of assets at a loss) Loss of goodwill and going concern value Employee layoffs Potential difficulties from broken contracts, leases etc. Possible adverse tax consequences
Sale to or merger with another company	Commonplace transaction Sale of stock is taxable at capital gains rates	Difficulty in locating a purchaser, Price may not be indicative of long-term value of Company

TABLE 5.5 (continued)

Alternative	Advantage	Disadvantage
Continued operation of the Company with the intention of selling it in the future	May get higher price in future	Doesn't solve management's real problem. Difficulties in retaining key operating personnel.
Employee Stock Ownership Plan	Provides ready, willing and able buyer Offers liquidity for stock at going concern value Provides capital gains treatment on sale of stock (permits withdrawal of excess cash at capital gains rates) Management retains effective control for a long period or indefinitely Employees share in capital growth of the company	Complexity of transaction Employee relations may be strained, resulting in interference with management Uncertainty of stocks future value Encumbrance on Company (including future buyback of shares)

Step 2: Analyzing Covered Payroll and Cash Flow

Once these advantages and disadvantages were laid out for management, the next step was an analysis, as we have seen previously, of the Company's covered payroll and impact of the ESOP on its cash flow.

The following section deals with some important technical considerations regarding the use of ESOPs.

5.7 TECHNICAL REQUIREMENTS FOR ESOPS

Accounting. The American Institute of Certified Public Accountants and the Securities and Exchange Commission both take the position that when an ESOP borrows, the obligation assumed by the employer (i.e., the guarantee to make contributions to the ESOP sufficient to amortize the ESOP loan) should be reflected on the employer's balance sheet as a long-term liability. The offsetting debit to this liability is recorded as a reduction of shareholder's equity. Thus in the case of a 100 percent ESOP purchase, such as in Okinite, shareholder's equity is reduced initially to zero. The liability should be reduced and the reduction in the shareholders' equity is restored or added back as the ESOP repays the debt obligation.

The impact of this accounting treatment was shown in an earlier example on page 98.

Allocation and distribution. The participants in the ESOP receive their stock interests according to the same complex ERISA rules that govern other forms of stock compensation and employee benefit plans. The employee must first become a "participant" in the plan, which is generally accomplished by his being a full-time employee for one year or more. Thus the company may exclude part-time employees from participation. A useful measure of this is 1000 hours of service per year.

The stock or cash that is contributed to the ESOP is "allocated" each year to the separate accounts of each participant. However, stock that has been pledged as security for borrowings by the ESOP cannot be allocated until such time as the debt associated with it has been paid off. The yearly allocations are usually in proportion to employee compensation, although duration of service (seniority) may also be a factor. Thus an employee who earns $16,000 per year may receive an allocation twice as large as an employee who earns $8,000 per year. The distribution can also be made on a per-capita basis or in any reasonable manner that does not unfairly discriminate in favor of higher-paid employees. That is, relative compensation provides a limit on the amount of discrimination that can take place.

Actual receipt or control of the stock is determined by one of several "vesting" schedules provided in ERISA:

• Full vesting on a prescribed graduated basis after 15 years of service.

• Full vesting after ten years of service, or

• Full vesting under the "Rule of 45," which gives an employee with at least five years of service 50 percent of his accrued benefit when the sum of his age and years of service totals 45.

When the employee leaves the company, he or she has the right to the value of the vested portion of his or her account, in one of two forms; either the right to the actual shares or a distribution of the fair market value of the shares in cash. Usually in a closely held company the latter is preferable for both employer and employee. The cash distribution is required by ERISA, which requires that shares received that are not regularly traded in a securities market must have a "put" option, allowing the employee to require the Company or the ESOP to purchase back his shares at fair market value. The Company or ESOP is, however, permitted to buy these back in installments over a five-year period.

Dividends. While stock is held in the ESOP, any dividend paid on it can be immediately passed through to the employees to provide them with additional income. Alternatively, it can be held in the Plan as cash, for the purchase of additional shares, or be used to repay debt incurred by the Plan. These are all matters of Trustee's discretion or they can be provided for explicitly in the Plan document.

Voting. Voting rights on publicly traded shares allocated to participants' accounts must be passed through to the participants. Those that are unallocated are voted by the Trustee. For nonpublicly traded shares it is necessary to pass through the vote on allocated shares on those significant corporate issues that require (either by law, corporate charter, or by-law) a greater-than-majority vote of the shareholders, such as merger or dissolution.

5.8 CAVEATS ON ESOPS: FOUR PROBLEM AREAS TO KEEP IN MIND

ESOPs can be a useful tool for improving cash flow in two situations: the transfer of ownership of a closely held corporation and the divestiture of a division or subsidiary. However, because of the negative impact on earnings per share it might appear that ESOPs have no place in a public corporation. The following chapter shows that this is not the case.

Four problem areas should be kept in mind. The first is that *employees must be educated about ESOPs so they can evolve into ownership,* especially in smaller firms that are heavily dependent upon two or three key employees. Second, *ESOPs by themselves are not ideal retirement plans* because the assets are not diversified and the rate of employer contributions is generally not fixed. This point is significant. Frequently, in an effort to consummate an ESOP transaction, management has attempted to convince employees to discontinue a pension plan in favor of an ESOP or to convert existing pension plan assets into ESOP assets. This is something that should not be undertaken lightly.

Third, *ESOPs are complicated and expensive.* A typical ESOP may cost $15,000 to $20,000 to design and implement, plus roughly $10,000 for administration and yearly valuation of employer securities contributed to the Plan. The penalties for failure to comply with the legal complexities of ESOPs can be heavy. However, the design costs are comparable to the costs for any other deferred compensation plan, though many other types do not require yearly valuations.

Finally, *ESOPs result in a hidden long-term liability for companies*. As vested employees retire from the company and exercise the put option on the stock they have received from the Plan, the company must plan ahead so that it has adequate liquidity to meet the obligation to re-purchase these shares.

chapter 6

How Public Companies Can Use ESOPs, TRASOPs, and Payroll-Based Stock Ownership Plans as Financing Tools

The discussion of Employee Stock Ownership Plans in Chapter 5 was directed at both closely held and public companies. Transfers of ownership and the purchase of shares from an owner/founder are of particular interest to the private concern, whereas divestitures more often pertain to the public conglomerate. The subject of capital formation is of concern to all corporations, whether public or private.

This chapter deals primarily with the use of Employee Stock Ownership Plans in public companies, both as a vehicle for going private and as a device in resisting a takeover attempt. In addition, a discussion is included here on Tax Reduction Act Stock Ownership Plans and the new payroll-based tax credit ESOPs. These devices have been and will continue to be used extensively by public companies.

6.1 HOW ESOPS PURCHASE STOCK FROM A PRIVATE SHAREHOLDER OF A PUBLIC COMPANY

As in the situations considered in the previous chapter involving the purchase of shares from stockholders of privately held companies, an ESOP can purchase shares from individual holders of publicly traded shares. §408e(1) of ERISA applies here as well, requiring that the stock cannot be purchased from a party-in-interest for more than adequate consideration, defined as the prevailing market price for a publicly traded security.

If the stock that is not publicly owned is held by more than a few shareholders, it is usually necessary for the ESOP to make an informal "tender" to all the "private" shareholders to purchase their shares on the same terms and conditions on a pro-rata basis. It is not uncommon for corporations themselves to repurchase stock on a privately negotiated basis at a price above current market under Rule 13e-2 in situations where the public market price is abnormally low. However, §408e(1) of ERISA mandates that these shares would then have to be contributed to the ESOP at the lesser market price.

The purchase of shares from the "private" shareholders is often the first step in making the entire company private. This is considered in the following section.

6.2 HOW TO USE AN ESOP TO GO PRIVATE

The term "going private" has often been loosely used to characterize the delisting of a security from a national securities exchange. It has also referred to a security or company becoming exempt from the jurisdiction of the SEC. We will use the latter definition, which means that a company reduces the number of its shareholders to less than 300 and must deregister under §12g(4) of the SEC Act of 1934.

6.2.1 The Benefits and Drawbacks of Going Private

There are numerous motivations for a public company to go private. These include the acquisition of shares at a bargain price, retiring outstanding shares in order to increase earnings per share, providing the company with greater flexibility in conducting its business without the pressures of public scrutiny, reducing the costs of public reporting and shareholder relations, and optimizing estate planning objectives of the principal shareholders.

As in every use of the ESOP, the benefits must be weighed against the cash-flow drain resulting from the cost of repurchasing the shares. Two new considerations develop with going private transactions: the risk of shareholder objections and litigation, and the lack of market for the once publicly held shares of the principal shareholders.

6.2.2 Using an ESOP

An ESOP may be used to accomplish a going private either by purchasing shares on the market until the number of shareholders is gradually reduced below 300 or by making a tender offer of sufficient size to reduce the number of shareholders at once to less than 300. In this regard individual participants in the ESOP (with the exception of those who have received shares upon retirement) are not regarded as individual shareholders. The ESOP is considered one shareholder.

The ESOP can accomplish the purchase by financing the re-acquisition of shares with pretax rather than after tax dollars. The company frequently could not afford to go private if it had to purchase the shares with aftertax dollars.

6.2.3 How Pamida, Inc. Went Private

In January of 1981, Pamida, Inc. of Omaha, Nebraska, sold all the assets of its discount store business to a new company, New Pamida, Inc. (New Pamida), which was to be owned indirectly by eligible employees of New Pamida through an ESOP. Pamida, Inc. operated 188 general merchandise discount stores in 13 Midwestern and Rocky Mountain states.

The sale of substantially all of the Company's assets and business (except certain retained assets) plus the assumption of substantially all of the liabilities and obligations, was for cash of $41,623,520. After consummation of the sale of assets, the company offered to purchase from its shareholders all of the outstanding public shares of the Company's common stock, resulting in the Company going private. Shareholders who did not tender all of the shares remained shareholders of the Company, which then operated as a closed-end investment company (i.e., a company engaged primarily in the business of investing, reinvesting, or trading in securities of other issuers).

On October 9, 1980, the day prior to the company's announcement that there would be an offer to purchase outstanding shares at $6.00 per share, the closing price of the Company's Common Stock on the New York Stock Exchange was $4.50. On November 26, 1980, the closing price was $5.38. Prior to the announcement of the proposed transaction, the Company's stock had not sold for more than $4.88 since before November 1, 1978.

Pamida's Financial Position. The following table summarizes the financial position of the company.

TABLE 6.1 Summary Financial Statements of Pamida, Inc.

Summary Statements of Earnings

	Years Ended January 31	
	1979	*1980*
Revenues (000's)	$ 318,833	333,463
Net income (000's)	528	3,053
Net income per common share	.06	.33
Average common shares outstanding	9,259,232	9,256,260
Book value per share at end of period	$6.85	$7.15

Summary Balance Sheet

	October 31, 1980	*Proforma After Sale Transaction*
Total assets (000's)	$152,312	$49,242
Total liabilities (000's)	$ 84,745	$ 119
Working capital (000's)	$ 61,379	$49,123
Total stockholder's equity (000's)[1]	$ 67,567	$49,123
Book value per share[1]	$ 7.30	$ 5.22

[1]There was a net loss from the sale of Company's assets of $18,977,000, resulting from a gross loss of $27,353,000 from sale below book value, less recovery of $8,376,000 in income taxes.

How the ESOP Came About. The ESOP concept evolved in the following manner. Mr. Witherspoon, who owned or controlled approximately 44 percent of the Company's stock, desired to retire from the Company's discount store business, yet he wanted to assure stability and continuity of management for the Company's discount business and to preserve the jobs of the company's employees. There were preliminary proposals received by the Company from third parties for the Company's stock or assets at prices between $3.00 and $4.00 per share. Mr. Witherspoon did not pursue such proposals because he did not believe that they represented a fair price for the Company or its stock.

New Pamida, Inc. was then formed solely to act as the purchaser in this transaction, and its management was to consist of the Company's present senior management with the exception of Witherspoon, and the new private company would be owned by its eligible employees through the vehicle of an ESOP. This transaction and the expected employment and compensation arrangements between New Pamida and certain of the existing senior management employees of the Company, along with the potential ownership position of management and the employees of the Company, were expected to provide substantial incentives for such management personnel to remain in the employ of New Pamida, thereby assuring the necessary stability and continuity.

Financing. The total net cash amount paid to the Company by New Pamida was $40,866,000 ($41,623,520 less expenses of $757,520). Such funds were provided from the following sources:

- Cash plus short-term investments of the Company $26,000,000
- Miscellaneous assets retained   272,000
- New industrial development revenue bonds   4,500,000
- Nine-year bank loan at prime plus 3 percent   10,094,000
     $40,866,000

The bank loan was provided by a group of five commercial banks, and was secured by a pledge of the promissory note of the New Pamida ESOP given to New Pamida in partial payment for the stock of New Pamida to be owned by the ESOP and by a pledge of such stock.

In addition to the cash portion of the purchase price, New Pamida assumed liabilities of the Company of approximately $47,000,000.

At the closing of the transaction, all of the outstanding shares of

New Pamida common stock were issued to its ESOP, for a consideration of $19,019,000. The ESOP paid such purchase price in cash to the extent of $19,000 (which it received as an initial contribution from New Pamida), and the balance of the purchase price was represented by the ESOP's interest-free, nonrecourse promissory note in the principal amount of $19,000,000, payable in installments over a nine-year period as follows: $570,000 the first year, $1,520,000 the second year, $1,710,000 the third year, $1,900,000 the fourth and fifth years, $2,228,000 the sixth, and $3,040,000 the seventh, eighth and ninth years.

The payment of the note by the ESOP was secured by a pledge of the New Pamida common stock acquired by the ESOP. Shares were to be released from the pledge annually as the ESOP made payments under the note, and such released shares were to be allocated to the individual accounts of the ESOP participants in accordance with the terms of the ESOP. The note was to be paid by the ESOP with funds derived from annual contributions to the ESOP that New Pamida intended to make.

Proforma Summary Balance Sheet. The following is a proforma summary balance sheet of New Pamida after the transaction. Particularly noteworthy is the near-zero net worth: this transaction was accomplished with essentially 100 percent leverage.

TABLE 6.2 New Pamida Summary Proforma Balance Sheet

Total assets (exclusive of non-recourse note receivable from ESOP)	$77,330,000
Liabilities Assumed (net of refinancings)	$47,253,000
Other Liabilities	500,000
New Long-Term Debt	25,000,000
New Capitalized Lease obligations	4,500,000
Total Liabilities	77,253,000
Stockholders' Equity	77,000[1]
Total Liabilities and Equity	$77,330,000

[1]$77,000 consists of the initial ESOP contribution of $19,000 plus approximately $58,000 connected with the sale of warrants.

The transaction is summarized in the following exhibit.

EXHIBIT 6.1 Going Private Using ESOP

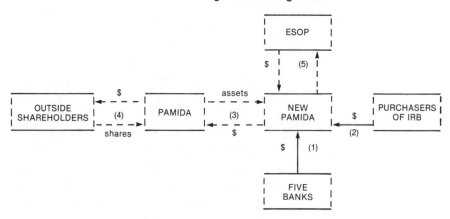

Steps in Going Private Using an ESOP

1. Five banks lend New Pamida $10,094,000.

2. New Pamida issues industrial revenue bonds for $4,500,000.

3. Simultaneously with (1) and (2), New Pamida purchases the assets and net of cash, and assumes the liabilities of Pamida.

4. Pamida, using its cash and miscellaneous assets of $26,272,000, along with the $10,594,000 received from New Pamida, pays its shareholders $40,866,000.

5. Simultaneously with the above, New Pamida issues all its outstanding shares to its ESOP, in exchange for cash of $19,000 and notes of $19,000,000.

6.2.4 Restrictions on ESOP Stock Purchases

When the ESOP purchases shares on the market, it is restricted by the volume and price limitations under SEC Rule 13-2, just as if it were a company purchasing its own shares. The amount that can be purchased on any one day is limited to 15 percent of the average daily volume on the exchange in the four preceding calendar weeks or one round lot per day, whichever is greater.[1] Also, for a security whose principal market is a registered national securities exchange, no bid can be made at a price higher than the last sale or highest current bid, whichever is higher. If not listed on a national securities exchange, no bid can be

---

[1]These limitations may be avoided if the ESOP is controlled by an independent trustee, as is the case, for example, of the Sears Roebuck Stock Plan.

made higher than the mean between the highest current bid and the lowest offer.

Another restriction that must be considered is that purchases do not violate Rule 10 b-5, which prohibits purchases from being used for the purpose of manipulating the stock price to benefit the corporation or insiders. This is an issue that lurked in the background during Continental's attempt to prevent a takeover by Texas Airlines and will be discussed in the next section. A different rule with similar prohibitions is §406(a) (1) (D) of ERISA, which prohibits the use of plan assets for the benefit of a party-in-interest.

How to Surmount These Prohibitions. Both of these prohibitions are largely obviated if the ESOP is engaged in a systematic program of purchasing shares in the market. The plan should provide for adequate flexibility as to the timing of purchases even though shares are purchased on a systematic basis. Whereas most plans allow for a contribution at year end, in the case of open-market purchases it may be desirable to make contributions and purchases quarterly or monthly.

6.3 USING AN ESOP TO RESIST A TAKEOVER ATTEMPT

Assume that a defending company (Defender) is the target of a takeover bid by another raiding company (Raider), and that the raiding company owns roughly 25 percent of the stock. Defender's directors and principal shareholders control 30 percent of the stock, with the remaining 45 percent broadly held among public shareholders. In order to ward off Raider and maintain control, the Defender can establish an ESOP and issue new shares to it, thus diluting the position of Raider and maintaining control in the hands of the insiders.

6.3.1 Beware of These Potential SEC and ERISA Problems

This tactic was employed by Continental Airlines in 1981. However, there are some very serious potential SEC and ERISA problems that arise in this type of maneuver. These arise when the objective of the directors in establishing the ESOP appears to be for their maintaining control rather than for the "exclusive benefit" of the employees. Would there be an ESOP without this defensive action? A frequent ancillary question is whether the Trustee of the ESOP violated the prudent-man rule by paying more than adequate consideration for the shares. Frequently the price may be inflated because of the competing bids for the shares without regard for the dilutive effect of the issuance of the new shares.

There are several important precedents involving the use of ESOPs to resist a takeover attempt. In 1974, E-Systems Inc. successfully conducted a competing tender offer using an ESOP. Then, in 1975, the case of *Klaus v. Hi-Shear Corporation* highlighted some of the SEC and corporate law problems involved. In that case a leveraged ESOP was used as a defensive measure to defeat a takeover bid. It was effective because it saw itself as a candidate in advance. However, in *Podesta v. Calumet Industries, Inc.* (1978), the timing of the adoption and funding of the ESOP became the determining factors. In the later case the ESOP was subject to question because it was established in the proxy contest after the Form 13D had already been filed.

6.3.2 How Continental Airlines Used an ESOP to Deter a Takeover

Another problem for the fiduciary in takeover situations is the question of whether the fiduciary who has purchased the stock using the ESOP can hold the stock when there is another tender at a higher price. This concern, however, did not deter the directors of Continental Airlines. There never was a more closely followed contest for control involving an ESOP than the takeover attempt by Texas International Airlines of Continental Airlines in 1981.

In the early months of 1981, Texas Air had paid $93 million, or an average of $12.50 per share, for 7.5 million Continental shares, giving Texas a 48.5 percent holding; the vast majority (6 million) of these were obtained from a tender offer at $13/share. The Civil Aeronautics Board limited the voting power of these shares until the impact of the potential merger on airline competition could be thoroughly examined.

In April Texas offered the Continental Board $13/share for the remaining 51.5 percent or the equivalent of $14/share on a tax-free basis. Continental not only rejected this offer but announced that nine of its lending banks, led by First National Bank of Chicago and Security Pacific National Bank, had pledged more than $185 million to finance an Employee Stock Ownership Plan. The financing package included a commitment from the Pilot's Retirement Fund for $40 million. The ESOP was to receive 15.4 million newly issued shares, giving it 51 percent of all outstanding shares, and reducing Texas' holding to less than 25 percent.

The proceeds from the sale of the shares to the ESOP were to be used to repay existing debt and to reduce Continental's long-term debt to $28 million from $213 million. In addition, Continental expected between $25 million and $30 million in annual interest expense that would in effect be borne by the 11,000 employees who had agreed to a 15 percent pay cut over the next four to seven years to pay for the stock.

In June, Texas engaged in several legal maneuvers, including a request for a preliminary injunction blocking the issuance of shares to the ESOP. The New York Stock Exchange would not continue Continental's listing if the new stock issuance to the ESOP were not submitted to a shareholder note. Continental's position was that the shareholders had already authorized the issuance of 50 million shares.

As an alternative to retaining its listing, Continental sought to have the shares issued in California. It had been encouraged on July 10 when a California Supreme Court Judge in Los Angeles denied Texas' request for an injunction to block the issuance of the 15.4 million shares. Continental's strategy in asking the California Corporations Commission to sponsor the stock issue of new special shares that could not be traded on the New York Stock Exchange was to get the ESOP implemented quickly so that Texas would have to attempt to overturn it. Thus Continental was racing for a favorable decision in California against approval of the merger by the Civil Aeronautics Board.

Largely as a result of the denial of Texas' request for an injunction, it appeared that Texas might sell its shares back to Continental. In mid-July the stock closed at $9.25, whereas Texas had purchased the bulk of its shares for $13. Texas had used its Continental stock to secure a $50-million loan from Manufacturer's Hanover in February, the terms of which required the market value of pledged stock to be at least 150 percent of the loan value outstanding.

Then on July 14 California's Commissioner of Corporations, Geraldine Green, issued a ruling that "Continental's plan isn't fair, just, and equitable." The crux of her decision was that the plan could not be implemented without a proper note of all the shareholders, including Texas. Now there was only one alternative left for Continental, which was to override the Commissioner's ruling by going directly to the state legislature.

Meanwhile the Civil Aeronautics Board was reaching a decision on the appropriateness of the merger. In March the CAB had allowed Texas to acquire up to 48.5 percent of Continental's shares, but required that such shares be placed in Trust. The Trustee was allowed to vote on most matters, and the CAB permitted Texas to try to vote all of its holders against the ESOP. Continental itself rebuffed this attempt, refusing to conduct a shareholder vote on the plan.

On August 20th the CAB recommended allowance of Texas' takeover of Continental, but would not allow a shareholders' meeting until President Reagan confirmed the CAB's decision (for which he had until October 13).

On August 24, by a vote of 56 to 20, the California Assembly passed a bill exempting Continental from the state law that Commissioner Green had applied in blocking the ESOP. If the California Senate had approved the bill and Governor Edmund Brown, Jr. had signed it, the Continental employees could have controlled the company before Reagan ruled on the merger.

Two Death Blows to Continental. At this point two death blows were delivered to Continental. The bank consortium that had offered to finance the ESOP takeover withdrew its offer. Secondly, the critical bill could not get off the floor of the Senate. Finally, on September 8th, the CAB permitted Texas to buy up to 67 percent of Continental shares, thus giving Texas enough (50 percent) to force a shareholder meeting under state law in Nevada, where Continental was incorporated. Then Texas purchased 300,000 additional shares, giving it 50.3 percent of the outstanding shares. A shareholder meeting was requested for October 19 (for the purpose of electing new directors), and the battle for control of Continental was over.

On March 24, 1982, Texas Air Corporation, parent of Texas International Airlines, and Continental announced an agreement under which Texas Air's 51 percent ownership of Continental would be increased to total ownership through exchanges of stock. Each share of the 49 percent of Continental's common stock not held by Texas was to be exchanged for four-tenths of a share of Texas Air's common and $4 of a new issue of Texas Air preferred stock. The new issue was to pay an annual dividend of 15 percent of the stock's liquidating value.

6.4 TRASOPS: A BENEFIT PAID FOR BY UNCLE SAM

6.4.1 Legislative History

"TRASOP," another form of employee stock ownership plan, is an acronym for Tax Reduction Act Stock Ownership Plan. The Tax Reduction Act of 1975 increased the standard investment credit from 7 percent to 10 percent, so that a company with, let's say, a hundred-million-dollar capital expenditure program could obtain ten-million dollars in tax credits. This Act also allowed a company to claim an additional 1 percent Investment Tax Credit for the 1975 and 1976 tax years, if an amount equal to the 1 percent were contributed to a TRASOP. The TRASOP had to invest in company stock that was to be allocated to the employees in amounts proportional to their total compensation up to $100,000.

The two-year time frame created by the legislation was problematic because the TRASOP was very costly to set up, did not provide a very large benefit, and was costly to administer. There were also several burdensome technical requirements, such as immediate vesting, pass-through voting, and the unusual seven-year holding period.

The Tax Reform Act of 1976 and the Tax Reduction Act of 1978 addressed some of the problems in the earlier TRASOP legislation. These Acts extended the favorable tax treatment of TRASOPs through 1983 and they allowed a TRASOP Company to recover some of the costs of setting up the plan from the additional investment credit. The Acts also made available an option allowing an additional ½ percent tax credit for company contributions to the TRASOP that were matched by employees.

The Economic Recovery Tax Act of 1981 changed the 1983 termination date for TRASOPs from 1983 to December 31, 1982. As a result of this Act, the investment tax credit type ESOP is to be replaced by a payroll-based tax credit employee stock ownership plan in subsequent years. A tax credit for a company's contributions to an employee stock ownership plan after 1982 will be calculated on the basis of wages paid in calendar years 1983 through 1987, after which the payroll-based plans will expire.

The rationale for replacing the investment-based tax credit ESOP with the payroll-based tax credit ESOP was the belief that payroll-based contributions would provide a greater incentive for labor-intensive companies to make ESOP contributions.

6.4.2 Is a TRASOP Right for You?

Until the advent of payroll-based tax credit ESOPs, companies with large capital expenditure budgets relative to the number of employees have been most likely to benefit from TRASOPs. A general rule of thumb has been the following: If 1 percent of the qualified capital expenditures divided by the number of eligible employees is more than $100, a TRASOP is considered worth pursuing. This has included quite a large number of major companies: 90 percent of the nation's 50 largest utilities now have TRASOPs and 85 percent of the largest petroleum refiners. Roughly 44 percent of all industrials with over $1 billion in sales have TRASOPs.

A November, 1981 survey by Hewitt Associates indicates that nearly half of America's major companies expect to adopt or switch to the new payroll-based tax credit ESOPs. A significant portion of these already have the investment-based tax credit ESOP.

It is evident that American business has realized that employee ownership has tremendous appeal, and this has been coupled with the fact that the benefit has not been costing the company anything. It has been paid for by Uncle Sam. The following is a sampling of companies that have instituted TRASOPs:

TABLE 6.3 Trasop Companies

AT&T	Eastman Kodak
Alcoa	Koopers
Anchor Hocking	Kraft
Burlington	Mobil
Beatrice Foods	Memorex
Continental Oil	Merch
Con Ed	Niagara Mohawk
Collins & Aikman	Newmont Mining
Crown Zellerbach	Olinkraft
Continental Group	Philip Morris
Duquesne Light	Polaroid
du Pont	Pittston
Eltra	Scott Paper
Federal Paper Board	St. Regis Paper
Florida Gas	Southern New England Telephone
Florida P&L	Southern Pacific
General Dynamics	Stanley Works
Getty Oil	Standard Oil of Ohio
Goodyear	Westvaco
Gulf Oil	Weyerhauser

6.5 TECHNICAL REQUIREMENTS OF TRASOPS

TRASOPs must satisfy the same general requirements that apply to ESOPs. In addition, there are special rules imposed only upon TRA-SOPs. The employer must elect the 11 percent investment tax credit each year, on or before the due date for filing the corporation's income tax return for the taxable year in which the credit is earned. For most corporations the tax return for the fiscal year is due in September of the following year. The timing of the transfer of the amount of the 1 percent credit to the TRASOP and the application of funds to the purchase of employer securities is also critical. Funds must be transferred and securities must be purchased on or before the 30th day following the due date for filing the corporation income tax return. The employer must agree, as a condition to receiving the additional 1 percent investment tax credit, to transfer forthwith to the plan, employer securities having an aggregate value at the time of the claim of 1 percent of the amount of the qualified investment for the taxable year.

A TRASOP can exclude nonsalaried employees. Only those employees who are required by the coverage requirements of Section 410 of the Internal Revenue Code need participate. The typical annual contribution in the plans for those companies listed above runs between $100 and $300 for each employee.

Limitations on Allocations to Employees. There are specific limitations on the allocations to the employees through a TRASOP. Each participant must be allocated stock attributable to the employer's contribution in the proportion that his or her salary is to total covered compensation. The amount allocated is subject to §415 of the Internal Revenue Code, which limits additions to an employee's account under defined contribution plans to 25 percent of annual pay. Aggregation rules will apply, but the allocation may be extended over whatever period necessary to bring the allocation within the limits.

An employer may further restrict the allocation by placing a maximum on the compensation to be considered in determining the allocation of stock. Total compensation up to a stated limit lower than $100,000 may be used if desired. Some companies place a $100 cap on eligible compensation that is considered in calculating share allocation. This effectively insures that each employee receives the same number of shares regardless of compensation.

Vesting and Withdrawals. Employees participating in a TRASOP become vested immediately and the employee must be allowed to direct the voting of the stock. Employees may make withdrawals prior to termination of employment, but in-service withdrawals of amounts cannot be made until 84 months (7 years) after they are credited to the participant's account, except for instances of death, disability, or termination of employment.

Tax Treatment. Because the TRASOP will be a qualified plan, a lump sum distribution at retirement is given favorable tax treatment. The lower of cost or market price of the stock at the time of distribution is considered ordinary income for the participant, but might be subject to the beneficial treatment of $\frac{1}{10}$ averaging. If the market value is higher than cost when the stock is distributed, that unrealized appreciation will be a long-term capital gain when the stock is sold. The holding period and cost basis for any further gain or loss begins with distribution.

For example, assume that the cost to the qualified plan was $800 and that market value at the time of distribution is $1,000. The unrealized appreciation at the time of distribution is thus $200, which would be treated as long-term capital gain. If the stock is held and subsequently sold three months after distribution at a price of $1,300, the additional $300 of gain obtained subsequent to receipt of the share would be accorded short-term capital gain treatment. If the stock had been sold nine months after the distribution date, the $300 would have been a long-term capital gain.

If the cost to the qualified plan had been $800 but the market value at the time of distribution had been $600, the recipient would have ordinary income of $600. His cost basis for any further gain or loss would be $600.

6.6 TWO WAYS THAT LARGE PUBLIC COMPANIES CAN BENEFIT FROM TAX CREDIT ESOPS

For a smaller company, the benefits of a TRASOP have probably not been sufficient to justify the additional administrative costs. However, for a larger company, there are greater inherent tax advantages despite the more restrictive requirements relating to investment credit ESOPs as compared to ESOPs generally. Since the employer receives a tax credit instead of a tax deduction for qualifying contributions, the tax benefit of the contribution is effectively doubled.

The tax advantage to the large, publicly owned company is achieved in one of two ways. If the company contributes cash to the plan, the cash can be used to purchase employer securities on the open market. A stock ownership benefit is provided at zero cost to the plan participants.

A second alternative is for the company to contribute newly issued or treasury stock to the plan, again resulting in stock ownership for the participants plus a capital infusion for the company.

Case 6.1, which follows, shows the tax-shelter benefits of a TRASOP. It is a TRASOP combined with an ESOP. An existing ESOP may be amended to meet the TRASOP requirements. However, amounts transferred to the plan for tax credit purposes must be credited to an account separate from the regular contributions to the plan.

For example, MCI Communications Corporation established a combined ESOP/TRASOP in 1979. MCI has contributed stock equal to 5 percent of covered compensation to the ESOP for each year that the plan has been in existence. For the first year of operation, the TRASOP contribution was equal to 1 percent of qualified investment, which worked out to roughly 3 percent of participating employee's compensation. Last year the TRASOP contribution equaled 8 percent of covered compensation.

The shift from the investment-based TRASOP tax credit to the payroll-based credit is an unfavorable development for a capital-intensive company such as MCI. Under the payroll-based credit requirements, it will have to limit its tax credit contribution to .5 percent of payroll.

CASE 6.1 USING A TRASOP COMBINED WITH AN ESOP TO TAX SHELTER REPAYMENT OF A BANK LOAN

A corporation needs $20,000,000 for the purchase of equipment and borrows that amount from a bank. It has a qualified payroll of $40,000,000. The company makes annual cash contributions to its ESOP/TRASOP equal to 10 percent of its payroll (although up to 25 percent is permitted) and additional cash contributions of 1 percent of the equipment cost (TRASOP credit). The company issues new shares that it then sells to its ESOP/TRASOP and receives the cash that it has contributed for that year in exchange for the shares. This cash is used to service principal and interest payments on the bank debt.

EXHIBIT 6.2 Use of a Combined ESOP/TRASOP

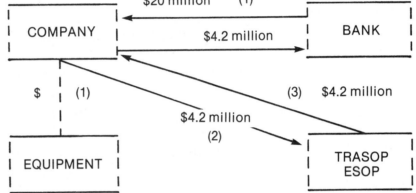

Steps in the Use of a Combined ESOP/TRASOP

1. Company borrows $20 million and purchases equipment.
2. Company makes deductible cash contributions to ESOP and receives ITC for 1 percent of equipment cost for contribution to TRASOP.
3. ESOP purchases newly issued shares from Company.
4. Company repays bank borrowings with proceeds from sale of shares to ESOP/TRASOP.

CASE 6.2 THE MATCHING FUND TRASOP

A company with a TRASOP may also obtain an additional one-half percent investment tax credit if it makes a contribution of additional cash or securities and such contribution is matched by an equal contribution by employees. It would take place in the following manner.

A company establishes a TRASOP without an ESOP and pur-

7.10 TECHNICAL CONSIDERATIONS FOR DEEP DISCOUNT DEBT

Thus far the discussion of original issue deep discount bonds has been fairly general and historical. Sections 7.10 through 7.12 consider their technical underpinnings.

Original issue discount, which is the difference between the principal amount of the debt securities at stated maturity and their issue price, is an indication that the coupon rate is not a sufficiently high rate of interest for the bond to bring their face value in the open market. The difference between the face amount or par value of the security and the actual amount of proceeds represents additional interest that will be paid as part of the face value at maturity. Thus the periodic interest expense, let's say semi-annual, includes the coupon payment plus an expense representing amortization of an appropriate amount of discount.

7.10.1 Advantages to the Issuer and Borrower

Deep discount bonds have the advantage to the issuer of significantly lower after-tax costs and a substantially higher annual cash flow over the life of the issue. The borrower has the use of the full amount of the proceeds with no need to pay back any funds as principal before maturity, and little or no interest. In addition, the borrower realizes an annual tax savings as a result of deducting the amortized discount.

Prior to the Tax Equity and Fiscal Responsibility Act of 1982 (TEFRA), borrowers were allowed under Treasury Regulation 1.163-4(a) to prorate the discount and take it in equal installments as an interest-expense deduction over the life of the obligation. The borrower's tax advantage for a discount bond was greater than a conventional bond because the present value of the deductible interest expense was higher with the discount bonds.

The advantage to the borrower was highlighted by a comparison of a 20-year conventional bond with a 16 percent coupon to a 20-year deep discount bond with the same yield to maturity (16 percent), but a coupon of 7 percent. The deep discount bond would have to be priced at $46.34 to yield 16 percent. Assuming a 46 percent tax bracket, the borrower's annual after-tax cost would be 8.64 percent on the conventional bond, but on the deep discount bonds the annual cost would be 7.95 percent. The deep discount bond resulted in an after-tax savings of 69 basis points.

Lower coupons and longer maturities increased the tax savings to the borrower. It is also significant that higher market rates of interest increase the potential tax savings. If the expected market yield to maturity were 10 percent instead of 16 percent, then the after-tax savings on a 20-year 7 percent coupon deep discount bond would be only 9 basis points (as opposed to 69 basis points) per annum. This helps to account for the widespread interest in deep discount bonds among borrowers during recent periods of excessive interest costs.

The following table illustrates the increase in tax savings through a decrease in coupon on a 30-year bond. The bonds are issued to yield 14 percent.

TABLE 7.2 Costs to Issuer of Bonds Issued to Yield 14%

	Coupon			
	0%	5%	10%	14%
Pretax Cost	8.48	12.30	13.52	14.0
After-tax (@46% Tax Rate)	4.58	6.64	7.3	7.36

The initial holder of an original issue deep discount bond is required for tax purposes to include a ratable portion of the discount as ordinary interest income, notwithstanding the fact that the notes do not provide for any periodic payments of interest. Any subsequent purchaser of the notes must similarly account for a portion of the original issue discount as interest income on a ratable basis, but the amount of the aggregate discount to be included would be reduced by the amount, if any, by which the price paid by the subsequent purchaser of the note exceeds the issue price increased by the amount of original issue discount attributable to the period prior to purchase.

Because of the application of the original issue discount rules, a tax-paying holder of the notes would receive interest income each year well in advance of the receipt of any cash flow. The holder would receive no cash flow (except in the case of redemption or an event of default) until maturity. This would reduce the holder's after-tax return on a discounted cash-flow basis below the after-tax return available on conventional bonds. The reduced after-tax yield makes these securities attractive primarily to nontaxpaying investors such as pension funds.

It should be pointed out that the lender may take on added risks with discount bonds because of the postponement of cash inflows over the life of the bonds. For this reason the issuer might be required to offer the lender risk-and-yield premiums.

The unusual tax treatment of deep discount bonds has resulted in these being attractive investment vehicles for foreign investors as well. Although foreign investors are generally subject to a 30-percent withholding tax on U.S. interest income, the amount withheld can never exceed the amount of the coupon.

7.10.2 The Adverse Effects of TEFRA

The advantages of deep discount bonds as a means of raising capital were adversely affected by the passage of TEFRA. For bonds issued after July 1, 1982, TEFRA required that the deduction attributable to the amortization of discount be computed under a formula that takes into account the compounding of accrued interest. The entire discount will still be deducted over the life of the bonds, but because of the compounding effect, the deduction in the early years is cut sharply.

For example, if a bond is issued with net proceeds of $1,000 and a yield of 15 percent, the amortized discount in the first year would only be $150 (i.e., 15 percent × $1,000), whereas in the second year it would be $172.50 (i.e., 15 percent × $1,150).

7.10.3 Attempts to Circumvent TEFRA

In response to the adverse impact of TEFRA upon the tax advantages of deep discount debt, several issuers, including Exxon and General Motors Acceptance Corp. (GMAC), attempted to design new debt instruments that would circumvent TEFRA.

Exxon developed a new instrument called a deferred interest debenture, which was issued in conjunction with a tax-free reorganization. The debt instrument was to pay $1,000 upon maturity in 30 years, have a face value of $270, and accrued interest of $730.

By definition under the tax code, there was no original issue discount involved in the issuance of such securities. This resulted in the same tax benefits to Exxon as it would have received prior to TEFRA for deep discount debt. Interest could be deducted each year even though none of it was payable until maturity.

In response to the deferred interest debenture, Congress passed a Technical Corrections Act to eliminate the loophole, requiring that the deferred interest be treated as original issue discount. The amendment was effective for securities issued after December 13, 1982.

7.10.4 The Tax Reform Act of 1984

The Tax Reform Act of 1984 made further changes to the Original Issue Discount rules. In order to curtail the mismatching of deductions with income, the rules were expanded so that they became applicable to obligations issued for nonpublicly traded property. Prior to the passage of this Act, the OID rules were applicable to obligations issued for property, such as stock, which was publicly traded in an established market, and to privately placed bonds. The rules would subsequently apply to the purchase of seller-financed property.

The Act contained a number of additional OID provisions intended to eliminate the abusive use of deep discount debt, including the prevention of the use of discount bonds as a basis for tax-sheltered transactions in which taxes are deferred and ordinary income is converted into capital gain.

7.11 ACCOUNTING FOR DEEP DISCOUNT DEBT

There have been two methods of amortizing the discount for accounting purposes. The simpler method involves a straight-line allocation of discount over the life of the bond. Under this method, the amount of discount to be amortized at each interest payment date (quarterly or semiannually) is the total discount to be amortized over the life of the bond divided by the number of interest payment dates. The account on the balance sheet "Discount on Notes[8] Payable" is treated as a contra-liability. It is a deduction from the liability account "Notes Payable."

The Preferred Method. Although the straight-line method had been generally accepted under GAAP, the preferred approach is the *effective interest method.*[9] The straight-line method results in a changing rate of interest each period because the effective liability (i.e., par value less unamortized discount) is changing each period. The effective interest method of amortization calculates an interest charge each period that results in a constant interest rate. The total interest charges over the life of the bonds will be the same as when the straight-line method is used, but the charge per period will increase for the bonds issued at a discount. The effective interest for a particular period is determined by multiplying the net liability at the start of the period (i.e., notes payable less discount payable) by the effective yield rate on the note at the time of issue (as opposed to time of interest payment).

Thus the effective interest will increase for each period over the life of the bond, as will the net liability. However, the current yield, calculated as the effective interest for a particular period divided by the net liability at the beginning of that period, will always be the same.

7.11.1 Conventional and Deep Discount Notes Compared

The following is a comparison of a $15,000,000 discount note with a 7 percent coupon and a $10,000,000 conventional note with a 17 percent coupon. Seventeen percent is the yield to maturity of the discount

---

[8]These may also be bonds or debentures.
[9]Opinion No. 21 of the Accounting Principles Board of the AICPA.

note as well. The proceeds are $10,078,989. The term of the notes is five years with semi-annual interest payments.

TABLE 7.3 Comparison of Conventional and Deep Discount Notes After-Tax[1] Cash Flows

	7% Discount Note			Conventional Note		Zero Coupon Note	
Period	Principal	Coupon	Discount	Principal	Coupon	Principal	Discount
0	10,078,989	—		10,000,000		10,034,445	—
1		283,500	226,367		(459,000)	—	550,416
2		283,500	226,367		(459,000)	—	550,416
3		283,500	226,367		(459,000)	—	550,416
4		283,500	226,367		(459,000)	—	550,416
5		283,500	226,367		(459,000)	—	550,416
6		283,500	226,367		(459,000)	—	550,416
7		283,500	226,367		(459,000)	—	550,416
8		283,500	226,367		(459,000)	—	550,416
9		283,500	226,367		(459,000)	—	550,416

[1]Assuming a 50% marginal tax bracket.

The after-tax internal rate of return of the 7 percent discount note is 10.19 percent, which compares quite favorably to the 9.18 percent rate of return for the conventional note. The IRR for the zero coupon issue is 11.01 percent.

7.12 WHY DEEP DISCOUNT DEBT IS ATTRACTIVE TO BORROWERS AND BUYERS

Borrowers have issued deep discount bonds at yields to maturity lower than yields on comparable conventional bonds. This is surprising in view of the fact that the tax savings to the borrower from the deep discount bond should have allowed it to offer these bonds at higher rates than conventional bonds.

7.12.1 Two Features That Attract Buyers

There are several other characteristics of the deep discount bond that provide the incentives for the purchaser of the bond despite the lower yields. These features are call protection and the elimination of reinvestment risk.

Call Protection. Unlike most conventional bonds, which have call protection for at least the first five years of the bond's life and often as long as ten years, there is much less risk to the investor that an original issue deep discount bond will be called. This is true even though deep discount bonds are usually callable at any time. Because of the large discrepancy between the issue cost and face amount of the deep discount bond, it would be unprofitable under most circumstances for the issuer to call the bonds before maturity. There would have to be a very significant drop in market rates of interest of conventional bonds so that the interest on these would be comparable to the low coupon on the deep discount bond.

The effect of a call being exercised is that the investor's yield to maturity is disrupted. If the call has been exercised because there has been a drop in interest rates—as is usually the case—the investor would have to reinvest the proceeds in a new lower-yielding bond. *Caution:* Conversely, the lack of flexibility in calling a deep discount bond is a disadvantage to the issuer. This must be weighed against the tax advantages.

Lesser Reinvestment Risk. The coupon payments received by the purchaser of a bond, whether in a conventional or deep discount issue, must be reinvested at the time they are received. The future rates of reinvestment are unknown at the time the bond is purchased. However, the reinvestment risk on a deep discount bond will always be less than that for a conventional bond of comparable yield because the coupon payments will always be smaller with the deep discount bond. In the extreme case of the zero coupon bond there will be no reinvestment risk.

7.13 HOW COMMERCIAL BANKS ADAPTED THE OID TO BANK LOANS

In order to compete effectively against OID notes, a number of the banks adapted the OID structure to bank loans, offering a floating rate modification. The loans were three to five years in maturity, with the interest broken down into two parts: a discount note and a floating usage fee.

Thus a loan priced at prime might be broken down into a discount note discounted quarterly at a rate of 12 percent per annum, let's say, plus a floating usage fee, payable quarterly in cash (just as normal interest would be paid in cash), with the usage fee equal to the difference between prime and 12 percent. The 12 percent interest on the discount rate would be capitalized so that no interest on this portion of the loan would actually be paid until maturity. The cash-flow benefits to the borrower allowed the bank to offer better priced loans than conventional loan structures.

7.13.1 Straight and Discounted Bank Loans Compared

A five-year term loan with a face amount of $20 million would result in net proceeds to the borrower of roughly $10,956,000 if it were discounted quarterly at an annual rate of 12 percent. A straight loan would result in a higher all-in cost to the borrower 30 to 50 basis points per year over the life of the loan. The following exhibit shows the comparison of a straight bank loan to a discounted bank loan.

TABLE 7.4 Discounted Bank Loan Proceeds of $10,956,000

| | ($000) | | | |
| | Straight Bank Loan | | Discount Loan | |
Year	After-Tax Interest Cost	After-Tax Cash Flow	After-Tax Interest Benefit	After-Tax Cash Flow
0	—	10,956	—	10,956
1	1,193	(1,193)	821	321[3]
2	1.076[1]	(1,076)	821[2]	399
3	956	(956)	821	503
4	836	(836)	821	642
5	836	(11,792)	821	(19,360)

[1]Assumes declining interest rates and a 46 percent tax bracket.
[2]The discount is amortized on a straight-line basis so that the principal amount increases. However, declining interest rates result in constant interest costs.
[3]The net cash flow for the discount loan includes a usage fee charged by the bank to cover the difference between the specified floating rate and 12 percent.

The internal rate of return for the normal bank loan is 9 percent whereas it is 8.68 percent for the discounted loan. This comparison was done when the prime rate was near 20 percent. If projected interest rates were to decline more rapidly than assumed here, the spread between the two loan structures would be even greater. The discount loan is more attractive in each case.

chapter 8

Unconventional Debt, Part Two: How to Use Blended Rate Financing, Floating Rate Notes, and Swaps to Cut Interest Costs, Realize a Tax Savings and Obtain Favorable Repayment Terms

In the previous chapter, we saw how extendable notes allowed for adjustments in the rate of a debt instrument in order to protect both the issuer and the buyer during periods of erratic interest rates. Similarly, as discussed in Section 7.5 for McDonnell Douglas, a rate-averaging technique was used to achieve the same objective.

Blended rate financings, floating rate notes, and adjustable rate preferred stock are also techniques that have been developed to provide similar types of protection.

8.1 HOW BLENDED RATE FINANCING GIVES CORPORATE BORROWERS THE BEST OF TWO WORLDS

The attractiveness to a corporate borrower of a particular rate structure and maturity will vary in relation to the existing rate environment as well as to expectations of the future behavior of the financial markets. Floating rate debt may result in too much potential exposure to the borrower in a volatile rate environment, whereas long-term fixed rate financing in a moderate or high-rate environment may inhibit the company's ability to refinance under more favorable terms, should there be a significant drop in interest rates.

The blended rate concept approaches a company's financing needs through the use of multiple sources of funds, and attempts to blend the best characteristics from each source rather than use one source exclusively. This is frequently accomplished by combining bank loans with private placements to institutional lenders. The bank loan is generally easier to obtain on a floating rate basis, although banks will give fixed rate loans from time to time. However, fixed rate bank loans are usually at a premium and for a shorter duration than those of institutional lenders. The term of a fixed rate bank loan will be four to eight (and occasionally ten) years.

8.2 COMBINING FLOATING RATE AND FIXED RATE DEBT TO OBTAIN A LONGER TERM AND LOWER INTEREST

The effect of combining or blending a private placement with a floating rate bank loan is to achieve a much longer average life and a more even maturity schedule than a bank term loan, while preserving a lower effective interest rate than afforded by a private placement.

8.2.1 Private Placement and Blended Financing Compared

Private placement. For example, assume that an industrial company seeks to borrow $15 million at a fixed rate of interest in the private placement market, and can obtain a loan with the following terms:

TABLE 8.1 Terms of a Typical Private Placement

Amount	$15 million		
Maturity	20 years		
Average Life	12.5 years		
Expenses	$131,250		
Coupon	9.25%	9.375%	9.5%
Effective Cost	9.375%	9.501%	9.627%

In the above financing, the costs of the private placement will have added approximately 12.6 basis points to the overall cost of the debt. The debt had a sinking fund of $93,750 beginning at the end of the fifth year, which would return approximately 94 percent of the issue to the lender prior to maturity.

One of the advantages of the private placement is that the fixed rate limits the borrower's exposure to very high interest rates and allows it to calculate exactly how much debt service will be required for the loan. Conversely, the fixed rate prevents the borrower from attaining the savings that would result from a drop in interest rates.

The fixed rate, which may be difficult to obtain for a long maturity, locks in a rate but is probably not readily refundable because of pre-payment penalties and refunding restrictions. Even when available, it may result in an unacceptably high rate to the issuer.

The following table shows the yearly cash flows for a 15-year private placement.

TABLE 8.2 Cash Flows for a $15 Million Private Placement

Periods Ending 5/30 (1) and 11/30 (2)	Interest Payment at 9 3/8%	Principal Payment	Principal Outstanding During Period	Fees and[1] Expenses	Net Cash Outflow (Inflow)
1978-Closing	.00	.00	15000000.00	134,250.00	(14868750.00)
1979 (1)	703125.00	.00	15000000.00		703125.00
(2)	703125.00	.00	15000000.00		703125.00
1980 (1)	703125.00	.00	15000000.00		703125.00
(2)	703125.00	.00	15000000.00		703125.00

TABLE 8.2 (continued)

Periods Ending 5/30 (1) and 11/30 (2)	Interest Payment at 9 3/8%	Principal Payment	Principal Outstanding During Period	Fees and[1] Expenses	Net Cash Outflow (Inflow)
1981 (1)	703125.00	.00	15000000.00		703125.00
(2)	703125.00	.00	15000000.00		703125.00
1982 (1)	703125.00	.00	15000000.00		703125.00
(2)	703125.00	.00	15000000.00		703125.00
1983 (1)	703125.00	.00	15000000.00		703125.00
(2)	703125.00	937500.00	15000000.00		1640625.00
1984 (1)	659179.69	.00	14062500.00		659179.69
(2)	659179.69	937500.00	14062500.00		1596679.69
1985 (1)	615234.38	.00	13125000.00		615234.38
(2)	615234.38	937500.00	13125000.00		1552734.38
1986 (1)	571289.06	.00	12187500.00		571289.06
(2)	571289.06	937500.00	12187500.00		1508789.06
1987 (1)	527343.75	.00	11250000.00		527343.75
(2)	527343.75	937500.00	11250000.00		1464843.75
1988 (1)	483398.44	.00	10312500.00		483398.44
(2)	483398.44	937500.00	10312500.00		1420898.44
1989 (1)	43943.13	.00	937500.00		439453.13
(2)	43943.13	937500.00	937500.00		1376953.13
1990 (1)	395507.81	.00	8437500.00		395507.81
(2)	395507.81	937500.00	8437500.00		1333007.81
1991 (1)	351562.50	.00	7500000.00		351562.50
(2)	351562.50	937500.00	7500000.00		1289062.50
1992 (1)	307617.19	.00	6562500.00		307617.19
(2)	307617.19	937500.00	6562500.00		1245117.19
1993 (1)	263671.88	.00	5625000.00		263671.88
(2)	263671.88	937500.00	5625000.00		1201171.88
1994 (1)	219726.56	.00	4687500.00		219726.56
(2)	219726.56	937500.00	4687500.00		1157226.56
1995 (1)	175781.25	.00	3750000.00		175781.25
(2)	175781.25	937500.00	3750000.00		1113281.25
1996 (1)	131835.94	.00	2812500.00		131835.94
(2)	131835.94	937500.00	2812500.00		1069335.94
1997 (1)	87890.63	.00	1875000.00		87890.63
(2)	87890.63	937500.00	1875000.00		1025390.63
1998 (1)	43945.31	.00	937500.00		43945.31
(2)	43945.31	937500.00	937500.00		981445.31

[1]Assumes legal and printing expenses of $25,000 and $12,500, respectively, and a 5/8% private placement advisory.

Blended financing. The blended concept enhances the borrower's ability to deal effectively with a high-rate environment. When a bank is available to offer a floating rate term loan in conjunction with the longer term debt obligation, the structure of the total financing might appear as follows:

TABLE 8.3 Blended Rate Financing

	Bank Participation	Private Placement	Blended Total
Amount	$5 million	$10 million	$15 million
Maturity	8 years	20 years	—
Average Life	6.5 years	12.5 years	10.5 years
Expenses	—		$100,000
Interest Rate	—		
	*	9.25	9.205
	*	9.375	9.305
	*	9.5	9.405

The bank debt here serves as a "collar"—that is, a ceiling and a floor. As is shown in Table 8.3, the bank loan carries a floating interest rate tied to prime with a minimum rate of 8 percent and a maximum rate not greater than the private placement interest rate. The ceiling remedies the major disadvantage of floating rate loans—unlimited exposure to potentially high interest rates. It limits the borrower's exposure while offering the benefit of lower interest rates that might exist over the life of the floating-rate portion of the loan.

Based on the projections as developed at the time of this analysis, the effective cost of blended financing would be 9.205 percent for a 9.25 percent coupon, 9.305 percent for a 9.375 coupon, and 9.405 percent for a 9.5 percent coupon. (Obviously the year 1982 did not conform to the projection).

TABLE 8.4 Projected Blended Financing Costs

Projected Average Bank Pricing	Private Placement Coupon		
	9.25 percent	9.375 percent	9.5 percent
8.0%	9.038	9.132	9.225
8.5%	9.165	9.259	9.352
9.0%	9.293	9.386	9.480
9.25%	9.356	9.450	9.544

The bank participation is for 8 years, which combines with the 20-year life of the private placement to give a blended average life of 10.5 years. The bank has an annual sinking fund of $1.25 million beginning at the end of the fifth year, retiring 75 percent of the bank debt prior to maturity. The private placement assumes a level annual sinking fund payment of $625,000 beginning at the end of the fifth year and retiring roughly 94 percent of the issue prior to maturity.

Table 8.5 shows the detailed cash flows for the blended financing.

8.2.2 Three Advantages of Blended Financing

The blended financing appeared to offer three distinct advantages to the company: interest rate savings, a limitation on interest rate exposure, and substantially greater financing flexibility.

Interest rate savings. At the time of the financing, interest rates were at their highest level in more than three years. Thus, it was expected that interest rates were going to come down, and the floating rate nature of the bank's participation would therefore result in a lower effective cost than a long-term fixed rate placement negotiated at their existing rates. There is roughly a 20 basis point savings, assuming the private placement is accomplished at 9.375, which would result in a $315,000 pretax savings in cash flow.

Limitation on interest rate exposure. One advantage of the straight private placement is that the fixed rate limits the borrower's exposure to increases in interest rates and allows the borrower to lock into its debt service costs. (Conversely, the fixed rate prevents the borrower from realizing savings from a drop in interest rates.)

With a blended alternative that includes an interest collar on the floating bank debt, the ceiling on the bank debt would be at the rate of the simultaneous private placement, and the floor would be set at 8 percent. The ceiling identifies the maximum rate the borrower would pay on the floating rate portion of the loan. Since this ceiling is set at the same rate as the private placement, the blended rate financing will never result in a higher cost than the straight private placement.

Financing flexibility. An additional benefit from the blended financing is its flexibility. The term loan from the bank has no prepayment penalty. Thus, there is the ability to prepay to bank loan and at time when rates are lower. It is likely that interest rate fluctuations would allow this to occur within a three to five-year time frame. Not only could there be an effective cost savings on the financing, but the average life of the loan could be extended as well. That is, if it is assumed that the refunding occurs with a financing having a 20-year term, the impact of refunding is to extend the final maturity and

TABLE 8.5 Cash Flows for a $15 Million "Blended" Financing

Period Ending 11/30 (2) and 5/30 (1)	Institutional Lender ($10 Million)					Bank Loan ($5 Million)				Combined Cash Outflow (Inflow)
	Interest Payment at 9 3/8%	Principal Repayment	Principal Outstanding During Period	Fees and Expenses[1]	Net Cash Outflow (Inflow)	Interest Payment[2]	Principal Payment	Principal Outstanding During Period	Net Cash Outflow (Inflow)	
1978-Closing	.00		1000000.00	100000.00	(9900000.00)	.00	.00	5000000.00	(5000000.00)	(14900000.00)
1979-1	468750.00	.00	1000000.00		468750.00	234375.00	.00	5000000.00	234375.00	703125.00
-2	468750.00	.00	1000000.00		468750.00	234375.00	.00	5000000.00	234375.00	703125.00
1980-1	468750.00	.00	1000000.00		468750.00	207500.00	.00	5000000.00	207500.00	676250.00
-2	468750.00	.00	1000000.00		468750.00	207500.00	.00	5000000.00	207500.00	676250.00
1981-1	468750.00	.00	1000000.00		468750.00	201250.00	.00	5000000.00	201250.00	670000.00
-2	468750.00	.00	1000000.00		468750.00	201250.00	.00	5000000.00	201250.00	670000.00
1982-1	468750.00	.00	1000000.00		468750.00	212000.00	.00	5000000.00	212000.00	680750.00
-2	468750.00	.00	1000000.00		468750.00	212000.00	.00	5000000.00	212000.00	680750.00
1983-1	468750.00	.00	1000000.00		468750.00	222750.00	.00	5000000.00	222750.00	691500.00
-2	468750.00	625000.00	1000000.00		1093750.00	222750.00	1250000.00	5000000.00	1472750.00	2566500.00
1984-1	439453.13	.00	9375000.00		439453.13	165000.00	.00	3750000.00	165000.00	604453.13
-2	439453.13	625000.00	9375000.00		1064453.13	165000.00	1250000.00	3750000.00	1415000.00	2479453.13
1985-1	410156.25	.00	8750000.00		410156.25	112000.00	.00	2500000.00	112000.00	522156.25
-2	410156.25	625000.00	8750000.00		1035156.25	112000.00	1250000.00	2500000.00	1362000.00	2397156.25
1986-1	380859.38	.00	8125000.00		380859.38	56000.00	.00	1250000.00	56000.00	436859.38
-2	380859.38	625000.00	8125000.00		1005858.38	56000.00	1250000.00	1250000.00	1306000.00	2311859.38
1987-1	351562.50	.00	7500000.00		351562.50					
-2	351562.50	625000.00	7500000.00		976562.50					
1988-1	322265.63	.00	6875000.00		322265.63					
-2	322265.63	625000.00	6875000.00		947265.63					
1989-1	292968.75	.00	6250000.00		292968.75					
-2	292968.75	625000.00	6250000.00		917968.75					

1990-1	263671.88	.00	5625000.00	263671.88
-2	263671.88	625000.00	5625000.00	888671.88
1991-1	234375.00	.00	5000000.00	234375.00
-2	234375.00	625000.00	5000000.00	859375.00
1992-1	205078.13	.00	4375000.00	205078.13
-2	205078.13	625000.00	4375000.00	830078.13
1993-1	175781.25	.00	3750000.00	175781.25
-2	175781.25	625000.00	3750000.00	800781.25
1994-1	146484.38	.00	3125000.00	146484.38
-2	146484.38	625000.00	3125000.00	771484.38
1995-1	117187.50	.00	2500000.00	117187.50
-2	117187.50	625000.00	2500000.00	742187.50
1996-1	87890.63	.00	1875000.00	87890.63
-2	87890.63	625000.00	1875000.00	712890.63
1997-1	58593.75	.00	1250000.00	58593.75
-2	58593.75	625000.00	1250000.00	683593.75
1998-1	29296.88	.00	625000.00	29296.88
-2	29296.88	625000.00	625000.00	654296.88

¹Assumes legal and printing expenses of $25,000 and $12,500, respectively, and a ⅝% private placement advisory fee.
²Interest is as follows:

For the year ending 11/30:   1979 – 1980:   105% of prime
1981 – 1982:   108% of prime
1983 – 1984:   110% of prime
1985 – 1986:   112% of prime

The following was assumed as the prime rate:
For the year ending 11/30:   1979:   9.45%
1980:   7.90%
1981:   7.45%
1982:   7.85%
1983:   8.10%
1984 – 1986:   8.00%

average life of the total financing to levels significantly greater than those of the private placement.

There is no certainty that the company will be able to refinance at a lower interest rate during the three- to five-year period. However, historical fluctuations of interest rates would indicate that there is a strong likelihood that a low point in interest rates will occur within any given five-year period. This approach allows companies with an immediate long-term financing need to remain flexible so that they can benefit from lower rates in future years.

8.3 HOW TO ACHIEVE A COST SAVINGS AND FAVORABLE REPAYMENT TERMS THROUGH OTHER FORMS OF BLENDED FINANCING

The approach of drawing upon and combining the more attractive features of various debt instruments can be used quite effectively. An example of this, which does not involve floating rate debt, is the combination of a traditional fixed rate debt instrument with a delayed payment note in the form of zero coupon debt. It would be structured in the following manner.

8.3.1 How the Financing Is Structured

Assume that a corporation is seeking long-term financing for real estate but that there is a shortage of funds with terms beyond fifteen years. The borrower would like to maximize the term (ideally 25 years), but structure the transaction in such a way that the effective borrowing cost is near that of 15-year money.

The financing would be structured in two layers. The first layer would consist of 90 percent of the financing, let's say $18 million out of $20 million, through a traditional note with a 15-year term. Assume that the interest cost of this portion of the financing is 12.5 percent.

The second layer of the financing (the remaining $2 million) would consist of a 25-year note priced at one-tenth of its face amount of $20 million. That is, the note would be structured with a 90 percent discount so that it would have a face amount of $20 million and a price of $2 million. This second note would not require any payments of interest or principal for the first 15 years. At the end of 15 years, payments of principal and interest would begin and would continue during the remaining ten year life of the note.

The delayed payment note resembles a zero coupon note, but without a single balloon payment at maturity. Rather, there are a series of payments—really like a series of zero coupon notes maturing in years 16 through 25.

The effective interest rate on this second note would be roughly 13 percent. Thus, when this second note is combined with the other portion of the financing, it provides a *blended* cost near 12.75 percent. Thus there is a significant savings of 25 basis points as compared to a 13 percent rate for a straight 25-year financing.

Not only does this structure result in a savings through the blended cost of the financing, but the repayment terms on the two notes are such that the combined effect strongly resembles a single traditional 25-year financing with a 15-year principal deferral. Only interest payments are made during the first 15 years, after which there is a step-up as the repayments begin in the delayed payment note.

8.3.2 How the Blending Impacts the Issuer's Financial Statement

The two notes in combination have a balancing effect upon the issuer's financial statement. The outstanding balance on the zero coupon note grows each year as interest is accrued, whereas the 15-year note is amortized so that the reduction in its outstanding amount roughly equals the increase in the other note. The total combined long-term debt carried on the balance sheet is $20 million through year 15. At this point, only the 25-year note remains to be amortized and the $20 million liability begins to be reduced.

8.4 FLOATING RATE NOTES: ATTRACTIVE TO BOTH ISSUER AND INVESTOR WHEN INTEREST RATES ARE HIGH

Floating Rate Notes, which have numerous variations, tend to become popular during periods of high and volatile interest rates. This structure is attractive to the issuer who does not want to lock into excessive fixed interest costs and is willing to take the interest rate fluctuation risk during the life of the security. On the other hand, an investment in a variable rate security can provide the buyer with superior protection on principal, and at the same time a higher overall rate of return than an investment in a fixed rate security.

How it works. A typical note may have an interest rate fixed semi-annually that at each semi-annual period is calculated at some factor, let's say 65 percent, above the then current "interest yield equivalent" of the market discount rate for six-month U.S. Treasury bills, subject to a minimum interest rate per annum of 6.5 percent and a maximum of 19 percent.

"Interest yield equivalent" is a concept derived from the U.S. Treasury bill market. U.S. Treasury bills are issued and traded on a discount basis, the amount of the discount being the difference between their face value at maturity and their sale price. The per annum market discount rate on a U.S. Treasury bill (which may vary from the average auction rate for the same week) is the percentage obtained by dividing the amount of the discount on each U.S. Treasury bill by its face amount at maturity and amortizing the percentage on the basis of a 360-day year.

For determining the interest rate on the notes in the following example, the average weekly per annum market discount rate for six month U.S. Treasury bills would be used, prior to the semi-annual period for which the interest rate on the notes was to be determined. The resulting interest yield equivalent would be slightly higher than the reported per annum discount rates on which it is based.

8.4.1 How the Interest Yield Equivalent Is Calculated

The calculation below shows how the interest yield equivalent method would be applied for a six-month period. As previously discussed, the formula is based upon the weekly per-annum market discount rates by six-month U.S. Treasury bills published by the Federal Reserve Board. These rates will be assumed to be 9.26 percent and 9.39 percent, with an average 9.325 percent. This average per-annum discount rate is converted to its interest yield equivalent for U.S. Treasury bills having a face value of $10,000 at maturity, with 1982 days to run to maturity.

1. 9.325% (average of reported discount rates) × $100,000 (face amount) = $932.50
2. $932.50 × $182/360$ = $471.43 (amount of discount)
3. $10,000 − $471.43 = $9,528.57
4. $471.43 ÷ 9,528.57 = 4.947%
5. 4.947% × $360/182$ = 9.785% (interest yield equivalent)

Using the preceding calculation, the interest rate on notes which are .65 percent above the interest yield equivalent would be 10.43 percent.

8.4.2 Other Ways to Price Variable Rate Securities Off Treasuries

There are other ways in which variable rate securities can be priced off Treasuries. Gulf Oil Corp., for example, issued variable/fixed rate 30-year Debentures with the interest rate per annum for each semi-annual period at .35 percent above the weekly average yield to maturity of U.S. Treasury securities adjusted to a constant maturity of 30-years as constructed by the U.S. Treasury Department. Should the yield decline to 8 percent or less, the interest rate on the debentures would no longer be variable but would be fixed at 8.375 percent per annum until maturity.

8.4.3 How Tucson Electric Structured Its Security to Save Interest Costs on a Long Maturity Bond

The average weekly and daily yields to maturity of U.S. Treasury securities adjusted to a constant maturity of 30 years are taken from the market yields published by the Federal Reserve Board. Such yields are based on yield curves of the most actively traded marketable treasury securities constructed daily by the U.S. Treasury Department. The yield values are read from the yield curve at fixed maturities—for instance, 1, 2, 3, 5, 7, 10, 20, and 30 years. Using this technique, a yield may be estimated for a five-year maturity even if there is no outstanding marketable Treasury issue which has five years to maturity at the time of the calculation.

Tucson Electric introduced a new method of pricing variable rate securities. The company issued $75 million of 8.75 percent, 40-year Quarterly Tender Industrial Development Revenue Bonds. The rate on the bonds was to reset quarterly based upon a formula calculated as follows. The average rate for triple-A, government guaranteed, 90-day project bonds will first be calculated by an independent third party. Fifty basis points will then be added to this rate. Finally, a factor that varies between 90 percent and 100 percent will be applied. As an added inducement to buyers of the bonds, the securities will carry a put that is exercisable at each quarter.

The unusual structure of this security allows the issuer to sell a bond with a long maturity while obtaining savings on the interest rate. Tucson would have had to pay at least 10 percent on a fixed rate three-year security and over 13 percent on a 30-year security, whereas the initial coupon on the variable rate instrument was at 8.75 percent.

8.4.4 New Wrinkles in Floating Rate Notes

Convertible notes. Numerous features have been added to floating rate notes over the past three years. A floating rate note will frequently be convertible by the holder into a longer-term, fixed-rate debenture of equivalent principal amount, which may have a term as long as an additional 20 years. The issuer of a floating rate convertible note will include a redemption feature to protect itself against conversion by the holder into a fixed rate obligation during a period of high interest rates.

The issuer may also have the right to convert to the fixed rate obligation during a portion of the term of the floating rate obligation. The conversion privilege by the issuer will allow it to lock into a lower fixed rate at an opportune time. The conversion feature was used successfully in issues by Mellon National Corporation and Imperial Bancorp.

Tying the rate to prime. Another variation for floating rate notes has been to tie the rate to a bank prime rate instead of Treasuries. Aristar, Inc. issued 20-year floating rate notes using the following formula:

> The interest rate per annum . . . will be at a rate ½ percent above the "prime rate" of Morgan Guaranty Trust Company of New York on the last business day preceding the [interest payment date] subject to a minimum per-annum interest rate of 10 percent and a maximum of 15 percent.

Varying the constant. Sometimes the issuer will vary the constant that is added to the Treasury bill interest yield equivalent or the prime rate, let's say from 1 percent to .75 percent after the first year. Occasionally, as an inducement to the buyer of the securities, a floor may be imposed upon the interest rate, but there will be no ceiling.

The floating rate/stock warrant. Southmark Properties issued 40,000 Units of (1) $40 million variable rate notes due on February 1, 1987, combined with (2) 2,000,000 warrants. Each Unit consisted of $1,000 principal amount of Notes and 50 warrants. The Notes bear interest at inception of 17½ percent and then are transformed into a variable interest rate equal to 1.315 times the average for the prior three weeks of the weekly average yield to maturity of five years, with a cap of 22½ percent and a floor of 12½ percent per annum.

Each warrant entitles the holder to purchase one common share of Southmark at $7.50, which compares with the public sale price of the common at the time of issue of $5.00 per share. There was an alternate rate on the notes, which would be used if for some reason the five-year daily Treasury rate could not be obtained. This alternate rate would be calculated as 1.2 times the average prime interest rate during the period of the prior 15 business days of Marine Midland Bank and Trust Co.

Floating rate notes combined with warrants to subscribe to bonds. A variation of the floating rate/stock warrant unit is the floating rate note combined with warrants to subscribe to bonds. London & Scottish Marine Oil issued $75,000,000 of seven-year floating rate notes with warrants to subscribe to 13 percent ten-year bonds. Each $5,000 principal amount of the Notes was issued with five warrants, each warrant entitling the holder to subscribe to $1,000 of the Bonds. The interest rate on the floating rate notes was at ⅜ percent per annum above the London inter-bank offered rate (LIBOR) for six-month Eurodollar deposits. The warrants are exercisable for a period of roughly two- and one-half years from issuance.

8.5 ADJUSTABLE RATE PREFERRED STOCK: AN EXTRAORDINARY RETURN FOR CORPORATE PURCHASERS

An offshoot of floating rate debt securities is *adjustable rate preferred stock*. Although this is technically an equity security, it is included here because of its similarity to floating rate debt.

Adjustable rate preferred stock became popular beginning in July of 1982. Corporate purchasers of the preferred may exclude 85 percent of the dividend from taxable income, thereby receiving an extraordinarily high return.

Manufacturer's Hanover sold two issues totalling nearly $400 million. The first issue carried a dividend rate 50 basis points above the highest of three-month, ten-year and twenty-year Treasuries, at the buyer's option. The second issue was 60 basis points below these yields. The differential in the two dividend rates was due largely to the fact that the market had become more familiar with the concept of an adjustable rate preferred stock. Manufacturer's preferred used another feature derived from floating rate debt securities: it had a floor of 7½ percent and a ceiling of 15½ percent.

Republic New York Corporation, Chemical Bank, Aetna, and Enserch also came out with adjustable rate preferred issues in the ensuing months. Chase Manhattan added a wrinkle by offering an adjustable rate preferred in exchange for its then outstanding preferred.

The use of exchange offers for the retirement of debt securities is discussed in the following section.

8.6 USING SWAPS TO SAVE TAXES AND REALIZE LONG-TERM CASH SAVINGS

There are a variety of swap techniques. Under this general designation are common equity-for-debt swaps, preferred stock-for-debt swaps, and debt-for-debt swaps.

The exchange of newly issued equity for a company's outstanding debt is a method of improving a company's balance sheet, which has had widespread use. The high interest rate environment severely depressed the market value of many companies' low-yield bonds that had been issued years earlier. Thus numerous companies were able to redeem these bonds at a significant discount from face value.

The transactions were structured in such a way that the issuing corporation could avoid taxes despite the fact that its outstanding debt obligations were being repurchased at a discount. The exchanges also provided long-term cash savings by conserving cash that otherwise would have to be used to redeem the debt instruments. Early users of this technique included Quaker Oats Co., Wells Fargo and Co., and Bankers Trust New York Corp.

How it works. An investment banking firm, or some other independent party, purchased and accumulated those bonds that the issuer ultimately sought to repurchase. The holder of the bonds then traded them to the issuer for an equivalent amount of common equity.

The issuer itself could repurchase its debt at a discount and produce a profit. Such profit would have been taxable. However, by exchanging shares for its outstanding securities, as opposed to paying cash for them, the issuer avoided taxes on the extraordinary gain it incurred through the retirement of the outstanding debt obligation. This is because the swap qualified under the Tax Code as a corporate reorganization, which is nontaxable.

If, for instance, $10 million of debt obligations carried a 7 percent interest rate, they may have had a market value of 40 percent of their face amount, or $6 million. By issuing $6 million of equity in exchange for the debt, the debt could have been liquidated and the company would no longer have owed $10 million. Because the actual cost of removing the debt was only $6 million, the issuer realized a profit of $4 million.

The 1984 Tax Reform Act substantially restricted the avoidance of taxes through repurchasing debt at a discount. A corporation which issues stock and applies the capital to retire debt incurs discharge income. The income must be recognized to the extent the outstanding principal of the debt exceeds the fair market value of the stock. The rule does not apply, however, in qualified workout situations where there is a substantial threat of involuntary proceedings.

8.7 HOW THE SWAP HAS BEEN MODIFIED TO SOLVE FINANCING PROBLEMS

Although the first swap transactions involved the exchange of common equity for debt, subsequent deals have incorporated significant modifications.

8.7.1 Preferred Stock for Debt

Florida Coast Banks, in conjunction with Dean Witter, completed a swap using a convertible preferred stock for the equity portion. The bank exchanged 324,957 shares of the preferred for $4.5 million of outstanding debt held by Dean Witter. The primary motivation of the bank was to improve its capital structure. The convertible preferred was more attractive than common because the outstanding common was closely held and thinly traded.

8.7.2 Equity for Debt

Toledo Edison did the first equity-for-debt swap in conjunction with a public offering. It issued $35 million of 15⅝ percent first mortgage bonds and 1.5 million shares of common, using 946,293 of the shares in exchange for $25 million of outstanding mortgage bonds. The outstanding bonds were held by Merrill Lynch, which sold the common that it had received in the swap as part of the public offering.

8.7.3 Swapping Cash and Stock for Debt to Reduce the Dilution Factor

A modification to the technique included the use of cash as well as stock in exchange for the debt obligation. Burlington Industries exchanged $4 million in cash plus 206,000 shares of common for $11 million principal amount of outstanding debt. PPG offered $7 million of cash and 217,000 shares of common in exchange for $22 million of debt. Exxon issued 700,000 shares plus $17 million in cash for $56 million face amount of outstanding debentures.

How cash-rich companies benefit. The effect of using cash in place of shares was to reduce the dilution factor through the issuance of fewer shares. Thus the capital gain resulting from the transaction was spread over fewer shares of stock, increasing the per-share impact. The company's new shares could be issued at a higher price. This approach had appeal to well-capitalized companies with excess cash on hand, enabling them to buy in debt at discount, obtain a tax savings, and minimize the dilution factor of the straight equity-for-debt swap.

Caution. Although the use of cash reduced the dilution factor, it also reduced the benefit to the balance sheet. There is a tax-free capital gain calculated as the difference between the price paid for the debt and its face value as if it were a noncash transaction. Thus, if $30 million in bonds were purchased for $40 million, consisting of $20 million cash and $20 million in stock, the cash would be applied to retire the first $20 million in debt. The remaining $30 million of debt would be retired with $20 million of stock, resulting in a tax-free capital gain of $10 million.

The following table provides a sampling of some of the more noteworthy equity-for-debt swap transactions.

TABLE 8.6 Selected Debt/Equity Swaps

Company Name	Market Value of Shares	Principal Amount of Debt Securities	Extraordinary Gain
Bankers Trust	18.3 million	24.4 million	5.1 million
Crown Zellerbach	31.8 million	46.8 million	15.0 million
Ownes-Illinois	15.2 million	24.0 million	8.8 million
Proctor & Gamble	17.3 million	25.0 million	7.7 million
Phillip Morris	18.4 million	25.9 million	7.5 million
Exxon Corp.	43.0 million	71.5 million	28.5 million
Intil. Min. & Chem.	28.9 million	34.8 million	5.9 million
Sears Roebuck	25.5 million	40.6 million	15.1 million
J.C. Penney	49.0 million	70.0 million	21.0 million
Alcoa	39.4 million	58.9 million	19.6 million
Dow Chemical	81.0 million	137.0 million	56.0 million
Pfizer	20.4 million	28.0 million	7.6 million
American Can	4.1 million	8.7 million	5.9 million
Textron Inc.	11.9 million	17.6 million	5.7 million
United Technologies	127.0 million	16.5 million	92.5 million

8.8 USING DEFEASANCE TO ACHIEVE TAX SAVINGS AND AVOID THE DILUTION FACTOR

By defeasing their bonds, corporations could obtain some of the tax advantages of equity-for-debt swaps while avoiding the use of under-valued common stock and the dilution effect of these transactions.

A significant modification of the equity-for-debt swap is the debt-for-debt swap, commonly referred to as defeasance.

8.8.1 Using Defeasance With Taxable Bonds

Defeasance has been used historically to retire tax-free bonds, which are difficult to repurchase on the open market. Only recently has the technique been applied to taxable securities. The reason is that tax-exempt bonds have often contained provisions allowing the issuer to deposit in trust sufficient funds to pay all interest and principal due on the bonds. This has the effect of releasing the issuer from the indebtedness, thereby allowing the debt to be removed from the balance sheet.

8.8.2 Is Off-Balance Sheet Treatment Allowed?

It has not been possible to enter into a pure defeasance with taxable bonds because the indentures rarely include defeasance provisions. Proponents of the defeasance technique for taxable securities have argued that the economic substance of a transaction is a defeasance even though the bond is not technically defeased. The issuer is still bound by the indenture, but the debt should be removed from the balance sheet.

In defeasance, a company that seeks to remove an outstanding debt obligation purchases government securities that have identical cash flows to those of the debt issue. The government securities are placed in an irrevocable trust and the principal and interest received on these are dedicated to the satisfaction of the debt service on the particular issue.

Because there was a dedicated portfolio of government securities to service the company's debt security, it was argued that such debt may be removed from the balance sheet. The AICPA's June 1978 Statement of Position "Accounting for Advance Refundings of Tax-Exempt Debt" had been cited as a basis for the off-balance sheet treatment. However, this language was rather restrictive so that the off-balance sheet treatment of defeasance for taxable transactions was not universally accepted.

Tax treatment. Even when off-balance sheet accounting treatment was allowed, the issuer would generally remain liable for the debt obligations and there would probably be footnote disclosure. The difference between the value of the securities purchased for the trust and the outstanding debt would be accounted for as a current gain. FASB statement No. 76, Extinguishment of Debt, generally modified defeasance so that debt would not be extinguished unless the issuer were relieved of its primary liability and it was probable that it would not be required to make future payments. Technical Bulletin No. 84-4 further restricted defeasance reporting where assets were placed in trust at the time the debt was incurred.

The transaction would not result in a cancellation of indebtedness and would therefore be nontaxable. Tax would be due, however, as the government securities mature, since this is the point in time at which the debt is actually paid off. However, the transaction would result in a gain for the issuer due to the fact that the cost of the government securities is less than the principal amount of the debt removed from the balance sheet. Because there would be no immediate tax impact, the deferred tax liability account would be increased by the gain times the applicable tax rate. The after-tax gain is reflected in an increase in retained earnings. Cash and long-term debt are reduced and earnings per share are increased currently. Deferred liabilities are increased along with retained earnings and are reduced as taxes are paid.

8.8.3 Two Noteworthy Defeasance Transactions

A $515 million defeasance transaction was conducted by Exxon, resulting in a $130 million after-tax gain. Kellogg followed with a modification of the Exxon deal with what is referred to as a liability assumption transaction. It paid a group of corporations roughly $65 million to assume responsibility for payments on its $75-million debit issue. Kellogg guaranteed payment of the debt with an irrevocable letter of credit from Morgan Guaranty (in place of the irrevocable trust that was used in the more straightforward Exxon structure).

8.8.4 Advantages of Defeasance Over Repurchase of Debt for Cash

The defeasance of taxable debt has several advantages over the normal repurchase of debt for cash. The company may not have sufficient cash on hand to effect the straight repurchase, and the effect of the repurchase may be to drive up the market value of the debt. To the extent that the debt is repurchased at a discount, the gain would be immediately taxable as opposed to the tax deferral under a defeasance of tax-free debt.

chapter 9

Hybrid Securities, Part One: How Convertible Debt, Warrants, and Index-Linked Bonds Cut Borrowing Costs and Provide a Hedge for the Lender

9.1 EVOLVING FORMS OF HYBRID SECURITY

The preceding two chapters have considered various debt instruments that have arisen largely as a result of high rates of inflation and unstable borrowing costs. There are a number of other approaches that have evolved over time with the objective of softening the impact of inflation and also providing a hedge for a lender against radical swings in interest rates. These techniques, which fall within the subject of *hybrid securities*, require two chapters. Chapter 9 discusses convertible securities, debt with warrants, and indexing. Chapter 10 discusses various recent debt issues that have been linked to specific assets such as real estate, oil, gold, and silver.

Hybrid securities provide a hedge by combining certain features of equity with the more traditional debt instrument. Hybrid securities have features of both debt and equity: debt through the mechanism of a current coupon, and equity through a tie-in to fundamental economic values of the company or the overall economy. In exchange for offering a hedge to the lender, the borrower is able to reduce its current borrowing costs.

9.1.1 Convertible Debt and Warrants

Long-term debt obligations have traditionally been structured in a number of ways so that they can carry an interest rate significantly below existing market rates for long-term debt with normal coupons. One method, and perhaps the most widely used, is to issue debt convertible into common stock at fixed or determinable amounts. A second popular technique is to issue debt combined with warrants. These methods are considered in this Chapter.

9.1.2 Commodity-Linked Securities

Alternatively, the debt security may carry a reduced coupon because it offers alternate modes of payment in lieu of cash. These may take the form of rights to fixed amounts of commodities (hence the name "commodity-linked bonds") such as oil, coal or silver, or a specified percent of the appreciation in a specified asset such as real estate. The final amount of repayment for the borrowed funds may be solely dependent on the underlying asset's value or on the greater of a face amount or the value of the underlying asset.

The repayment may be made by delivering the required amount of the asset or cash, or some combination of these. This is usually accomplished by providing the bond holder with a right to convert the principal amount of the bond into a fixed quantity of the commodity. If the price of the commodity reflects the general price level of the economy, then the bond holder is provided with protection against unexpected increases in the rate of inflation.

Commodity-linked debt resembles a traditional debt instrument combined with an options contract for the particular commodity. The primary distinction between the two is that in the case of the commodity-linked security, the debt obligation is extinguished when the debt holder exercises his conversion privilege for delivery of the commodity. In the case of the pure options contract, which presumably is purchased separately from the bond, the debt obligation would not be extinguished upon exercise of the option.

Sunshine Mining's issue of silver-linked debt, which is discussed at length in Chapter 10, paid 8½ percent on a current basis, whereas the company would have paid around 14½ percent for a pure debt issue of comparable features.

Caveat: An obvious caveat for the purchaser is that if silver prices fail to rise sufficiently during the life of the debt, the purchaser will have received a lower return than he would have received from higher coupon traditional debt.

9.1.3. How Hybrid Securities Sidestep High Interest Rates

In the case of convertible securities or debt with warrants, the objective is to create a vehicle that will not involve high cash interest rates on a long-term basis. This objective also applies for commodity or asset based securities. However, in the later case it may better be expressed as the desire to substitute price inflation on a specified asset for the inflation element in a cash interest rate. The issuer obtains funds at a below market rate of interest in exchange for the opportunity to realize gain on the value of the underlying asset. The lender gives up several points in current cash return in exchange for the potential appreciation in the underlying asset.

In the case of Sunshine Mining, if the payments had been indexed to inflation as well as silver, the issuer would have been able to lower the coupon even further. We considered the indexing of coupons through the use of variable rate notes in Chapter 8. The final section of Chapter 9 takes the concept of indexing a step further by indexing redemption value as well as interest payments.

9.2 CONVERTIBLE SECURITIES OFFER A STABLE INCOME STREAM PLUS A CAPITAL GAIN FOR THE BUYER

Let us consider our first type of hybrid security. A convertible security, in either the form of a preferred stock or debenture, contains a provision that allows the holder to convert or exchange the security into a particular number of shares of the issuing company's common stock (per $1000 bond or per share of preferred stock) at the owner's discretion at specified terms. The remainder of this section deals exclusively with convertible bonds.

9.2.1 Convertible Bonds and How They Work

From the perspective of the purchaser of the security, the convertible bond offers a stable income stream through the coupon while the conversion feature offers a capital gain opportunity or "hedge" through a tie-in to the underlying equity of the issuer. That is, if inflation or other economic factors increase the inherent value of the issuer, the holder of the convertible bond can convert and thus participate in price movements in the underlying common stock.

Because of the potential gains arising from the convertibility feature, the coupon on convertible bonds is lower than the coupon on nonconvertible securities of the same issuer. However, the coupon rate on the convertible bond is usually higher than the dividend rate on the issuer's common stock.

The conversion terms may be expressed as a ratio or as a conversion price. The conversion ratio will indicate how many shares of common stock are received for each $1000 face amount of the debenture. If the conversion ratio is ten, then ten shares of common stock are received with the common stock price implied at $100 per share. If the conversion is defined in terms of price, it would be stated as convertible at $100. The following simple formula applies:

$$\frac{\$1,000 \, (\text{Face Amount of Debenture})}{\text{Conversion Price}} = \text{Conversion Ratio}$$

Conversion may be permitted immediately or not until some future date, and the privilege may expire after a certain period of time.

9.3 THE TWO COMPONENTS INVOLVED IN VALUING A CONVERTIBLE SECURITY

The value of a convertible security (its market price) is made up of two components: the value of the security as a pure debt instrument (its investment value) exclusive of its conversion feature, and the value attributable to the right of the holder to receive common stock upon conversion (conversion value). The first element of value—as a pure debt instrument—provides the holder with a floor in value regardless of a decline in the value of the issuer's common stock. On the other hand, the second element of value gives the holder the opportunity to benefit from a rise in common stock price. The combined effect of these two elements is to cause a convertible to sell at a premium above its value based upon either of these elements independently.

The convertible security's bond investment value is simply the price at which a straight debt instrument of that particular coupon and maturity would sell at in the existing bond market.

Example of Convertible Security Valuation. For example, let's assume that the investment value of a particular convertible security with a face amount of $1000 is $900. This occurs because its existing coupon of 10 percent is less than the comparable yields then prevailing in the market place. Thus the bond will sell at discount from par in order to offer a market yield. The investment value of a convertible security will rise or fall inversely in relation to prevailing market yields.

Let's further assume that the convertible security is convertible into 20 shares of the issuer's common stock at $50 per share per $1000 bond. If the current market price of the common stock is $40 per share, then the conversion value is $800. To find the conversion value, simply take the number of shares into which the bond is convertible and multiply by the market price per share of the common stock.

If the market price of the common rises to $60 per share, the bonds conversion value would be $20 \times 60 = \$1,200$. Thus conversion value of a convertible will rise or fall directly in relation to movements in the price of the common stock.

But Watch This: This relationship does not hold, however, as the conversion value approaches investment value in a declining stock market. In the above example, if the stock price were falling from $50 to $45, the conversion value would equal the investment value of $900 and the market value of the convertible would also decline. However, if the stock price continued to fall below $45, the market value of the convertible would resist decline and continue to trade above $900.

9.3.1 How the Conversion Premium Is Established

There is a subtle interrelationship between investment value, conversion value, and the actual market value of the convertible security. When a convertible trades above its conversion value, which is usually the case,[1] it is said to be selling at a premium over conversion value. This may be expressed either in a dollar amount, or more frequently,

---

[1]If the conversion premium is 0 percent, which is rare, the bond is said to be trading on a parity with conversion value. It is extremely unusual though not impossible for a convertible security to trade below parity.

as a percent. In the example so far given, if the market price of the common is $47 dollars, the conversion value would be $940 (i.e., 20 × $47). If the convertible bonds were selling at $987, then the conversion premium would be 5 percent above conversion value.

Another way to consider the conversion premium is to compare two securities that are convertible at two different conversion prices. Because the conversion premium reflects the opportunity of the security to benefit from a rise in the price of the common stock, the size of the premium will depend upon the difference between (1) the value of the security as a pure investment and (2) conversion value. For instance, let's assume that the investment value is $700 and that the market price of the common is $41 per share. If the conversion price is $47 (i.e., conversion ratio = 21.3), then the premium (above investment value) would be less than if the conversion price were $45 (i.e., conversion ratio = 22.2). This comparison can be shown as follows:

TABLE 9.1 Conversion Price Comparison

	Conversion Price $47	Conversion Price $45
Investment Value	$ 800	$ 800
Market Price Common	$ 41	$ 41
Conversion Value	$ 853	$ 910
Market Value of Convertible	$ 880	$ 940
Premium Above Investment Value	$ 80	$ 140

Because the conversion price is closer to the market price for the second security, allowing for a greater likelihood of benefiting from a rise in the market price of the common stock, it commands a greater premium above investment value.

Caution: The preceding comparison is simplistic because it assumes that all other indices of values are equal (which they never are). One must compare the market performance and prospects of the common stock of each issuer, as well as the dividend yield on the common as compared to the yield on the convertible. Is one company's market performance more erratic than the other, with greater fluctuations in both directions? A stock with greater potential, due to its underlying business prospects or those of its particular industry, would command a higher premium.

9.3.2. When to Consider Offering a Convertible

The various reasons that a company would consider offering a convertible are often similar in motivation to those of an issuer of a commodity-backed security. The use of commodity-linked securities, as we shall see, is really a special case in the use of convertible securities. By offering the purchaser a "sweetener" through an ability to share in the value of an underlying commodity, the issuer improves its ability to sell a security that might otherwise be difficult to sell. Such difficulty may exist because of a below market coupon on the debt instrument or other unattractive feature (such as a "call" provision), or because the debt market in general is poor.

A convertible security or a commodity-backed security may often address more than one of the preceding problems. However, there are some important differences in the use of the two types of securities. For the pure convertible there are frequently reasons that do not pertain to the commodity-backed security, such as (1) a need by the company to increase its common equity in its capital structure at a time when the market price is depressed, or (2) a desire by a company for more common equity while incurring gradual dilution (through conversion) rather than immediate dilution.

9.4 MODIFICATIONS OF THE CONVERTIBLE SECURITY

The financial markets in recent years have been quite favorable for convertible securities, but for different reasons at different times. For example, AGS Computers issued $10 million of convertible debentures in place of a planned 1.5-million share common stock offering. This was because the stock market was depressed at the time and the company was not satisfied with the price. The convertible debenture gave this rapid growth company the opportunity to sell investors on the possibility of receiving the company's common stock at a much higher value in the future.

Conversely, the convertible may be used when the equity markets are strong. Denny's offered $50 million of 9½ percent debentures convertible into common stock at roughly a 24 percent premium. Had Denny's offered nonconvertible debt instead, it would have carried a coupon in the 12 percent to 13 percent range. This was typical of a number of convertible deals done during surges in the equity markets. These deals with conversion premiums in the 20 percent range and rates under 10 percent aroused great demand even though investors did not expect to benefit from the conversion until at least four years from issuance. This compares to a two- to three-year horizon historically.

9.4.1 How Anacomp Raised Needed Capital by Combining a Deep Discount Bond With a Convertible Security

One underlying theme throughout this book has been the proposition that financial techniques are evolutionary. Parts and pieces of earlier techniques are selected and reshaped into new ones. An example of this, which combines the deep discount bond with the convertible security, is a hybrid security that was offered by Anacomp in February of 1982.

Anacomp was a high-growth software company, in an industry that traditionally raised as much capital as possible through public equity offerings. However, at the time that Anacomp required a significant capital infusion, the equity markets were plagued by low price/earnings multiples. Thus a pure common stock offering was not appropriate. Anacomp instead issued $50 million of 13.875 percent convertible debentures. The convertibility feature still allowed the issuer to trade upon the future growth potential of the company.

In addition, in order to increase the yield, the convertible debentures were discounted to $855 to yield 16.45 percent. The company's common stock at the time of the issue was trading at $11⅛. The conversion price for the debentures was set at $17½. Thus the debentures were structured to appeal to investors seeking a high yield to maturity (16.45 percent) coupled with the potential to share in upward movements in the price of the common stock in an industry noted for such movements.

9.4.2 Damson Oil Corp.: Another Variation

An interesting variation of the traditional convertible security was the issuance by Damson Oil Corp. of $25 delayed cumulative convertible preferred stock. The issue carried the potential for a high conversion premium, although the premium was not set at the time of issuance. Rather, the company retained the right to set the conversion price during the succeeding two years at 75 percent of the average market price for the prior 20 days, with a maximum of $15 and a minimum of $5.[2]

---

[2]The stock had traded above $20, although its price at time of issuance was around $8.

The issue initially carried a rather high dividend of 15 percent. However, once the conversion price has been set, the dividend drops to 10 percent. The 15 percent yield is guaranteed, however, for the first year.

Caution: This approach must be used discreetly because there are significant risks for the issuer. In the case of Damson Oil, if the company's stock price remains at its current level or even decreases further, it would have to issue a huge number of shares—perhaps 3.5 million—and suffer a huge dilution. If, on the other hand, the stock price approaches prior levels—let's say $20, then the conversion price would be around $15 (i.e., 75 percent × $20) and the company would only have to issue roughly 1.2 million shares. It all depends upon management's perception of the future performance of the company's stock.

9.4.3 Raising Capital at Low Cost Via an "Arcans"

Another modification of the convertible security is the adjustable rate convertible note (Arcans) which, as its name implies, takes two complex debt instruments and combines them. These gained popularity in late 1982 and early 1983, and not surprisingly allow companies to raise capital at a cost well below that of traditional debt or equity. Issuers have included Nicor, Borg Warner, Mapco and Hercules.

The interest rate varies in relation to the dividend on the company's common. Unlike the normal adjustable rate note that varies in relation to an index such as Treasury Bills, over which the issuer has no control, the interest rate on the adjustable rate convertible note will actually reflect the firm's performance. They have such strong equity features that care must be taken to construct them so that they are not challenged by the IRS as disguised equity and therefore not entitled to an interest deduction.

Borg Warner's Experience. The Borg Warner 20-year notes were issued at a cost to purchasers of $1,000, but carried only $550 face amount.[3] Interest payments vary with dividend payments with a floor of 47 cents per share (each note is convertible into 26.32 shares of common) on a quarterly basis for the first three years, and 65 cents thereafter. The interest payments will remain at least 7 cents per share higher than the dividend rate.

Thus the purchaser has a guaranteed minimum payment, which may rise with the issuer's performance. If the price of the common is below $20.90 (i.e., less than 45 percent below the conversion price of $38), then the holder has the right to $550 (the face amount) rather than convert.

---

[3]The Company carries $550 as debt and $450 as equity on the balance sheet.

9.5 HOW WARRANTS ARE USED TO MAKE AN OFFERING MORE SALEABLE

Warrants are frequently used as a sweetener in conjunction with the issuance of a debt security in order to make the offering more saleable.[4] Thus they are a frequent alternative to the use of convertible debt; they accomplish many of the same objectives and carry a number of similar features to convertible debt.

How It Works. A warrant gives the warrant holder the right to purchase common stock[5] at a specified price during a specified period of time. Sometimes the price at which the warrant may be exercised increases over time. In those situations where there is no step up in the exercise price, the warrants are usually exercised just prior to the expiration date.

The warrant usually entitles the holder to purchase one share of common stock, although in certain cases the warrant is exercisable into fractions of a share or more than one share. The warrant is surrendered to the issuer upon exercise, along with the exercise price in cash. In exchange, the warrant holder receives the specified amount of common stock. The holder of the warrant receives no current income and has no voting rights.

As in the case of a convertible security, which tends to sell at a premium over its pure investment value or pure stock value, the warrant will tend to sell at a premium over its intrinsic value. Its intrinsic value is the difference between its exercise price and the market value of the common stock at the time of the issuance. This difference represents the economic gain to the holder who exercises the warrant and then immediately sells the common stock at its existing market price.

A warrant will generally be worth at least its intrinsic value, since the warrant's exercise price represents a discount for the purchase of the common stock below its market price. Because of its other features, which will be discussed shortly, the warrant will invariably have a higher market value than its intrinsic value. In the extreme case, where the common stock is worth less than the exercise price on the warrant, the intrinsic value of the warrant is zero. This situation is quite unlikely because the warrant holder would not find the warrant attractive if its exercise price were higher than the market value of the common.

---

[4]They may also be used as part of a package with a debt instrument in order to obtain a better price for the debt (lower coupon), rather than improve sale ability. Warrants are sometimes offered separately or in conjunction with a common stock offering.

[5]The security that may be purchased is usually common stock but it may also involve the right to purchase other types of securities. For instance, there may be warrants to purchase additional bonds. If interest rates fall, the holder can purchase another bond offering an above-market yield.

9.5.1 Why Warrants Are Attractive to Investors

The attractiveness of warrants to an investor lies in the fact that they allow speculation in the common stock without paying the full market value of the common stock. The investor can actually leverage upon the investment in the warrant, obtaining the potential for a greater percentage appreciation in the warrant than if the investment were made directly in the common stock. On the other hand, it should be noted that there is also a greater potential depreciation in the warrant with a downward movement in the common stock.

For example, let's assume that the market price of a company's common stock is $100 and that the exercise price of its warrant is $90. The intrinsic value of the warrant would therefore be $10. If the market price of the common were to move up $10 to $110, the intrinsic value would have increased to $20, showing an appreciation of 100 percent. Conversely, if the market price were to drop from $100 to $95, this would be a decline of 5 percent in the value of the common stock, but a decline of 50 percent in the intrinsic value of the warrant.

9.5.2 Two Factors That Influence the Size of the Premium

Because of this greater opportunity for appreciation than a direct investment in the common stock, an investor will pay a premium for a warrant over its intrinsic value. The warrant's true or market value can thus be viewed as having two components: intrinsic value and premium. For instance, in our prior example of the warrant with an exercise price of $90 (intrinsic value of $10), an investor might be willing to pay $12 or $15, representing premiums of 20 percent and 50 percent respectively over the warrant's intrinsic value.

Issuers seek to achieve maximum premiums over intrinsic value in the pricing of the warrant. On the other hand, warrant holders seek to pay as little a premium as possible, since the less they pay in premium the greater the leverage the warrant provides.

The premium that the investor is willing to pay represents the cost of speculating in the common stock on a leveraged basis. It represents a hedge against downward movement in the value of the common stock: at most, the warrant holder stands to lose the purchase price of the warrant. However, if the stock price rises, the warrant holder stands to receive a profit at least equal to the intrinsic value of the warrant less the price initially paid for the warrant.

Anticipated Price Increases. Thus, a primary factor influencing the size of the premium is the market's expectation of future increases in the market price of the common stock. When the market price of the common stock is the same as the exercise price of the warrant, the premium is at a maximum. This is another way of saying that if the intrinsic value of the warrant is zero (since the intrinsic value is the difference between the market price and the exercise price), then the entire value of the warrant consists only of premium. When the premium is at a maximum, it indicates that the warrant holder has the greatest potential for upward appreciation because the market price of the common is low.

As the market price of the common stock rises, more of the value of the warrant resides in its intrinsic value (since the differences between market price and exercise price is increasing) and less in its premium. The premium varies inversely in relation to movements in the market price of the common stock.

Time Left Before the Warrant Expires. A second factor that significantly influences the size of the premium is the amount of time remaining before expiration of the warrant. The premium will decrease as the remaining exercise period becomes shorter. This is not surprising since the rationale for purchasing a warrant is to obtain leverage and to benefit from an anticipated rise in the value of a security of greater value (i.e., the common stock). If there is little time left for the common stock to move up in price, there is less potential benefit for the warrant holder.

If the exercise period is too long, the issuer will be unable to calculate accurately whether it will be able to use the capital that it would receive upon exercise of the warrants. Extended exercise periods may also interfere with future financings in which the company might wish to engage. The company may be required to buy back the warrants at a high price. In addition, the warrants are a continuing source of potential dilution upon the common stock.

9.6 HOW THE TRADITIONAL WARRANT WAS MODIFIED TO SOLVE FINANCING PROBLEMS

Let us first take two recent examples of the use of the traditional warrant. At a time when its stock price was depressed (at $9 from a high of $13) Nortek required some additional equity in its capital structure. Instead of issuing common stock, it offered 26,000 units, with each unit consisting of a 20-year, 15-percent subordinated debenture and 25-year warrants.

Intermagnetics General offered one million units of one share of common plus one warrant at a price of $13.50 per unit. Just prior to the issue, the company's stock price had reached an all time high of $16.00. Thus the warrants had tremendous appeal to investors as an equity play at a low price, while providing the issuer with the potential to raise further equity in the future (upon exercise of the warrants) without having to return to the equity markets.

9.6.1 Trans World Corp. and the Dual Option Warrant

A new approach to the use of the warrant was developed in 1982 with the use of the *dual option warrant*. This type of security can be converted into the issuer's common stock or a fixed income security such as preferred stock or bonds. Trans World Corp. sold 1.8 million units at $15.50 per unit (the common stock price at the time of issuance was 11⅝), with each unit consisting of one share of common and one warrant. The warrant is exercisable into common at $25.50 through December 31, 1986. Furthermore, there is a window period from May 16, 1983 to June 30, 1984 during which time the unit can be swapped for one share of $25 preferred stock with a coupon of 13.96 percent.

9.6.2 Why Swaps Are Better Suited to Big Companies

The swap feature provides a hedge for the investor against declines in the price of the common stock by allowing for conversion into a fixed income security. This hedge creates an exposure for the issuer because it may end up with the liability of a fixed income security. Thus it has more appeal to a larger company with sufficient capitalization to absorb this risk. This risk is mitigated to some extent by several factors: (1) the swap feature is delayed for one year, (2) the yield on the new preferred is below that of Trans World's existing preferred, providing a disincentive for the swap, and (3) the investor has an inducement to hold on and wait to convert to common for a full four and one half years because there is no call or acceleration provision. The issuer is also compensated for the risk of the swap by the units commanding a significant premium over the price of the common stock at the time of issuance.

9.6.3 How Altex Oil Solved Two Problems With One Combination Offer

Altex Oil was faced with the problem of having its outstanding warrants expire unexercised because of a deflated stock market. The market price of its common was $4¼ whereas the exercise price of the warrants was $5⅝. Because of its need for cash, the company offered new units of stock and warrants to holders of the expiring warrants as an inducement to exercise the warrants.

Each warrant holder was offered a combination of shares and warrants whose combined value was well above that of the exercise price of the warrants. This technique solved two immediate problems for the company. First, it allowed Altex to avoid the disadvantage of incurring a retroactive tax liability, which would have occurred upon expiration of the warrants, on the portion of its original financing that was attributable to the warrants. Second, as an alternative to simply issuing more common stock to raise the needed cash, the addition of warrants as part of the new units helps to lessen the dilution effect of the new common shares. It provides the investors with the potential (not realized through their earlier warrants) to capitalize on future gains in the company's common stock price.

9.7 CONVERTIBLE DEBT AND WARRANTS COMPARED

Before moving on to the subject of indexing, it would be useful to compare warrants coupled with debt to convertible debt.

From the buyer's perspective, the incentive to purchase these securities is similar. In each instance the buyer is purchasing the potential of earning very high returns if the underlying common stock increases in price. Because of this potential, the buyer is willing to accept a lower current interest rate on either the convertible debt or on the debt instrument issued in conjunction with the warrant.

Valuation. As far as valuation is concerned, in both cases the securities must be split apart and their units analyzed separately. The quality of the debt instrument should be considered with a determination made as to whether the timing is right regarding the buying of fixed income securities in general. This would include an analysis of the expected direction of interest rates in the near future. The objective is to determine the yield that the debt instrument should carry as a pure debt instrument. From this analysis one can isolate the risk incurred relative to purchasing the debt instrument as straight debt.

The second phase of the analysis is to determine how much the holder stands to gain from the underlying equity play. This turns on expectations as to the future price of the stock, which is embodied in the size of the premium.

In the case of convertible debt, the conversion parity price (purchase price divided by the number of shares into which the debt is converted) is determined. The minimum value of the convertible security (current market price of the common × the number of shares into which the debt can be converted) should not be too far below (a good range is 10 to 15 percent) the current market price of the debt. The current market price of the common stock should then be considered to determine that it is not too far below (15–20 percent) conversion parity. Finally the expected appreciation of the common stock between the time of purchase and the time of conversion should be substantial (i.e., significantly above conversion parity).

For a warrant, a similar approach is taken to determine if the warrant premium is reasonable in light of the expected volatility of the underlying common. A primary issue is whether the leverage ratio provides sufficient potential upside (or premium sufficiently low) so that if the common stock increases in value, the warrant will increase by a proportionately greater amount.

Dividend Yield. Another question that should be asked regarding both securities involves dividend yield. In the case of convertible bonds, the current yield should compare favorably with the dividend yield on the common stock. Also in the case of warrants there is a relationship between premiums and dividend yield on the underlying common stock. The higher the dividend yield on the common, the lower the premium, because the lost dividend income becomes more significant to the investor.

From the issuer's standpoint, a convertible security will ultimately improve the company's capital structure by elimination of the debt security and its replacement with equity. This is not so with a warrant, where the senior security to which it is attached remains outstanding after the warrant is exercised.

The company has more control over the future of the security in the case of convertible debt. This is because convertible debt is callable and thus the holder can be forced to convert at a time when the conversion value is sufficiently above the call price. The warrant may never be exercised, so that the issuer is uncertain as to whether it will receive the additional proceeds in the future. On the other hand, if the warrant is not exercised, the issuer can avoid dilution although it has obtained the proceeds from the issuance of the warrants.

9.8 INFLATION INDEXING: HOW TO OVERCOME THE DRAWBACKS BY INDEXING THE PRINCIPAL

In the preceding chapter we examined the use of variable rate loans. These loans, however, are not without their disadvantages to both the borrower and the lender. Some of these disadvantages have been remedied through the indexing of principal as opposed to merely indexing the coupon. The indexing may be based upon an inflation index (as for example with the variable rate notes discussed in Chapter 8), or it may be based upon the value of a commodity. Examples of the latter are real estate (an example of which is Koger Properties), oil prices (Petro-Lewis), or silver (Sunshine Mining and HMW).

When the borrower utilizes the variable rate loan, it is actually paying for anticipated declines in the value of the underlying principal through increased periodic interest payments. Thus the borrower may actually be incurring a higher debt cost on a current basis if inflation is greater than zero.

Conversely, if the principal is indexed, or if both coupon and principal are indexed, the debt cost will be leveled out over the life of the loan rather than being "front-loaded."

A second disadvantage of variable rate loans is incurred by a borrower whose pre-interest earnings are not "inflation resistant." That is, if a company's earnings are expected to grow with inflation, then there is little risk to the borrower in pegging its interest costs to an inflation adjusted index such as the consumer price index. However, if the company's pre-interest earnings are anticipated to stay barely even with inflation, then there is a serious additional credit risk imposed upon a lender that has its interest payments pegged to inflation.

The indexing of principal can reduce this credit risk, particularly if the index chosen is linked to a more stable element in the company's inherent business (such as oil in the case of Petro-Lewis) rather than an inflation index that reflects the vagaries of the overall economy.

A Word of Caution to the Borrower. The indexed loans bring certain disadvantages for the borrower. The final payment at maturity may be a significant multiple of the face amount of the loan if the underlying inflation index or product index increases substantially in value. The large payment at maturity may mean that the borrower has in fact overpaid for its capital. This risk theoretically has no limit, as opposed to a fixed interest payment or a predictable amortization of discount.

9.9 RETAIL PRICE INDEXING: HOW INDEX-LINKED BONDS PROVIDE A HEDGE AGAINST INFLATION

A series of index-linked securities was issued by the British government in 1982.[6] The most important feature of these bonds is that both the principal and the interest on them are indexed to the British General Index of Retail Prices, thus carrying an effective hedge against inflation. That is, the investor is assured of the "real" return, which he is offered upon purchase of the bonds if he holds them to redemption. The only risk to the purchaser is that the actual semi-annual payments of interest and the principal repayment at redemption will vary in relation to movements in the Retail Price Index (RPI).

---

[6]There were four issues of Index-Linked Treasury Stock: 2 percent due 1996, 2 percent due 2006, 2½ percent due 2011, and 2 percent due 1988.

How It Works. The British Government's approach to indexing was to link the payments of interest and principal to the RPI for the month eight months prior to that in which the payment in question falls. The reason for the eight-months' time lag is to allow the interest payment due at the end of any given six-month period to be fixed and ascertainable before that period begins. In order to compensate the bond holder for the additional eight-month lag of inflation, a corresponding eight-month lag from the time of issue is applied in determining the base RPI from which all calculations of interest and principal are scaled upwards.

For example, for the series issued in March of 1982, interest was to be paid each March and September with redemption in March of 1988. July 1981 is the month that fell eight months prior to the month of issue. Thus July 1981 was the base month for these bonds. The Retail Price Index for July 1981 was 297.1, which became the Base RPI for these bonds.

This series was to be redeemed in March of 1988. July of 1987 is eight months prior to the month of redemption. Thus the redemption value of the bonds would be calculated as:

$$\text{Redemption Value} = \frac{(\text{RPI for July 1987})}{100 \times (\text{RPI for July 1981})}$$

If one assumes a 12 percent per annum inflation rate comparable to that existing at the time of issuance, then the RPI for July of 1987 would be 583.9. This would result in a redemption value of 196.5. The redemption values for various inflation assumptions appear in the following table:

Rate of Inflation	Redemption Value
12%	196.5
10%	178.4
8%	161.9
6%	146.8
0%	108.7

The value of each interest payment is established in a similar manner. Interest is to be paid in March and September with the value of each payment linked to the RPI for the month eight months prior to that in which the payment falls. Thus the interest payment for September 1986 would be the RPI for January 1986 divided by the RPI for July 1981 (i.e., 297.1) for each $100 face amount of bonds.

9.9.1 How to Evaluate an Index-Linked Security

How then does one evaluate an index-linked security? This depends upon one's view of the future course of inflation. Based upon various inflation assumptions, a table can be constructed showing various interest and redemption values (Table 9.2).

9.9.2 Figuring the Premium Based on the Inflation Rate

The preceding yields should be compared to the yields of available conventional bonds. If one takes an optimistic view of inflation, the conventional market may in fact offer better yields. However, this ignores the fact that the inflation-linked security provides a hedge against inflation during the life of the security. This protection demands a premium in the price of the bond. As the inflation rate increases, this premium should increase during the life of the security.

For example, at the time of issuance of the 2 percent I.L. 1988, there existed in Great Britain an inflation rate of 9½ percent. In December of 1988, this security was trading at 97.625, for a yield to maturity of 12.748 percent. Nonindex-linked securities of comparable quality and maturity were trading to yield around 13.006 percent. The index-linked security would have to trade at around 96.41 in order to offer a similar yield. Thus, the 2 percent I.L. Treasury 1988 commanded a premium over conventional bonds of roughly 1.26 percent.

Let's now examine two sensitivities on the base case of a 9½ percent continuing rate of inflation. The first involves a lesser rate of inflation (7 percent). In the case of a 7 percent rate of inflation, the yield to maturity on the index-linked security would be 10.465 percent. The price at which the 2 percent I.L. 1988 would have to trade in order to offer a yield comparable to conventional bonds (i.e., 13.006 percent) would be 85.82. Thus the premium represented by its market price in December 1982 was 13.76 percent.

However, quite a different picture is presented assuming a 12 percent inflation rate. The yield to maturity on the 2 percent I.L. 1988 becomes 15.028 percent. In order to offer a yield comparable to conventional securities, the 2 percent I.L. 1988 would have to trade at 108.13. Thus it actually traded at a discount of 9.72 percent in December if one assumes this higher expected rate of inflation.

The analysis shows that as the expected rate of inflation increases above 9½ percent, the 2 percent I.L. 2,000 becomes a better buy than comparable conventional securities. Although short-term inflation rates will have a significant impact upon the price of index-linked securities, it should be emphasized that the possibility of rapid inflation at some period during the life of the security justifies a premium for the index-linked security as compared to conventional ones.

TABLE 9.2 Interest and Redemption Values (Face Amount $100—2% 1988 Bonds)

				Inflation				
Date	0%	2%	4%	6%	8%	10%	12%	14%
Interest Payments 9/82	.9996	.9996	.9996	.9996	.9996	.9996	.9996	.9996
3/83	1.0868	1.0886	1.0904	1.0922	1.0939	1.0957	1.0974	1.0991
3/84	1.0868	1.1105	1.1344	1.1587	1.1832	1.2080	1.2330	1.2584
3/85	1.0868	1.1328	1.1803	1.2292	1.2797	1.3318	1.3854	1.4407
3/86	1.0868	1.1556	1.2280	1.3041	1.3842	1.4683	1.5567	1.6495
3/87	1.0868	1.1788	1.2776	1.3835	1.4971	1.6188	1.7491	1.8885
3/88	1.0868	1.2025	1.3292	1.4678	1.6193	1.7848	1.9653	2.1622
Redemption Value 3/88	108.689	120.2539	132.9231	146.2834	161.9338	178.4800	196.5357	216.2221

30

From this set of data a second table can be constructed showing the price that should be paid to achieve various rates of return, or yields, for different future rates of inflation

184

TABLE 9.3 Market Values for Index-Linked Securities (Face Amount $100)

Inflation Rate	Yield to Maturity									
	9	10	11	12	13	14	15	16	18	20
6	100.44	95.40	90.65	86.17	81.93	77.94	74.16	70.59	64.03	58.16
7	105.27	99.88	94.99	90.28	85.84	81.64	77.68	73.93	67.04	60.87
8	110.32	104.77	99.53	94.59	89.92	85.51	81.35	77.42	70.18	63.71
9	115.60	109.77	104.27	99.08	94.18	89.56	85.19	81.06	73.47	66.68
10	121.11	115.00	109.23	103.78	98.64	93.78	89.20	84.87	76.90	69.78
11	126.88	120.46	114.40	108.69	103.29	98.20	93.39	88.84	80.49	73.01
12	132.89	126.16	119.81	113.81	108.15	102.81	97.76	92.99	84.23	76.39
13	139.18	132.11	125.45	119.16	113.23	107.62	102.33	97.33	88.14	79.92
14	145.74	138.33	131.34	124.75	118.52	112.65	107.10	101.86	92.22	83.60
15	152.58	144.82	137.49	130.58	124.05	117.89	112.08	106.58	96.48	87.44
16	159.73	151.59	143.91	136.66	129.83	123.37	117.27	111.51	100.92	91.45
18	174.97	166.03	157.60	149.64	142.13	135.04	128.34	122.02	110.39	100.00
20	191.55	181.74	172.48	163.75	155.51	147.73	140.39	133.45	120.69	109.29

chapter 10

Hybrid Securities, Part Two: Obtaining Financing Through Securities Backed by Real Estate and Commodities

The previous chapter discussed several hybrid securities that involved general indices of value: a company's inherent equity value in the case of convertible securities and warrants, and the overall performance of the economy in the case of inflation-hedged bonds that were tied to a price index.

This chapter considers hybrid securities where the debt instrument is linked to specific and identifiable assets such as real estate, silver, gold, and oil. The use of identifiable assets is especially attractive to those investors who have a particular expertise involving that asset. Conversely, there may be greater risk in linking the debt instrument to a specific asset as opposed to the overall performance of the company or the broader economy.

10.1 REAL ESTATE: HOW LENDERS HAVE USED EQUITY-LINKED LENDING TO HEDGE AGAINST INFLATION

Some of the earliest examples of equity-linked lending have occurred in the real estate area. Frequently a loan is coupled with an ownership interest in the real estate. For example, a mortgage for an office building might have a rate of 10 percent, but the loan includes a 50 percent equity interest in all gross revenues over fixed costs of the building for ten years. At the end of ten years the loan is convertible into a 75 percent equity position in the building, leaving the developer with 25 percent. The mortgage lender might also have an option to buy the remaining 25 percent at the then current market value.

Another form of equity interest occurs where the lender, in exchange for construction financing of an office building, will own the land when the building is completed and hold the mortgage on the building at 12 percent. In addition the lender receives fifty percent of all rental increases and 50 percent of the profits if the building is sold.

Citibank, Aetna Life Insurance Company, Prudential, and Equitable Life all have provided real estate financing in the form of *participating mortgages* or convertible mortgages, which are variations of the preceding examples. These lenders have provided fixed rate mortgages to the developer, typically ten to fifteen years in duration, at, let's say, 12 percent. In return the lender receives both a 50 percent interest in the cash flow and 50 percent of the capital appreciation when the building is sold. Thus the lender hedges itself against inflation. If inflation continues or rises, the property appreciates at a greater rate. If inflation decreases, the lender receives the benefit of an attractive fixed rate on the mortgage.

189

10.2 HOW REAL ESTATE APPRECIATION NOTES PROVIDED A CASH-FLOW ADVANTAGE TO THE KROGER COMPANY

The Kroger Company issued $30,000,000 of Real Estate Appreciation Notes due June 1, 2000. The appreciation in the notes was tied to the increase in the appraised value of the company's properties.

Kroger is engaged in the business of owning and operating office buildings located in suburban office centers. The Company's properties included 136 buildings containing 3,462,450 square feet of rentable space in 12 Sunbelt cities. The buildings were approximately 99 percent leased, with an average annual rental of $8.70 per square foot and an average offering price for new tenants of $10.65 per square foot.

The majority of the Company's leases are on a gross basis with terms varying from three to five years. Roughly 75 percent of the Company's gross rental revenues were derived under leases containing rental escalation provisions based upon changes in the Consumer Price Index, and approximately 17 percent were derived under leases containing escalation provisions based upon real estate tax and operating expense increases.

How the Notes Work. The Real Estate Appreciation Notes were to bear interest based on two components. The first interest component, called the *Fixed Interest Portion*, is calculated at an annual rate of 9 percent, payable semi-annually. Thereafter the notes are to bear fixed interest on the outstanding principal at the greater of 8 percent or the Capitalization Rate for Indexed Properties.

Capitalization Rate, which is determined as of December 31, is calculated by dividing the forecasted net operating income for the succeeding calendar year from the indexed properties by the index appraised value of the indexed properties at such date. Forecasted net operating income is estimated by an independent appraiser (meaning the American Appraisal Company, or another independent appraiser of nationally recognized standing as designated by the Company).

Indexed properties are all the commercial real properties owned by the Company at the time of the offering or thereafter acquired for the production of rental income that are located within (or no more than one mile from), and managed in conjunction with, Kroger Executive Centers. Kroger Executive Centers were any of the 12 suburban office centers in which the company owned buildings at the time of the offering, or any other suburban office centers developed by Kroger having the same characteristics of the Executive Centers with more than 3,000,000 square feet of rentable space.

Indexed appraised value of an indexed property was defined as the fair market value of the particular property, assuming that such property is free and clear of all mortgage indebtedness, as determined by an independent appraiser using the same methods as those used to determine the index appraised value of the Company's 136 office buildings as of December 31, 1981.

Fair market value was defined as the estimated price that a property might be expectd to bring if offered for sale in the open market, allowing a reasonable time to find a purchaser who buys with knowledge of all the uses to which the property is capable of being used. The office centers were valued using the direct capitalization method, the equity capitalization method, and the discounted cash-flow approach.

In the *direct capitalization method*, net operating income is forecast for the current year. Net operating income consists of gross rents less direct operating expenses other than debt service, income taxes, depreciation and amortization. A multiple (the inverse of the capitalization rate) is then applied to the net operating income to obtain the fair market value. The overall risk, as well as the leverage factor and debt structure, are reflected in the multiple.

Equity capitalization is a slight modification of direct capitalization, where a multiple (the inverse of the equity capitalization rate) is applied to the gross cash flow for the current year. Gross cash flow is net operating income, as defined above, less debt service. The resulting number is the equity value of the properties. The outstanding mortgage balance is added to the equity value to obtain the fair market value of the properties.

In the *discounted cash flow method*, the present value is calculated for future cash flows during a six-year period. To this value is added the residual value (value upon sale) at the end of the period, resulting in the total current equity value of the properties. The mortgage balance is then added to the equity value to give the total value of the properties.

Two further methods were used as a check: a *market approach* and a *cost approach*. In the market approach sales prices of recently sold comparable properties were analyzed. In the cost approach, the estimated cost for the reproduction of the existing Kroger properties was estimated.

In addition to the fixed interest component there is a further interest calculation for *additional interest*. Each December 31 the notes *accrue* additional interest at a rate equal to the percentage increase, if any, in the independently appraised value of the indexed properties during the year ending on such December 31, provided that at least a minimum of $500 of additional interest will accrue through December 31, 1987 on each $1,000 of original principal amount of the notes. On June 1, 1988 and June 1, 1994 the principal amount of the outstanding notes will be increased by the amount of additional interest accrued to the preceding December 31, and fixed interest thereafter will be payable on such increased principal amount.

Total fixed interest and additional interest may not exceed 25 percent per annum, compounded annually. However, a decrease in the index appraised value in any calendar year will not affect the amount of additional interest accrued for prior years.

If an indexed property is sold during any year for more than its index appraised value at the end of the preceding year, the index appraised value of the indexed properties determined at the end of the year of sale in calculating additional interest will include the sales price of such property only if the inclusion of such property at such sales price would increase the amount of additional interest that accrues for such year. If an indexed property is sold during any year for less than its index appraised value at the end of the preceding year, such property will not be included in calculating the additional interest for such year.

The additional interest will closely resemble an equity position—that is, it will be affected by the risks of ownership of real property. These risks include the uncertainties of cash flow to meet fixed obligations, adverse local market conditions due to economic conditions and neighborhood characteristics, availability and cost of mortgage financing, increases in real estate taxes and other operating expenses such as energy costs, as well as uninsured casualty losses. The values of the properties will also depend upon the ability to retain tenants, which will depend upon other factors such as surplus office space.

How Additional Interest is Calculated. The following table shows how additional interest would be calculated for a variety of appreciation rates:

TABLE 10.1 Calculations of Additional Interest ($1000 Principal Amount)

Case	Year	Appreciation of Indexed Properties	Additional Interest Accrued
I	1	10%	$100
	2	10%	$100 (10% × $1100)
II	1	10.6% (including sales price of properties sold at >10% appreciation rate in Index Appraised Value)	$106
III	1	10.0% (excluding sales of properties at <10% appreciation rate)	$100
IV	1	10%	$100
	2	10%	$110
	3	(5 %)	$ 0
	4	10%	$ 60.50 (5% × $1210)

TABLE 10.1 (continued)

Case	Year	Appreciation of Indexed Properties		Additional Interest Accrued
V	1–4	10 % per year		$464 (for 4 years)
	5	(10%)		$ 0
	6	5 %		$ 0
	7	10 %		$146.40
VI	1–5	[	]	$250
	6	<20%		$250
VII	1–5	[	]	$250
	6	25%		$312.50

In case V, the initial term ends after year six and the second term begins in year seven. Thus, no further "makeup" in appreciation is required in year seven and the additional interest calculation for that year is based upon the index appraised value at the end of year four ($1464). Cases VI and VII illustrate the point that there is a minimum requirement of $500 of Additional Interest for the Initial Term. The Company will, as a minimum, accrue for accounting purposes the $500 additional interest ratably over the six-year period. This minimum amount, however, will not be considered earned until the end of the initial term.

Thus the actual interest *paid* is calculated as follows:

Interest Paid (1982–1988) = original principal amount × 9 percent

Interest Paid (1988–1994) = [original principal amount + accrued Additional Interest through December 31, 1987]

×

[greater of 8 percent or Capitalization Rate as determined December 31, 1986]

Interest Paid (1994–2000) = [original principal amount + accrued Additional Interest through December 31, 1993]

×

[greater of 8 percent or Capitalization Rate as determined December 31, 1992]

The holder of the debt has the right to redeem at two specific dates: June 1, 1988, and June 1, 1994. The redemption price is equal to the principal amount plus all accrued fixed interest and additional interest. After June 1, 1995, the notes are redeemable at the option of the Company.

10.2.1 Tax Treatment of Real Estate Appreciation Notes

There are some interesting tax considerations resulting from the unusual character of the real estate appreciation notes. The fixed interest portion of the notes would be deductible by the Company as it accrues and be reportable (by an accrual basis tax payer) in gross income of the holder.

The Notes were issued at an original issue discount.[1] The stated redemption price of a note at maturity will be the original principal amount of $1000 increased by the $500 minimum amount of additional interest. Therefore the Company will amortize and deduct the original issue discount ratably over the term of the notes. Because the holder can require redemption on June 1, 1988, and on June 1, 1994, each of those dates may be treated as the maturity date of a separate obligation. Each note would, in effect, be treated as three separate six-year notes with the original issue discount deducted over the initial term of the note ending June 1, 1988. The holder of the note will be required to include the ratable portion of the original issue discount in gross income. An unresolved tax question at the time of the offering was whether the original issue discount rules could be interpreted to apply to the contingent portion of additional interest (i.e., that portion above $500 that depends upon the index appraised value of the properties).[2]

Thus the company not only priced the notes at a discount, but essentially guaranteed at least a 7 percent appreciation rate on top of the coupon. The effective rate to investors will be a minimum of 16 percent regardless of whether the property appreciates. The cash-flow advantage to the company derives from the fact that it has the use of the accrued appreciation for each six-year period before it pays it over to the investors.

---

[1] See Chapter 7.

[2] The Tax Reform Act of 1984 resolved this question. If there is OID and the taxpayer has elected to compute the discount using the constant interest method, the redemption price of the bond is treated as its "revised issue price" and the portion of OID includable in income is determined under the Regulations.

10.3 SECURITIES BACKED BY GOLD AND SILVER

10.3.1 The Rente Giscard 7 Percent Loan: A Noteworthy Precious Metal Index-Linked Security

One of the most noteworthy precious metal index-linked securities is the FF 6.5 billion Rente Giscard 7 percent loan, issued at par in January of 1973 by the French government. It was linked to the value of gold in order to protect against weaknesses in, or devaluations of, the French currency. The issue is redeemable in one installment in January, 1988.

The redemption price and annual coupon were not initially linked to gold. However, the indexing was triggered in 1978 as a result of the French franc floating freely through the demonitization of gold. The index then became based on the price of the "L'Ingot."

How It Works. Final redemption value and the annual coupon are both indexed to the average market price of the gold bar over the 30 trading days preceding the date of issuance. This price was FF 10,483. Thus the indexed coupon payable each year is calculated by taking the average price of the L'Ingot on the 30 trading days preceding January 1st (FF 94,529 for 1982) and applying the following formula:

$$\frac{FF\ 94,529}{FF\ 10,483} \times .07 \times FF\ 1000 = FF\ 631.22$$

The redemption price on January 1, 1988 would be calculated in the same manner. That is, the then current average price of the L'Ingot would be divided by FF 10,483, and the resulting ratio would be applied to FF 1000.

These securities remain among the most marketable of all French securities.

10.3.2 Sunshine Mining Company: The First Issuer of Silver-Indexed Bonds

In 1980, Sunshine Mining Company issued $25,000,000 of 8½ percent silver-indexed bonds due in 1995. Each $1000 face amount bond was to be payable at maturity or redemption at the greater of $1000 or the market price of 50 ounces of silver (indexed principal amount). If the indexed principal amount at such time is greater than $1000, the company may at its option deliver silver to holders of the debt electing to accept such delivery in satisfaction of the indexed principal amount.

The bonds were redeemable in whole on or after April 1985 at the option of the company, at the indexed principal amount together with accrued interest, if the indexed principal amount equals or exceeds $2000 for a period of 30 consecutive days. The bonds are secured by a security agreement entitling the holders to receive, upon default, 3.627 percent of the annual mining production of the Sunshine Mine. However, the security is limited by the number of ounces of silver per year sufficient to supply the total at the date of acceleration, and not more than 50 ounces of silver per $1000 face amount of outstanding bonds.

A further feature of the bond issue was a sinking fund for retirement of 7 percent of the issue each year beginning in 1982. Each holder whose bonds have been called for redemption through operation of the sinking fund has the right to elect not to have its bonds redeemed. The face amount of the bonds called by the company but not redeemed is added to the amount called for redemption in subsequent years up to an additional 7 percent of the issue in any year. The excess above the additional 7 percent will not be carried forward in subsequent years.

Because of the novelty of the silver-linked bonds as an investment security, certain mechanisms had to be created to ascertain the actual amounts due to the investors. The market price for the indexed principal amount was to be calculated as the average Market Price for the 15 trading days immediately preceding such date of determination of 50 ounces of silver. Market price for a particular trading day means the Spot Settlement Price published by the Commodity Exchange, Inc., or if not available the Chicago Board of Trade, or Handy and Harman, or the London Metal Exchange. The Spot Settlement Price itself had to be defined in two ways: (1) with respect to silver futures contracts— as the settlement price per ounce of silver with respect to the current or nearest delivery month as established daily at the close of trading on such date by the exchange on which such contract is traded, and (2) with respect to a person who customarily publishes quotes for the purchase or sale of silver, the last price per ounce published on such date by such person for currently deliverable silver.

With respect to the company's obligations under the sinking fund and redemption at maturity, Sunshine expects to satisfy these obligations out of its production of silver by delivering to the trustee of the bonds the required number of ounces of silver, or if the indexed principal amount exceeds $1000, the proceeds from the sale of its production of such number of ounces of silver.

If Sunshine satisfied its obligations by the delivery of silver instead of cash, the company may deliver the silver smelted, refined, or minted in any size, form or configuration (such as medallions) and it may even be inscribed. Silver must be delivered in units of whole ounces of no more than 1000 ounces each. All storage costs incurred after any maturity or redemption date, as well as insurance, transportation and delivery costs, and assaying charges and sales commissions, are the responsibility of the purchasers of the bonds.

The Company gave the purchasers of the bonds no assurance that the silver received would be in a form or quantity meeting the requirements of a particular exchange or that it would have an available market in which to sell such silver. (Silver is traded on exchanges in accordance with specialized requirements including minimum tradable amounts, so that holders receiving less than those traded quantities could experience substantial discounts in the sales of such smaller quantities.)

As already indicated, the indexed principal amount of the bonds is determined by reference to the market price of silver, which in turn is defined as the Spot Settlement Price quoted by the Comex. As of the close of trading on the day prior to the offering (April 9, 1980), the Spot Settlement Price of Silver on the Comex in New York was $16.00 per ounce. Thus 50 ounces of silver would have been valued at $800.

Prior to the time of the offering, the trading prices of silver had been characterized by unprecedented volatility. Following a very sharp increase in silver prices, particularly during the last quarter of 1979 and January 1980, the price of silver declined sharply from its high point. On March 26, 1980, the price of silver declined $4.40 to $15.80 per ounce, a decline of roughly 50 percent in two days.

The following table was set forth showing price ranges of silver (per ounce) as reported by Comex.

TABLE 10.2 Price Range of Silver

Year	High	Low	Contracts Traded[1] (5000 ozs. each)
1974	$6.19	3.26	1365915
1975	5.25	3.92	2902315
1976	5.14	3.83	3741908
1977	4.98	4.31	3540047
1978	6.32	4.81	3822085
1979			
1st Quarter	7.92	5.92	1152810
2nd Quarter	8.85	7.28	1362323
3rd Quarter	16.45	8.55	1081104
4th Quarter	34.45	15.30	481382
1980			
1st Quarter	48.70	10.80	282200[1]

[1]A futures contract as traded represents the right and obligation to receive or deliver in the specified month an aggregate of 5,000 ounces of silver. A futures contract expiring in the spot month requires the holder of a long position (obligation to purchase) to accept delivery within that month.

10.3.3 Tax Treatment of Sunshine's Silver-Indexed Bonds

The holder of the bonds will realize a capital gain (or loss) upon sale, maturity, or redemption of the bonds if the proceeds are in excess of the holder's basis. The Company may be required to recognize as ordinary income or as an ordinary loss the difference between the fair market value of any silver delivered upon the redemption or maturity of a bond and the company's adjusted basis in such silver. Furthermore, any amount paid by the company upon redemption or maturity of a bond in excess of its face amount may be deductible by the company as interest or as an ordinary business expense. (These ordinary income consequences to the company will not arise if the company elects to satisfy the indexed principal amount by the payment of cash—unless the company sells silver to obtain such cash).

10.3.4 HMW Industries: Another Issuer of Silver-Backed Securities

In 1981, HMW Industries, Inc. became the second issuer of silver-backed bonds, issuing $19 million of 8 percent silver-indexed bonds due in 2001. The bonds were issued at an original issue discount of 80 percent of face value.

How It Works. The Bonds are secured by a security interest in the Silver Inventory of Wallace Silversmiths, Inc. (a wholly owned subsidiary of HMW) equal to the Market Price (as of the date of offering) of the aggregate number of ounces of silver represented by the total "Silver Units." A Silver Unit was defined as 43 ounces of silver for each $1000 principal amount of bonds. On May 7, 1981, the Spot Settlement Price of an ounce of silver on Comex was $10.99, or $472.57 per silver unit as security for each $1000 for bonds.

Silver inventory had to be defined as all silver contained in any or all of the following goods of Wallace (including the products thereof owned by Wallace and the proceeds and insurance proceeds therefrom): all inventory, raw materials, work in process, or materials used or consumed in the business of Wallace, whether owned on the date of the offering, or thereafter acquired, and whether in the possession of Wallace, Wallace's warehouseman, any refiner that holds silver for the account of Wallace, or other bailees of Wallace. Furthermore, Wallace had to covenant to maintain its Silver Inventory at a level equal to at least 105 percent of the aggregate number of ounces of silver for which all outstanding bonds could be redeemed.

After May 1, 1983,[3] the holder could redeem its bonds for cash

---

[3]The Company is only obligated to redeem 20 percent of the issue per year until May, 1988, at which time it is only obligated to redeem 40 percent per year.

equal to the market price of a silver unit for each $1000 principal amount of bonds. In lieu of cash and at its option, HMW may satisfy its obligations to redeem such bonds by delivering silver units in kind.

Similar to the case of Sunshine, if the market price of a silver unit exceeds $2000 for 20 consecutive days, the Company may redeem for cash at the market price of a silver unit.

A sinking fund for 10 percent of the issue began in 1983. No holder will receive silver in satisfaction of any redemption (either holder initiated or HMW initiated) unless HMW and the holder have elected to receive it, and no holder will receive silver in satisfaction of any sinking fund redemption.

TABLE 10.3 Comparison of Silver Backed Securities

	Sunshine	*HMW*
Face Amount	$25,000,000	$10,000,000
Price to public	100 percent	80 percent
Coupon	8½ percent	8 percent
Term	15 years	20 years
Security	50 ounces of silver (indexed principal amount) for each $1000 face amount of bonds	43 ounces of silver (silver unit) for each $1000 face amount
Nonmandatory Sinking Fund	Up to 7 percent per year beginning in second year for cash equal to principal amount	Up to 10 percent of issue per year beginning in second year for cash equal to principal amount
Redemption by Company	In cash or silver equal to value of IPA, if indexed principal amount averages $2000 for 30 consecutive days	In cash or silver equal to value of a silver unit, if silver unit averages $2000 for 20 consecutive days
Redemption by Holder	None	Up to 20 percent of issue per year beginning in 2nd year, in cash or silver equal to value of Silver Unit.
Payment at Maturity	Greater of $1000 or Indexed Principal Amount	In cash or silver equal to value of silver unit

Thus HMW, by virtue of offering the bonds at a deep discount, offered a much higher yield to maturity than Sunshine's 8½ percent. However, Sunshine's bonds were secured by substantially more silver.

10.4 HOW PETRO-LEWIS RAISED CASH THROUGH OIL-INDEXED NOTES

In April of 1981, Petro-Lewis Corporation,[4] which was engaged in the oil and gas exploration and production business, issued $20,000,000 of 9 percent oil-indexed notes due 1986.

How It Works. Nominal interest on the notes was payable annually at 9 percent. In addition, Contingent Interest on each $1000 principal amount of the Notes is payable at maturity in an amount equal to the increase over $668.96 of (1) the average Crude Oil Price of 18½ barrels of crude oil for the three months ending February 28, 1986, or (2) if greater, the highest average Crude Oil Price of 18½ barrels of crude oil, up to a maximum of $1258 ($68 per barrel), for any calendar quarter through the quarter ending December 31, 1985. The $668.96 base price is the average Crude Oil Price of 18½ barrels of crude oil for the calendar quarter ending March 31, 1981, based on an average Crude Oil Price per barrel of $36.16.

Crude Oil Price was defined as the arithmetic average of the official or government posted selling prices, excluding special premiums, add-ons, and concessions (the "official posted selling prices"), for the following seven types of crude oil: Saudi Arabian light 34°, Kuwaiti 31°, Nigerian Bonny 37°, Venezuelan Tia Juana 26°, Indonesian Minas 34°, U.K. Forties 36.5°, and Mexican Asthmus 34°, as determined on a weekly basis from *Weekly Petroleum Status Report*, published by the U.S. Department of Energy. In certain events, alternative crude oils were to be substituted for the foregoing index crude oils, and alternative publications were to be used to determine the official posted selling prices of the index crude oils.

The seven types of crude oil used to determine Crude Oil Prices are produced by seven major exporters of oil. Table 10.4 was included in the prospectus to show the prices for these index crude oils on December 31 for each of the five years and on March 31, 1981, as well as the average prices on these dates.

An explanation was included after this table, which suggested that data should not be construed as a projection that crude oil prices would increase over the term of the notes. Further, it was emphasized that during the prior five years there were substantial increases in crude oil prices as a result of the Organization of Petroleum Exporting Countries, increasing dependence on OPEC as a source of crude oil, and world wide inflationary forces.

Petro will be required to certify prior to maturity of the notes the

---

[4] The notes were actually issued by Petro-Lewis International Finance N.V. and guaranteed by the parent corporation, Petro-Lewis Corporation.

TABLE 10.4 Prices of Index Crude Oils

Date	Saudi Arabian Light 34°	Kuwaiti 31°	Nigerian Bonny 37°	Venezuelan Tia Juana 26°	Indonesian Minas 34°	U.K. Forties 36.5°	Mexican Isthmus 34°	Average
December 31, 1976	$11.51	$11.23	$13.10	$11.32	$12.80	$ —	$13.35	$12.22
December 31, 1977	12.70	12.37	14.63	12.72	13.55	13.65	13.42	13.29
December 31, 1978	12.70	12.27	14.10	12.72	13.55	14.00	13.10	13.20
December 31, 1979	24.00	21.43	26.24	23.46	25.50	26.02	24.60	24.46
December 31, 1980	32.00	31.50	37.02	29.88	31.50	35.66	38.50	33.72

applicable average crude oil price for calculation of the amount of contingent interest. An independent economics consulting firm will verify the amount of such applicable average crude oil price and contingent interest. The independent economics consulting firm was not specified at the time of the offering, but was to be selected by the Company and reasonably acceptable to the trustee for the noteholder.

If Petro determines in good faith at maturity that, as a result of governmental regulation (including reimposition of U.S. crude oil price controls) or taxes (including increases in the U.S. Windfall Profit Tax), its ability to obtain the benefits of increases in crude oil prices is materially impaired, the maximum amount payable for each $1000 principal amount of the notes, including principal, accrued nominal interest and contingent interest, will be $2500.

The noteholders had a right of early maturity on November 1, 1983. If the election was made, the holders were paid $1182 for each $1000 principal amount of their notes, which, together with nominal interest previously payable, was equivalent to a 14 percent interest yield to maturity. No contingent interest was payable on any note maturing early pursuant to a holder's election.

Tax Treatment of Oil-Indexed Bonds. Because of the use of an Antilles Corporation (Petro N.V.) as the issuing entity (which was subject to the Income Tax convention between the United States of America and the Kingdom of the Netherlands, as extended to the Netherlands Antilles), the offering allowed for an early redemption by Petro in the event of certain changes affecting United States or Netherlands Antilles taxation. Such redemption would be at principal amount plus accrued nominal interest and contingent interest.

Changes in the tax law would result in the issuer paying "Additional Interest" to the holders in sufficient amounts so that every *net* payment of principal or interest, after withholding tax for any present or future tax, assessment, or other governmental charge subsequently imposed by the Netherlands Antilles or the United States (or any political subdivision or taxing authority of these) will not be less than the amount originally provided for in the offering.

The additional interest protection was meant to provide protection against a future Netherlands Antilles tax for a foreign or nonresident entity in relation to the Netherlands Antilles. As to future United States tax, the Additional Interest protection was meant to apply to a foreign or nonresident entity in relation to the United States.

At the time of the offering, Petro's counsel gave the opinion that (1) payments of principal and interest on the notes would be exempt from U.S. Federal income taxation unless the recipient were a resident of the United States, and (2) such a nonresident noteholder would not be subject to United States federal income tax on gain realized on sale, maturity, or redemption.

Similarly, an opinion was offered with respect to Netherlands Antilles tax law to the effect that: (1) payments of principal and interest to Antilles nonresidents would not be subject to Netherlands Antilles income or withholding tax, and (2) such nonresidents would not be subject to Netherland Antilles income tax on gain realized on sale, maturity, or redemption of the Notes.

10.5 HOW OTHER INDUSTRIES CAN TAP THE POTENTIAL IN COMMODITY-LINKED DEBT

There is untapped potential for the use of commodity-backed securities in other industries as well.

Timber Industry. For instance, a number of structures have been developed for companies with holdings of severely undervalued timberland. A joint venture structure[5] is frequently employed with the objective of providing the lender/investor with a share in the earnings of the timberlands, while the tax benefits remain with the owner/issuer.

Coal. In the coal industry, Seminara Coal Corp. came up with the concept of offering securities convertible into coal. The security was a preferred stock, offered in units of $1360 each, with the shares carrying a 16 percent annual dividend. After four years the preferred could be converted into 33 tons of coal per unit. Until that time, the preferred is convertible into common. Although the investor would technically be entitled to receive 33 tons of coal, as a practical matter the company would pay the investor the coal's value in cash, after deducting 5 percent for shipping and selling expenses.

Tucson Electric and Public Service of New Mexico closed an indexed financing related to coal in 1982. These utilities created a jointly owned captive coal company and sold participations in the trust. The investors were to receive a royalty that was adjustable each quarter by the rate of change in the GNP deflator, with the proviso that the royalty could not fall below a set rate. At the time of issuance the investors were receiving a rate around 14 percent, which would always at least equal inflation plus 3 percent.

Another technique related to coal involved Rio Verde Energy, which sold five-year convertible debentures, each with a face value of $60,000. These carried a 7½ percent coupon plus a royalty of 2 ½ cents for each ton of coal produced, up to a maximum of 2 million tons or $50,000. The 2.5-cent royalty continues to be payable even after the bonds are redeemed or converted, until the 2 million ton limit is reached.

---

[5] See Chapter 1.

Depending upon the amount of time to reach the 2 million ton limit, the rate of return to the investor will vary significantly. If this were to be reached within five years, the return based on royalties alone would be roughly 16.5 percent. Adding the 7.5 percent from the coupon, the total return would be near 24 percent. If only 1 million tons were mined in the first five years, then the total return during this period would drop to 15.75 percent.

Hybrid Securities to Diversify Debt. It should be emphasized that all of the various debt instruments that we have considered might be used by the same company. They are not mutually exclusive. By diversifying among numerous types of loans and deep discount, variable rate, blended rate, CPI indexed, product indexed, and so on, borrowers can achieve a balanced portfolio that improves the stability of their debt service costs.

10.5.1 Keep This Trade-Off in Mind

Although hybrid securities offer certain advantages to purchasers, the holder is usually trading a known current return in the traditional debt instrument for a bond with a lower current return. A significant portion of the yield of the hybrid security is paid late in its life. This trade-off depends on the investor's views as to the future direction of the underlying equity—whether it is measured by a specific asset or the overall economy.

chapter 11

Tax-Inspired Financing: Exchange Offers, Royalty Trusts, Safe Harbor Leasing, and the Net Operating Loss Acquisition

Taxes have been a significant consideration in virtually every financing technique discussed in this book. We saw in the discussion of off-balance sheet financing in the first four chapters that significant tax planning was required in order to achieve the desired financial reporting and economic objectives of the particular transaction.

The employee stock ownership plan and the tax reduction act stock ownership plan considered in Chapters 6 and 7 were, at once, employee benefit plans and financing vehicles. Both of these devices were created by tax legislation.

Deep discount debt relied upon various provisions of the Internal Revenue Code to create tax deductions in the raising of debt, while at the same time reducing the current cash outlays of the borrower. R&D Partnerships, which are discussed in the following chapter, are also a product of tax legislation.

This chapter discusses several financing mechanisms that have been quite popular in recent years and that have a significant tax component: (1) the oil and gas exchange offer, (2) the royalty trust, (3) the net operating loss acquisition, and (4) the tax benefit transfer lease. The oil and gas exchange offer and the royalty trust are frequently found in the same transaction. The tax benefit transfer lease, also known as the safe harbor lease, is limited to equipment leasing. The net operating loss acquisition can be used in most types of corporate acquisition.

11.1 HOW EXCHANGE OFFERS PROVIDE TAX AND FINANCIAL BENEFITS FOR INVESTORS AND GENERAL PARTNERS

In an oil or gas exchange offer, limited partners in oil or gas drilling partnerships are offered the opportunity to exchange those interests either for cash, or in recent years, for a more liquid interest in an existing or newly formed entity. The new interest is usually a marketable security such as common stock, but more complex instruments have been utilized, such as convertible subordinated notes.

Exchange offers range from simple and traditional deals between a single general partner and his limited partners, to broader ventures such as Integrated Energy (discussed subsequently in greater detail), where a new company is formed out of a number of unrelated partnership programs. Notable transactions have been done by Ensource, Templeton Energy, Towner Petroleum, Wainoco, Sovran Energy, Howell Petroleum, Visa Petroleum, and numerous others.

11.1.1 Cash Tender Offers Have Given Way to More Tax-Advantaged Exchange Transactions

Earlier exchange offers were primarily cash tender offers that were made to limited partner investors in a particular drilling fund by the same exploration company that acted as general partner. The amount of cash paid was calculated as the discounted present value of the projected future revenues of the partnership. With recent surges in interest rates, the discount rates have increased substantially, thus making the cash tender offers less attractive. A further disadvantage to the cash tender offer was the ordinary income tax that applied to the offer.

More recent exchange offers, such as the transaction conducted by the Apache Petroleum Company, have involved the exchange of stock or publicly traded depositary units in royalty trusts for the partnership interests. In this manner, the ordinary income tax consequences are avoided while the investor receives substantial liquidity with the new security. Without the swap, the investor would be locked into long-term ownership of a depleting asset.

11.1.2 Three Notable Exchange Offers: Integrated Energy, Ensource, and Templeton

Integrated Energy's complex transaction in 1981 involved the exchange of $485 million of oil and gas interests for common stock, 80 percent of which were producing properties. Roughly 75 percent of the interests tendered were in large, private deals. These interests generated over $40 million per year in revenues. The consolidation of these interests provided a significant cash flow that could be used by Integrated to obtain leverage for further expansion.

In the case of the Ensource exchange offer, Ensource specified the 26 properties that would qualify for the offer after a detailed review of over 175 different properties. Unlike other stock swaps, there was no initial public offering of Ensource shares. All of the stock went to the investors who participated in the exchange. In the Templeton Energy exchange offer, which did involve a public offering, partnerships managed by three different sponsors were involved. The deal was structured so that it would unwind if it failed to net at least $10 million from the stock issue.

Although Ensource and Templeton may appear complicated, they were relatively straightforward in relation to Integrated. Integrated did not identify and negotiate for specific properties in advance of the exchange offer. Rather, it issued a blanket call for interests in exploration, development and production activities, proven reserves, and undeveloped leaseholds.

The owners of the various properties were solicited and asked to request an evaluation of their properties from Integrated. The evaluation was to indicate the amount of stock that would be exchanged by Integrated for the property. After the solicitation process had been completed, Integrated was to put together a final prospectus that would summarize each accepted interest. On the basis of the final prospectus, each potential participant would decide whether to accept the exchange offer.

11.1.3 When to Make an Exchange Offer

Exchange offers are generally made to investors when the tax advantages that initially brought the investor into the partnership are exhausted. These tax benefits include the investment tax credit, intangible drilling costs, and depletion and depreciation. That is, the investment has reached the point where it has begun to generate taxable income at ordinary income rates. Cash distributions to the partners may be partly sheltered, with as much as 25 percent being tax free because of continued oil and gas depletion allowances and depreciation write-offs.

How the Investor Benefits. The exchange gives the investor a means of converting the other 75 percent that is not sheltered (taxed at ordinary income rates) into long-term capital gains. This result is due to the fact that an investor, who has exchanged interests in a partnership held for more than one year, can sell the stock of the newly formed company immediately, and the sale should qualify for the more favorable capital gains treatment. *Note*: The exchange, although usually tax free, could result in some ordinary taxable income if the investor had debt incurred by the partnership in excess of his own individual tax basis.

Not only is the investor attracted to the immediate exchange offering of a particular company, but in addition, for a company that offers a series of oil and gas drilling programs, an investor will be more attracted to subsequent programs with the knowledge that the sponsoring company may offer an exit vehicle through the use of an exchange offering.

11.1.4 Two Valuation Problems in Exchange Transactions

A critical issue in structuring an exchange offer involves the determination of the exchange value of the interests offered. Because it cannot always be determined in advance which interests will be tendered, the valuation of the stock in the new entity is at best imprecise. One approach is to set an approximate value on the stock of the new company, assuming that certain interests are tendered, and then employ a formula that calculates the number of shares to be exchanged. It is difficult to develop an exact value because there are numerous variables that are difficult to pin down.

The engineering analysis of proven oil or gas reserves, for example, may employ different methods and have wide margins of error from property to property. Even if the valuation is sound, there is the uncertainty about what might happen to the stock in the after market.

The valuation of the general partner's interest in properties presents further problems. The general partner, by virtue of its controlling position in a limited partnership, is usually offered a discount for the stock it receives as compared to the limited partners. The discount enables the general partner to end up with a disproportionately large share of the new company in relation to the limited partners.

11.1.5 New Twists to Exchange Offerings

In 1982, Conquest Exploration added a new twist to oil and gas exchange offers by combining the offer with a simultaneous public units offering. Conquest offered 3.5 million units of one share and two warrants. Because the partnerships that Conquest wanted to obtain were encumbered with a substantial debt burden, the new equity raised in the public units offering was used to reduce the partnership debts. The original owners of the partnerships were protected against dilution resulting from the units offering by giving them the first right to buy the units.

An interesting modification was added by Energetics to help it sell an offer to exchange limited partnership interests in oil programs for stock in a new company. Of particular concern to Energetics was the negative impact on the stock price that frequently occurs after an exchange offer.

To prevent a precipitous drop of the stock price following the exchange, Energetics offered to sell shares of common stock of the new company on behalf of the limited partners 60 days after the exchange. The general partners and the underwriter would not be allowed to sell shares in the underwriting, and would not be able to sell shares for a year thereafter. Stock of the limited partners not sold in the underwriting could only be sold at staggered intervals during the year.

As an added inducement for the limited partners to take part in the exchange, the limited partners were entitled to receive up to 20 percent of their interests in preferred stock of the new company, which had a yield of roughly 13 percent.

11.1.6 Using Exchanges in Real Estate Transactions

The exchange offering technique was applied to real estate by MCO equities, a subsidiary of MCO Holdings. In late 1981 MCO began to structure an exchange offering of shares in a new company for real estate interests and holdings. The owners of those real estate interests were to become shareholders in the new company.

Other applications in the real estate area have included both divestitures and sale/leasebacks of real estate by corporations. Divesting properties through the exchange offer provides several advantages over an outright sale. At a time of poor market conditions, the seller might be forced to sell below the property's appraised value. Alternatively, the seller might have to take back a purchase money mortgage instead of cash. If the property has not been held for the required period of time, the seller might also have to absorb the negative tax consequences of recapture of depreciation or investment tax credits. These problems can be avoided in the exchange offer, where the seller receives a liquid security, and generally avoids recapture in a tax-free exchange.[1]

11.2 USING DEPOSITORY UNITS IN AN EXCHANGE OFFER

An unusual transaction vehicle was employed in an exchange offer by Apache Petroleum Company in February of 1981: $180 million of depository units were issued in a tax free exchange for certain interests in Apache Oil and Gas programs undertaken from 1959 through 1978. The units were publicly traded, limited partnership interests in Apache Petroleum Company.

Apache was structured around a corporation which, directly and through its wholly owned subsidiaries, organized and managed oil and gas exploration and development programs. This managing corporation was the general partner in a number of partnerships, thirty-three in total, organized to explore for and develop petroleum properties.

---

[1]The Tax Reform Act of 1984 revamped the tax-free swap rules, restricting the qualification of certain partnership interests as like-kind property, and therefore barring tax-free exchange treatment.

How It Worked. In order to effect the exchange offer, the managing corporation created two limited partnerships as follows:

EXHIBIT 11.1 The Apache Petroleum Exchange Offer

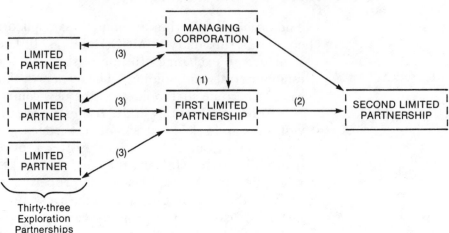

Thirty-three
Exploration
Partnerships

1. First Limited Partnership was formed in which the Managing Corporation was the sole general partner, maintaining at all times during the life of First Limited Partnership at least a 1 percent interest in each material item of income, gain, loss, deduction, or credit. Managing Corporation acquired its general partnership interest by contributing cash to First Limited Partnership. The limited partners consisted of participants in the 33 exploration programs who elected to take part in the exchange offer.

2. Second Limited Partnership was formed in which the Managing Corporation was the sole general partner, maintaining at all times during the life of Second Limited Partnership at least a 1 percent interest in each material item of income, gain, loss, deduction, or credit. Managing Corporation acquired its general partnership interest by contributing cash to Second Limited Partnership. First Limited Partnership was the sole limited partner of Second Limited Partnership.

3. Managing Corporation and First Limited Partnership made an exchange offer to the limited partners in each of the 33 development and exploration programs. The holder of an interest in any of these programs was offered the right to exchange his interests under any of the following three options:

a. An exchange directly with Managing Corporation in return for cash plus an installment note payable by Managing Corporation over three years

    b. An exchange with First Limited Partnership in return for an interest in First Limited Partnership, or

    c. An exchange partially with Managing Corporation and partially with First Limited Partner.

4. After the exchange with the holders of the interests in the 33 development programs, Managing Corporation exchanged those interests acquired for cash and notes with First Limited Partnership in return for limited partnership interests.

5. First Limited Partnership then contributed the interests in the development programs that it acquired in return for partnership interests to Second Limited Partnership in return for a limited partnership interest in Second Limited Partnership.

6. After Second Limited Partnership had acquired interests in the various development programs, each program distributed a pro-rata portion of its assets in liquidation of the interests held by Second Limited Partnership.

Holders of interests in the 33 development programs were not required to participate in the exchange transaction, and it was anticipated at the time that each program would remain in existence after the exchange. A participant was also entitled to contribute cash to First Limited Partnership to the extent of his pro-rata share of liabilities in the particular development program.

The limited partnership interests in First Limited Partnership were required to be delivered to a depositor in return for a depository receipt representing ownership of the interests. The depository receipts were to be publicly traded. A limited partner could hold a partnership unit directly as opposed to holding the receipts, but it could not be transferred except at death or by operation of law.

Tax Aspects. The primary tax objective of this transaction was that it be treated as a tax-free exchange. The relevant provision of the Internal Revenue Code was Section 721, which provided that no gain or loss would be recognized to a partnership or to any of its partners in the case of a contribution of property to the partnership in exchange for an interest in the partnership. Therefore no gain or loss was recognized to First Limited Partnership or to any partner in First Limited Partnership upon his contribution to First Limited Partnership of an interest in one of the development programs or an interest in one of the programs plus cash in exchange for one or more units in First Limited Partnership.

No gain or loss was recognized to Second Limited Partnership or to First Limited Partnership upon First Limited Partnership's contribution of interests in the development of programs and cash to Second

Limited Partnership in exchange for a partnership interest in Second Limited Partnership.

In order to come within Section 721, the new partnership had to qualify as such. There was an issue as to whether First Limited Partnership and Second Limited Partnership really were an association, resulting in taxation as a corporation. Both of these partnerships were associated with the objective of carrying on a business and dividing the gains from that business. In order not to be classified as associations taxable as corporations, both entities could not have a preponderance of corporate characteristics such as continuity of life, limited liability, centralization of management, and free transferability of interests.

Because both First and Second Limited Partnerships were created in conformity with their appropriate state limited partnership laws, they were deemed by the Internal Revenue Service to lack the corporate characteristic of continuity of life. Furthermore, because the Managing Corporation that was the general partner of both limited partnerships had substantial assets exclusive of its interests in First and Second Limited Partnership, where such assets could be reached by the general creditors of both partnerships, both limited partnerships lacked the corporate characteristic of limited liability. Since First and Second Limited Partnership lacked the corporate characteristics of continuity of life and limited liability, these entities did not have more corporate than noncorporate characteristics. Therefore, the entities were classified as partnerships for federal income tax purposes.

Status of Investors. Of equal importance was the status of the investors admitted to First and Second Limited Partnerships. Under Section 761 of the Internal Revenue Code, the term "partner" designated a member of a partnership. Thus the owners of the units in First Limited Partnership and of depository receipts representing such units who were admitted as limited partners in First Limited Partnership, as well as any assignee or purchaser of the unit or receipt, were classified and treated as partners for federal income tax purposes.

One Unintended Consequence. Although the terms of the exchange offer indicated that the development programs undertaken since 1959 would not be terminated, one unintended consequence of the exchange offer was the possible termination of several of these programs by operation of the tax law. Internal Revenue Code Section 708 provided that a partnership would be considered as terminated if within a 12-month period there was a sale or exchange of 50 percent or more of the total interest in partnership capital and profits. Thus, if as a result of the contribution of interests in the development programs to First Limited Partnership, 50 percent or more of the total interests in partnership capital and profits of a particular program was sold or exchanged within a given 12-month period, such a program would be deemed terminated as a partnership.

11.3 ROYALTY TRUSTS: ACHIEVING LIQUIDITY AND TAX-SHELTERED INCOME FROM NATURAL RESOURCES

Royalty Trusts allow for liquidity and tax-sheltered income from natural resources.

Advantages of Royalty Trusts. Unlike a limited partnership interest, which has been the predominant form of investment security in natural resources and which is not freely transferable, the trust unit's of beneficial interest are transferable and marketable. As distinguished from dividends on common stocks, the trust's share of production income avoids taxation at the corporate level, allowing the income stream to be paid out directly to the holders of the trust's units of beneficial interest. The improved tax treatment allows the full underlying value of the petroleum assets to be more favorably reflected in the price of the trust units than in relatively illiquid partnership interests or in common stocks.

11.3.1 Drawbacks to Royalty Trusts

One drawback to investing in the trust, as opposed to a corporation involved in numerous ventures, is that the trust's assets are being depleted without replacement, giving the income stream a limited life.

11.3.2 How a Royalty Trust Works

The basic components of the royalty trust are shown in the following schematic diagram.

EXHIBIT 11.2 Components of the Royalty Trust

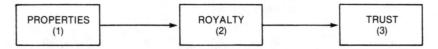

1. *Properties*: It is difficult to generalize about the suitability of petroleum properties for a Royalty Trust. Revenues are generated either from oil or natural gas production. Certain early trusts in the 1950s were formed to hold overriding royalties

on unexplored properties. More recent trusts have received royalties from mature producing properties or a combination of developed and unexplored properties. Some properties have long remaining lives with gradual yearly declines in production while others have short lives with rapid declines in production.

2. *Royalty*: Certain royalties permit the recipient to share in the gross revenues from production, net of certain taxes such as severance taxes, and the windfall profits tax. Other royalties entitle the holder to revenues net of production expenses and drilling costs.

3. *The Trust*: The trust administers the royalty interests in the mineral properties. The royalty stream is payable to the trust and results in trust income. The trust generally qualifies as a grantor trust within IRS guidelines, which means that it is not a taxable entity so that the unit holders report income and deductions of the trust on their own returns. Cost depletion of the properties is distributed pro rata to the unit holders so that a significant portion of the income from the trust will be nontaxable as a return of capital. Thus the trust income (net of trust administration expenses) is distributed to the unit holders of the trust.

11.3.3 How Royalty Trusts Are Used

In Exchange Offers. Royalty Trusts have been used in exchange offers[2] where the oil and gas interests are held in trust with publicly traded units in oil and gas royalty trusts. As we saw in the case of Apache Petroleum Company, the transferable depository units were exchanged for limited partnership interests in a series of partnerships in a tax-free "wrap-up" or exchange.

To Provide Liquidity. Marine Petroleum Trust and Tidelands Royalty Trust were also organized to provide liquidity that was unavailable to a partnership while avoiding the double taxation of corporate dividends.

To Permit Shareholders to Better Realize the Values of the Underlying Assets. Trusts have also been created by companies such as Mesa Petroleum and Southland Royalty in order to allow shareholders to better realize the values of the underlying assets.

---

[2]Discussed at length in Section 8.6.

Example. Mesa Petroleum started the royalty trust concept when it spun-out the Mesa Royalty Trust Company in 1979. Mesa formed its trust in order to shrink the size of the parent company. Such shrinkage was expected to facilitate reserve growth from a smaller base, while at the same time transfering the underlying asset value to the Mesa shareholders. The 1-for-1 distribution of shares in the new Mesa Royalty Trust resulted in a substantial increase in Mesa Petroleum Company's stock.

Since their formation, the trust units traded separately on the New York Stock Exchange from the shares of stock of Mesa. The sole asset of the trust was a 90 percent net overriding royalty interest that was carved out of Mesa's working interests in certain producing oil and gas properties in the Hugoton and Panoma-Council Grove fields of Kansas, the San Juan Basin of northwestern New Mexico and southwestern Colorado, and the Yellow Creek field in Wyoming. The royalty entitled the holder to 90 percent of the excess of gross revenues from production over operating and capital costs.

In May 1984, Mesa Petroleum Co., through a wholly owned subsidiary, MRT Holding Co., offered to purchase for cash all the 16,295,151 outstanding units of beneficial interest of Mesa Royalty Trust. The offer was prompted by the fact that existing market prices for the units at the time of the offer reflected an undevaluation of the Trust's assets, primarily as a result of reduced levels of natural gas demand and concern about natural gas prices. The offer provided the unit holders with an opportunity to realize a price approximately 25 percent above market.

The objective of the offer was to obtain enough units so that the purchaser could have the option of selling the royalty and terminating the trust. The proceeds from any sale of all or any part of the royalty, after payment of expenses and reduction of liabilities, were to be distributed to the remaining unit holders.

The receipt of cash pursuant to the Mesa offer was a taxable transaction. The unit holder received a capital gain equal to the difference between the amount of cash received for such unit and his tax basis. Such tax basis was less than the original cost basis for the unit due to depletion. The net long-term capital gain was a tax preference item for purposes of computing the 20 percent alternative minimum tax.

Southland Royalty followed Mesa and spun out two trusts in 1980. Southland had similar motivation to Mesa in desiring to reduce the capitalization of the parent in order to facilitate reserve growth. As a result of the spin off, Southland's shares, which sold as low as $23 prior to the spin off, were selling in the low $50s after the transaction. Southland set up two trusts—the San Juan Basin Royalty Trust and the Permian Basin Royalty Trust, and channeled through them to shareholders a royalty stream of roughly $100 million. The underlying properties were old, mature holdings that had exhausted their depletion allowances, but that had significant production lives remaining. These properties had relatively low development and exploration expenses. Thus the earnings of these properties when received by Southland were taxed at high corporate tax rates because Southland had little related expenses with which to shelter the income.

How Mesa and Southland Avoided the Problem of High Corporate Taxation. The creation of the trusts by both Mesa and Southland avoided the high corporate taxation problem by building in a new cost depletion basis around the assets. In the case of Southland, stock holders received one unit in each trust for each share that they held of Southland's stock. Roughly half of the combined cash flow generated by the units was to be sheltered by depletion. For a combined market value for the units of $31, $26 was considered a return of capital and therefore nontaxable, and $5 was considered an ordinary income dividend.

The distribution of the interests in the two new trusts resulted in a reduction of roughly $100 million in Southland's revenues. This was offset to a large extent by higher oil prices and increased production, as well as the acquistions of P&O Oil Corp. and certain assets of Shenandoah Oil. Furthermore, the distribution of the cash-generating units allowed the company to discontinue dividend payments, resulting in a cash-flow savings of roughly $13.2 million per year.

Both the Mesa and Southland Trusts were created when the sponsoring corporation's common stock was selling significantly below the value of the underlying assets. The trusts gave shareholders a direct interest in the underlying asset's production income before corporate taxes, and also created a step-up in tax basis of the properties.

To Raise Equity Capital. Royalty trusts have also been used to raise equity capital—as in the case of the Houston Oil Royalty Trust—rather than distribute assets to shareholders. Houston Oil and Minerals, now merged with Tenneco, created its first trust in 1980 in order to raise $60 million dollars for debt repayment. At the time, both the debt and equity markets were tight and the trust presented an attractive alternative as a financing vehicle. It allowed Houston Oil to raise capital without resulting in dilution to the shareholder base.

To Liquidate or Sell Corporate Assets. Another use of Royalty Trusts has been in the liquidation or sale of corporate assets. An example of the later use was the merger agreement between Houston Oil and Minerals and Tenneco. In this transaction the two companies agreed to merge following distribution of a trust with a 75 percent interest in the net profits of its proved domestic properties and a five percent overriding royalty interest in its exploration properties.

Example. OKC Corporation considered the use of the Royalty Trust as a vehicle for distribution of assets to its shareholders as the final step in its plan for liquidation, but ultimately decided upon a limited partnership format as the transition entity that allowed for maximum development of certain early stage properties coupled with the tax benefits discussed previously. The early stage properties would not command a premium upon sale until more fully developed and were thus worth more to the OKC shareholders when maintained in a limited partnership for further development.

11.4 USING NET OPERATING LOSSES TO CUT TAXES IN AN ACQUISITION

In this age of acquisitions and divestitures of companies[3], a pivotal consideration is the tax attributes of the property to be acquired. Particularly if a large amount of leverage is employed, as in a leveraged buy out, whatever tax dollars might be saved can be employed in servicing or reducing the debt burden. Frequently the creative use of these saved tax dollars can convert a marginal or difficult acquisition into a less risky and profitable one.

One means of reducing taxes in an acquisition is with the use of a net operating loss (NOL). When Company A acquires Company B, Company A may be able to retain the NOL of Company B if the transaction meets certain requirements under Section 381 of the Internal Revenue Code.

Best Approach. Generally, the preferred approach is to structure the transaction so that it qualifies as a tax-free acquisition of assets in which no gain or loss is recognized by Company B.

11.4.1 How to Use a Triangular Merger to Avoid a Reduction in NOL

Alternatively, if the transaction is a nontaxable acquisition of Company B's assets in exchange for stock of Company A, the net operating loss of Company B would be proportionately reduced whenever Company

---

[3]For an overview of merger and acquisition activity, see the *Handbook of Mergers, Acquisitions and Buy Outs*, Prentice-Hall, Inc., 1980.

B's shareholders receive less than 20 percent of the outstanding stock of Company A. One way of avoiding this negative result, especially in the acquisition of small loss corporations by larger publicly held companies, has been with the use of the so-called triangular merger.

In this type of transaction, a subsidiary corporation is used as the acquiring entity. Instead of Company A acquiring Company B directly, A forms A-sub. A-sub acquires the assets of Company B. The Company B shareholders receive Company A stock, which is treated as A-sub stock for tax purposes. Because the A-sub stock represents 100 percent of the total outstanding stock of A-sub, the 20 percent requirement is easily satisfied and the net operating loss is not reduced.

Drawback. The drawback to this type of transaction is that A-sub rather than Company A succeeds to the NOL. Thus the NOL may only be utilized to offset future taxable income of A-sub. The use of a consolidated tax return for Company A and A-sub is not permitted in this instance.

11.4.2 An Alternative Move: Purchase the Stock

An alternative to acquiring the assets of a tax loss corporation is to purchase the stock in a taxable transaction. The NOL would only be lost if 50 percent of stock of Company B changed hands in the transaction, and Company B had not continued to carry on a trade or business in substantially the same way as that conducted before the transaction. The change in ownership requirement is an objective one. However, the change in business limitation is not as clear. A number of factors must be weighed in making a factual determination, including changes in the company's plant and equipment, product line, location, employees, customers, and all other relevant factors.

Tax Note. If the acquisition of a loss corporation falls successfully within any of the preceding categories, it must still be demonstrated that the acquisition was not made for the primary purpose of tax avoidance. This is the Section 269 requirement of the Internal Revenue Code, which has been used by the Internal Revenue Service to disallow net operating loss transactions where it finds that an acquisition has occurred for the principal purpose of avoiding federal taxation.

A rather complex method of utilizing tax losses in acquisitions was developed during the past few years, utilizing a partnership rather than a corporate structure. This structure is discussed in the following section.

11.5 USING A PARTNERSHIP STRUCTURE TO REALIZE A TAX ADVANTAGE FROM OPERATING LOSSES

In April of 1982, an investor group headed by Harold Geneen and Ira Hechler, together with top members of management, purchased substantially all of the assets and assumed substantially all of the liabilities of Leslie Fay, Inc. (a manufacturer of women's apparel) for an amount equal to $15.50 per share or approximately $55 million. The entity formed to purchase the Leslie Fay assets was a partnership that consisted of two general partners. One partner was Louis Marx Toy Co. (Marx), a company with a tax-loss carry forward of approximately $35 million, and the second partner was a new corporation (Lesfay) formed by Leslie Fay's management, Hechler, Geneen, and certain subordinated lenders to the transaction. Lesfay was the managing partner responsible for day-to-day operation and management of the partnership. Each general partner contributed a small amount of capital to the partnership with the remaining funds provided by a group of senior lending institutions and subordinated lenders.

The partnership had a stated life of 40 years, unless terminated sooner by mutual agreement of the partners. Although each partner contributed the same amount of capital, Marx was to receive an allocation (as distinguished from a distribution) of 90 percent of all profits and losses during the first three and one-half years of the partnership, and Lesfay was to receive a ten percent allocation. Thereafter, for the remaining term of the partnership, Marx was to receive a ten percent allocation and Lesfay was to receive a 90 percent allocation. In addition, each partner was to receive certain cash distributions for the purpose of paying overhead expenses and taxes, and to provide some interim return on their respective capital contributions. The cash distributions were structured as follows.

For each fiscal year during the initial period, cash distributions were expected to be made to Lesfay and Marx in the following amounts:

1. an amount sufficient to enable both Lesfay and Marx to meet their respective current operating expenses (including certain claims of Marx creditors that continued under the Marx Plan of Reorganization) and certain taxes

2. an amount sufficient to enable Marx and Lesfay to pay the amount of any interest and principal required to be paid on any amounts borrowed and contributed by them to the capital of the joint venture, and

3. if and to the extent approved by the joint venture, an amount

out of available net income, generally in the ratio of 90 percent to Marx and 10 percent to Lesfay.

For each fiscal year during the Final Period, guaranteed payments and distributions were expected to be made to Lesfay and Marx as follows:

1. an amount sufficient to enable each of Lesfay and Marx to meet their respective current operating expenses (including certain claims of Marx creditors that continued under the Marx Plan of Reorganization) and certain taxes

2. an amount sufficient to enable Marx and Lesfay to pay the amount of any interest or principal required to be paid on amounts borrowed by them and contributed to the capital of the joint ventures

3. an amount sufficient to enable Marx to receive the balance of its capital account as it existed at the end of the initial period over a period of 25 years, together with interest thereon at the rate of seven percent per annum, and

4. if and to the extent approved by the joint venture, an amount out of available net income generally in the ratio of 90 percent to Lesfay and 10 percent to Marx.

EXHIBIT 11.3a

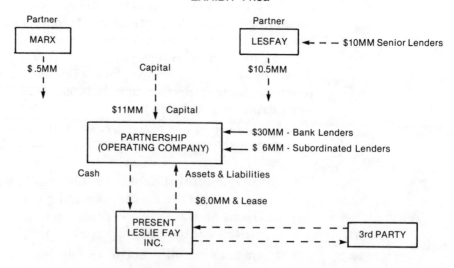

Since a partnership structure is not common for this type of transaction, an analogy to the above for purposes of clarity would be a parent corporation with two subsidiaries. The similar schematic diagram would be as follows:

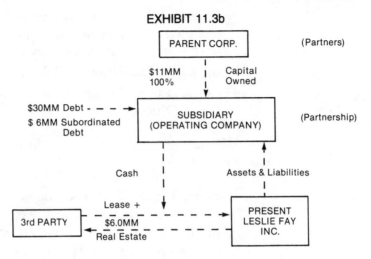

EXHIBIT 11.3b

11.6 BRO-DART: USING A LIMITED PARTNERSHIP STRUCTURE

In another transaction similar to Leslie Fay, Bro-dart Industries sold substantially all the company's assets in May, 1983, for a net amount equal to $9.10 per share. The structure employed in the transaction differed from the earlier deal in two material respects. First, instead of a general partnership, a limited partnership was employed. Second, the limited partner supplying the tax loss was a financial institution— Goldome Bank for Savings. Goldome was a mutual savings bank based in New York.

How It Worked. The limited partnership was called Broco, with Nubro, Inc. as general partner; 49.9 percent of the shares of Nubro common stock were owned by members of the executive group of the former company, and the remaining shares by a third party and a syndicate of subordinated lenders led by Bankers Trust Company.

The allocations of income and distributions of cash under the partnership agreement resembled that of the earlier transaction. However, the initial period—during which net income and loss of Broco was to be allocated 90 percent to Goldome and 10 percent to Nubro— was for roughly four and one-half years. The allocation of net income and loss was reversed during the final period, which ran for 36 years.

During the initial period, cash distributions were to be made by Nubro and Goldome as follows:

1. in amounts sufficient to enable each of Nubro and Goldome to meet their respective estimated event operating expenses and anticipated federal, state, and local taxes

2. in amounts sufficient to enable Nubro to pay the amount of any interest and principal required to be paid on any amounts borrowed and contributed by it to the capital of Broco

3. the sum of $250,000 to Goldome, and

4. excess cash in the ratio of 90 percent to Goldome and 10 percent to Nubro.

During the final period, cash distributions were expected to be made as follows:

1. in amounts sufficient to enable Nubro and Goldome to meet their respective anticipated taxes

2. in amounts sufficient to enable Nubro to pay the amount of any interest and principal required to be paid on amounts borrowed by it and contributed to the capital of Broco

3. an amount sufficient to enable Goldome to receive the balance of its capital account that would exist at the end of the initial period, over a period of 25 years, together with interest at the rate of 7 percent per annum

4. excess cash in the ratio of 90 percent to Nubro and 10 percent to Goldome.

The transaction required the repayment of Bro-dart's existing debt, working capital requirements, and the payment to Bro-dart's shareholders of $9.10 per share for a total of $33 million.

The source and application of the funds were estimated to be approximately as follows:

TABLE 11.1 Bro-Dart Sources and Uses of Funds ($ thousands)

Source of Funds:	
Term loan facility from banks	$18,000
Net Proceeds from sale of Pennsylvania Properties	4,100
Subordinated notes	3,500
Tax Refund carryback	1,500
Cash on hand	400
Revolving credit facility	2,500
Refund of year of sale estimated tax payment	500
Investment of Nubro	2,250
Investment of Goldome	250
	$33,000

TABLE 11.1 (continued)

Application of Funds:	
Payment to holders of the Company's Common Stock ($9.10 per share)	$21,500
Prepayment of the Company's long-term debt	5,700
Payment of the Company's short-term debt	2,500
Recapture of investment tax credit	400
Taxes on accumulated earnings of foreign subsidiaries	200
Payment of fees and estimated expenses	2,700
	$33,000

11.7 SAFE HARBOR LEASING: AN ALTERNATE MEANS OF BUYING A TAX LOSS

The Economic Recovery Tax Act of 1981 (ERTA) substantially increased the depreciation and investment tax credit benefits available to owners of depreciable assets. Not all taxpayers, however, could utilize these benefits to the same extent. The ability to maximize these benefits was dependent upon the asset owner's level of taxable income and amount of tax liability. If a taxpayer incurred a loss in a taxable year, it could not utilize the depreciation or investment tax credit allowances except in future profitable years or unless such losses or credits could be carried back to prior profitable periods as net operating loss or tax credit carrybacks.

ERTA's new leasing rules, however, also allowed those taxpayers who were not able to maximize the investment incentives that it created to transfer the right to such benefits to profitable business. It created the ability for companies to sell unused tax benefits to other companies through the use of a "safe harbor" lease, in which the only money changing hands was the payment for the credits. Such payments ranged from as little as 10 percent of the equity value of the leased property for shorter term leases to as much as 35 percent for long-term lease periods.

11.7.1 The Benefits of Safe Harbor Leasing

The result of safe harbor leasing was to effectively reduce the cost of new equipment by 15 percent to 20 percent for a company that would ordinarily owe little or no tax. The tax credits on the new piece of equipment, which could not be fully utilized by a marginally profitable company, could be transferred along with the "tax title" to the equipment to a tax paying company. The profitable company could use the tax benefits to shelter income. The unprofitable company would have the use of the equipment and it would either receive a payment for the tax benefits or a lease on favorable terms.

11.7.2 Requirements for Safe Harbor Transactions

Real estate was excluded from such transactions. The leased equipment had to be new and leased within three months of being placed in service. The lease term could not exceed certain standards. Also, both parties had to elect to have the safe harbor rules apply.

Under the new code provisions, the lessor had to maintain a minimum investment in the qualified lease property that was not less than ten percent of the adjusted basis of the property. This investment had to be maintained from the time the property was first placed in service under the lease, and thereafter throughout the term of the lease. Minimum investment was defined as the amount the lessor had at risk with respect to the property, but did not include any amount received as financing from the lessee, or a related party of the lessee. Thus, the lessor could not include the amount of any financing received from the lessee in a sale-leaseback arrangement.

The lessor's put option or the lessee's call option on the qualified leased property did not affect the amount the lessor had at risk. If the lessor retained a put equal to the value of the minimum investment and borrowed the remainder of the purchase price on a nonrecourse basis, the lessor could be almost completely protected from the economic risk of purchasing the property. Furthermore, the investment tax credit alone was probably sufficient to cover the lessor's down payment.

Lease Term. The term of the lease, including any extensions, could not exceed the greater of (1) 90 percent of the useful life of the property, or (2) 150 percent of the existing class life of the property. This allowed lessors to lease the qualifying lease property for substantially its entire useful life. The lease term in most cases would probably have been at least equal to the term of any loan that would have been used to finance the acquisition of the property.

11.8 HOW AN ACTUAL SAFE HARBOR LEASE TRANSACTION WAS STRUCTURED

The following example shows how an actual transaction was structured for XYZ Co., involving $21 million of operating equipment that was acquired by XYZ. XYZ acted as lessee and the equity investor/lessor was comprised of two institutional investors. XYZ was marginally profitable whereas the two institutional investors were substantial taxpayers.

The equipment consisted of two separate categories of Section 38 property within the meaning of the Internal Revenue Code. Roughly $18,750,000 had a 16-year life, and $2,250,000 had a six-year life.

Structure

1. The transaction qualified as a lease within the meaning of Section 168(f)(8) of the Internal Revenue Code as amended in the Economic Recovery Tax Act of 1981.

2. All the equipment was placed in service by the lessee on or after January 1, 1981 but before November 13, 1981.

3. A trust purchased tax ownership of the equipment from the lessee for an amount equal to its adjusted basis to the lessee (the equipment cost) and leased it back under a net lease arrangement.

4. The equity investors contributed a specified percentage of equipment cost to the trust. The balance of the equipment cost was financed under a nonrecourse loan from the lessee to the trust (the trust note).

5. The lessee was to make lease payments to the trust over the lease term in an amount at least sufficient to service the trust note.

6. Legal title to the equipment was at all times to remain with the lessee.

11.8.1 Lease Terms and Conditions

1. *Lease Term:* Five (5) years from closing date for both categories of equipment.

2. *Lease Payments:* Semi-annual in arrears beginning six (6) months from the closing date.

3. *Closing Date:* On or about November 13, 1981.

4. *Net Lease:* The lease was to be a net lease with the lessee responsible for all maintenance, insurance, taxes (except income taxes of the lessor or equity investors), and other charges or expenses related to the ownership or use of the Equipment.

5. *Terms of Trust Note:*

   a. Interest rate: assumed to be 17 percent per annum

   b. Maturity: equal to lease term

   c. Amortization: mortgage type or optimized structure

6. *Voluntary Termination:* Lessee had the right, any time after the fifth anniversary of the closing date, to terminate the lease with respect to any unit of equipment (provided, however, that such voluntary termination was with respect to a material percentage of original equipment cost) by paying to the lessor an applicable termination value, which was calculated to preserve the lessor's expected net economic return.

7. *Additions, Modifications and Repairs of Equipment*: During the lease term, lessee could make any additions, modifications, or repairs to the equipment consistent with prudent business practice. Lessee could make any additions, modifications, and repairs to the equipment that were required by any governmental authority with jurisdiction over the lessee's operations. Lessee would indemnify lessor for the consequences, if any, of the inclusion in lessor's gross income of such addition, modification, or repair.

8. *Sublease:* Lessee had the right to sublease (a) without prior notice to lessor any unit of equipment to any of its subsidiaries, affiliates, and unrelated entities with which the lessee had working interests in properties and (b) with prior consent of lessor, which consent could not be unreasonably withheld if the proposed sublessee was a substantial, reputable, and creditworthy entity, and units of equipment that constitute a material percentage of equipment cost.

9. *Tax Assumptions:*

   a. The lease was a lease as described in Section 168(f)(8) of the Internal Revenue Code, as amended by the Economic Recovery Tax Act of 1981 (the Act).

   b. The equipment was "qualified leased property" as defined in Section 168 (f)(8)(D)(96) of the code, as amended by the Act.

   c. Lessor would be entitled to and would claim the full 10 percent Investment Tax Credit on the total equipment cost.

   d. The equipment was eligible for depreciation over five (5) years under the Accelerated Cost Recovery System of the Code, as amended by the Act.

   e. Lessor would be entitled to income tax deductions for the full amount of interest payments made with respect to the debt during the lessor's tax year during which such payments were accrued or made.

   f. The equipment was at all times to be located within the United States of America.

10. *Income Tax Indemnity:* Lessee was to indemnify lessor for any loss or delay in tax benefits caused by reason of any act or omission to act by lessee or any misrepresentation on the part of the lessee.

11. *Transaction Costs:* Lessee was responsible for payment of all transaction costs that were customary and reasonable for a transaction of this nature. Lessee could pay these directly or could request that lessor included them as part of equipment cost. Transaction costs included fees and disbursements of lessor's and lessee's counsel, and special counsel required by any party to the lease, trustee's counsel, placement fees, printing costs, and any other related fees and charges in reasonable amounts.

12. *Placement Agent's Compensation:* For performing its services in this transaction and for making this investment opportunity available to XYZ, Inc., the lessor paid the Placement Agent on the closing date a fee equal to one half of one percent of equipment cost.

13. *Other Equipment:* It was contemplated that as much as five million dollars ($5,000,000) in equipment would be acquired by the lessee after the closing date but prior to December 31, 1981. It was anticipated that this equipment would be included under the Lease pursuant to an amendment to the documentation.

11.8.2 How Equipment Manufacturers Can Benefit From Tax-Planning Alternatives Created by ERTA

In summary, a number of interesting tax-planning alternatives were created by ERTA. For example, ERTA benefited manufacturers of equipment who sought to lease the property rather than sell it, in order to retain the residual value. These manufacturers frequently could not utilize all the tax benefits associated with leasing such equipment, especially those involved with larger items such as ships or airplanes. These parties were enabled to use sale-leaseback arrangements either with the ultimate purchaser of the equipment, or with substantial tax paying financial intermediaries. In such cases, the manufacturer could sell the property to the financial intermediary for the amount of the debt financing, and the lessee/user would pay rentals to the lender under the same repayment schedule as if the manufacturer had borrowed the money, reduced by the economic value of the tax benefits (which had been passed on to the financing source).

In those instances where the financial intermediary did not have substantial taxable income, the manufacturer could look to sell the property to the lessee/user, transferring the tax benefits in that manner. If the lessee could not fully utilize the tax benefits, it might arrange to lease the property from a substitute lessor that could act as lessor, and receive a small fee for this accommodation.

11.9 THE CURTAILMENT OF SAFE HARBOR LEASING

Under the Tax Equity and Fiscal Responsibility Act of 1982 (TEFRA) Safe Harbor Leasing was modified as of July 1982 and repealed as of January, 1984. Since January of 1984, certain tax lease transactions have been permitted for leases of special purpose property, leases with commencement dates within ninety days of the property being first placed in service, and with fixed price purchase options of at least ten percent of original cost. An election to take advantage of these provisions subjects the lessee to a 40 percent limit on the amount of equipment it can lease, and a 50 percent limit on the amount of tax liability which the lessor can reduce. For transactions since September, 1985, the lessor may claim full tax benefits associated with equipment ownership.

chapter 12

How to Raise Capital for Small, High-Risk Ventures Through R&D Limited Partnerships

This chapter discusses a popular technique used in the raising of capital for small, high-risk ventures. The corporation obtains off-balance sheet financing and risk avoidance by using this device. There is a significant tax element involved in R&D limited partnerships. Reference should be made to the discussion of tax planning in Chapter 3 and also to the discussion of limited partnerships in Chapter 4.

12.1 WAYS BUSINESSES BENEFIT BY SPONSORING R&D LIMITED PARTNERSHIPS

A research and development limited partnership (R&D partnership) is a financing vehicle used to obtain research and development funds by a sponsoring corporation or inventor at a relatively low cost and with limited risk, while the limited partner investors who provide the financing obtain tax deductions for the expenditures of the R&D partnership and the potential to earn a high return taxed at capital gains rate.

12.1.1 How R&D Partnerships Provide a Remedy for High Financing Costs

R&D partnerships have arisen for a variety of reasons: business and economic, financial reporting, and tax. From a financing standpoint, the traditional sources of risk capital for research and development projects have been venture capital sources. Venture capitalists demand high rates of return in relation to the degree of risk involved. Inflation and high interest rates have pushed the costs of financing, especially for protracted research and development programs, to the point where the sponsoring company's or inventor's rate of return is often insufficient to justify investing in the project.

The limited partnership structure in an R&D partnership can provide a remedy for high financing costs. It allows the inventor to obtain research financing by offering substantial upside to the investor through the eventual sale of the results of the research. Furthermore, because of the tax benefits to investors (discussed in detail in 12.3), the investors in R&D partnerships are willing to take financial risks that may be unacceptable to investors in comparable investments without tax advantages. By increasing the potential rate of return to the investor through the use of tax benefits, there is less cost and therefore a greater potential rate of return to the inventor or sponsoring corporation.

The inventor/sponsor acts as general partner in the limited partnership and thereby retains significant control over the entire development process by virtue of the lack of participation by the limited partners in the management of the business. The control is retained by the corporation despite the fact that the research and development expenditures are funded by an outside partnership rather than from corporate funds. As owner of the technology, the R&D partnership licenses the rights to the technology back to the sponsoring corporation for a royalty based on sales. The sponsoring corporation bears virtually no risk from failure to produce a salable product or process from the R&D expenditures.

12.1.2 How Companies Can Obtain More Favorable Accounting Treatment by Sponsoring R&D Partnerships

A second reason has to do with the favorable accounting treatment. Research and development limited partnerships provide a funding source for new product development that does not impair the sponsoring company's balance sheet from a financial reporting standpoint. Until 1972, companies engaged in new product development were allowed to capitalize research and development costs for financial reporting purposes and deduct those costs over the life of successful projects. However, the accounting rules were changed in 1972 to require companies to expense research and development costs in the current year for financial reporting purposes.

The current accounting rule requiring the expending of research and development costs has a negative impact on the company's profit and loss statement for expenditures made for new product development. The impact of the accounting rules in place since 1972 has been to discourage expenditures on research and development.

Research and development limited partnerships (R&D partnerships) transfer research and development expense from a company's profit and loss statement to a separate partnership. Companies using these partnerships can expend their research and development budgets without incurring the adverse financial accounting consequence. The sponsoring company essentially subcontracts with the partnership to perform the research and development for it.

12.1.3 Tax Benefits That Accrue to R&D Limited Partnerships

The third reason has to do with the tax benefits of the R&D limited partnership. The limited partners in the R&D partnership take significant tax deductions and also share in the revenues, if any, of the products developed and sold by the partnership. The investors typically can deduct 85 to 90 percent of the initial investment (net of commissions and offering costs). If the research results in a salable product, the royalty payments to the investors are taxed at long-term capital gains rates, even if less than one year has elapsed since the investment.

It is not uncommon for the investors in the R&D partnership to share not only in the potential revenues of the partnership, but in future growth of the sponsor company as well. The offering of partnership units often includes warrants for common stock in the company whose research the partnership is financing.

12.2 THE EVOLUTION OF THE R&D LIMITED PARTNERSHIP AS A DEVICE FOR RAISING CAPITAL

R&D limited partnerships were used only on a small scale in the 1970s. An example was Energy Sciences Corp., a maker of weapons and communications devices, which first began raising capital through a series of R&D partnerships in 1974. These early R&D partnerships generally raised only several million dollars at a shot.

12.2.1 How Lear Fan Research Limited Partnership Raised $25 Million for Aircraft Development

The use of R&D limited partnerships began in earnest for large, established companies at the beginning of the decade. Lear Fan Research Limited Partnership was formed in April, 1980, to raise $25 million for the development of the Lear Fan 2100 aircraft, a turbine powered business aircraft. Each $150,000 investment for one limited partnership interest resulted in deductions of $49,500 in 1980, a $70,500 deduction in 1981, and $30,000 of deductions in 1982. The investors paid $50,000 at closing with the remainder in the form of installment notes of $100,000 to be paid in the amount of $70,000 in 1981 and $30,000 in 1982.

A production entity called "Limited" received an option from the Lear Fan Research Limited Partnership to acquire results of the research and development. Limited would manufacture the new planes and would pay the partnership a royalty for each plane sold during the next 25 years.

Assuming that the expectations for development and sale of the planes were met, an investor in the 50 percent tax bracket would receive a return on investment as shown in the following table.

TABLE 12.1 Returns to an Investor in Lear Fan Research Limited Partnership ($000)

Year	Investment	Tax Deduction	Potential Cash Distribution	Potential Tax Savings (Liability)	Annual Net Cash Flow	Cumulative Cash Flow
1980	50	49.5	—	24.75	(25.25)	(25.25)
1981	70	70.5	—	35.25	(34.75)	(60.0)
1982	30	30.0	6.9	13.6	(9.5)	(69.5)
1983	—	—	40.0	(8.0)	32.0	(37.5)
1984	—	—	87.3	(17.5)	69.8	32.3
1985	—	—	107.5	(21.5)	85.9	118.3
1986	—	—	89.8	(17.9)	71.8	190.1
1987	—	—	75.5	(15.1)	60.4	250.5
1988–1997	—	—	754.9	(150.9)	603.9	854.4
1998–2007	—	—	723.4	(144.7)	578.8	1433.2

12.2.2 How Trilogy Opened Up the Market Via a Public Offering

In 1981 Storage Technology Corp., the manufacturer of computer peripheral equipment, raised $90 million through the private placement of interests in two R&D partnerships to develop a main frame computer and an optical, or laser, disk. As opposed to the private market, Trilogy Ltd., also in the computer field, announced that it would raise $55 million through a public offering of R&D limited partnership units.

The Trilogy offering opened up the market for R&D partnerships to the same medium to high net-worth individual investors who had traditionally purchased oil and gas and real estate partnerships. Prior to the Trilogy public offering, R&D partnership interests were limited to investors willing to invest $150,000 or more. However, the public offering of Trilogy Computer Development Partners involved the sale of units of only $5,000, with a minimum investment of two units of $10,000.

12.3 HOW R&D LIMITED PARTNERSHIPS ARE STRUCTURED

In an R&D limited partnership, the sponsoring entity typically has control of or obtains a process or invention that it contributes to the partnership. It then acts as general partner while the limited partners invest capital through the purchase of limited partnership interests to finance the necessary research or development. The partnership then expends funds for research, resulting in a write-off or tax loss that is passed on to the limited partners. When and if the invention or process is developed, the general and limited partners share in the revenues generated from the sale of the product.

12.3.1 Using a Research Corporation to Control Development and Save Cash

More recent R&D partnerships work in tandem with a research corporation to which the partnership contracts out the substantial portion of the research. The research corporation is typically controlled by the investor or sponsoring corporation. This allows the investor or sponsor to exercise significant control over the development effort and to protect proprietary information. The research corporation also results in significant cash savings for the R&D partnership through the reduction of start-up costs and capital expenditures by virtue of utilizing existing facilities.

EXHIBIT 12.1 Structure of an R&D Partnership

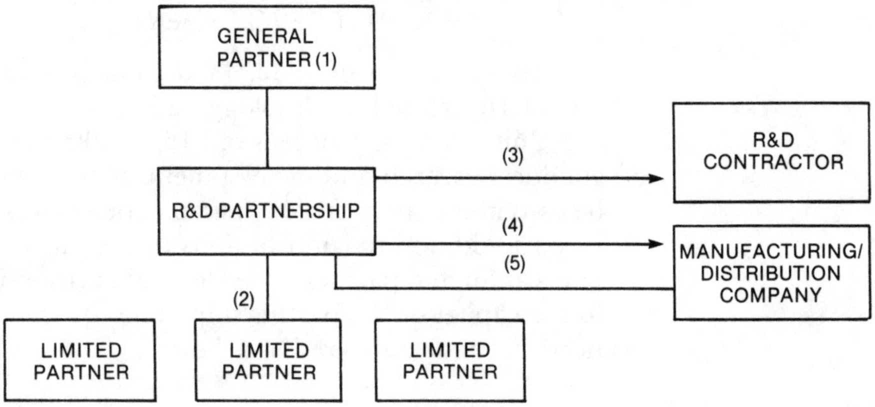

1. The General Partner manages the R&D Partnership in exchange for a fee and an interest in the profits and assets of the Partnership. The General Partner is frequently affiliated with the Manufacturing/Distributor of the product.
2. The Limited Partners provide the capital for the R&D Partnership. Typically the Limited Partners receive all or a significant portion of the operating losses and cash flow of the Partnership until some stipulated return on the capital, and a reduced percentage of cash flow thereafter.
3. The R&D Contractor is the entity that performs the research and development for the Partnership under the R&D Contract.

The contract generally provides for prepayment of the R&D work in the year in which the limited partners make their investment. This allows immediate deductibility of these expenses under Section 174.

4. The Manufacturing and Distributing Company is the entity that manufactures the product either under license from the R&D Partnership or by option or right of first refusal, they market or distribute the final product. It should be noted that the General Partner, the R&D Contractor and the Manufacturer/Distributor are frequently combined in one company.

5. The Manufacturer/Distributor makes royalty payments to the R&D Partnership as compensation for its right to license the product.

The following detailed example shows the use of a series of research companies by Diversified Technology Partners, Ltd.

CASE 12.1 HOW DIVERSIFIED TECHNOLOGY PARTNERS, LTD. USED A SERIES OF RESEARCH COMPANIES TO FINANCE NEW PRODUCT DEVELOPMENT

In September of 1982, 3330 Units of Limited Partnership Interests of Diversified Technology Partners, Ltd. were offered at $5,000 per Unit, for total proceeds of $16,665,000. Diversified was formed to conduct research and development in connection with technology to be used in the commercial application of a diversified group of products.

In addition to contributions to the partnership by purchasers of Units as limited partners, the General Partner[1] contributed $1,948,500 to the capital of the partnership. The source and application of partnership funds appeared as follows.

Source of Funds	Amount	Percent
Gross Offering Proceeds (Limited Partners' Capital Contribution)	$16,650,000	89.5%
General Partner Contribution	1,948,500	10.5%
Total Partnership Capitalization	$18,598,500	100.0%

[1]The General Partner was BEHR Technology Management Group, Ltd., 1982, an affiliate of Bateman, Eichler, Hill, Richards Incorporated, the Selling Agent.

USE OF FUNDS

Research and Development Projects:

Use of Funds Research and Development Projects:

Contractor	Project Cost			
1. Anderson Jacobson, Inc.	8,800,000 (55.3%)			
2. Quixote Corporation	4,000,000 (25.2%)			
3. Digilog Inc.	2,000,000 (12.6%)			
4. Velo-Bind, Inc, Incorporated	1,100,000 (6.9%)			
Total	$15,900,000 (100.0%)	$15,900,000	85.5%
Selling Commissions		1,322,000	7.2%
Offering and Organizational Expenses		600,000	3.2%
Partnership Working Capital		600,000	3.2%
Financial Advisory Fee		166,500	.9%
Total		$18,598,500	100.0%

Allocation of profits, losses, and cash distributions. Profits, losses and cash distributions of the Partnership were to be allocated to the Limited Partners and the General Partner before and after payout (receipt by the Limited Partners of cash distributions equal to their capital contributions) as follows:

	Limited Partners	General Partner
Before Payout	95%	5%
After Payout	85%	15%

Diversified was attempting to introduce to the marketplace seven new products with a broad range of commercial applications. Research and development on these products was being conducted through four independent research and development projects with four publicly held companies:

1. A project with Anderson Jacobson, Inc., (a manufacturer of proprietary computer terminals and data-communications equipment) involving the development of two third-generation Pri-

vate Branch Exchange telephone systems capable of transmitting both voice and data.

2. A project with Quixote Corporation (a developer, manufacturer, and marketer for computer-assisted transcription systems and related supplies, shorthand machines and highway safety products) involving the development of a process for the mastering and replication of laser-read or deodiscs.

3. A project with Digilog, Inc. (a developer and manufacturer of electronic products for a variety of applications in the information processing and telecommunications industries) involving the development of three products designed to monitor and assess the information flow through data communications networks, which typically include computers, telephone lines, and related equipment.

4. A project with Velo-Bind, Inc. (a manufacturer of patented office binding equipment and related supplies, and a supplier of custom graphics services for cover identification and decoration) involving the development of a proprietary new product designed for use in the office environment.

How each R&D project was structured. Each research and development project was structured essentially as follows:

a. Pursuant to a research and development agreement, Diversified was to engage a research company (Anderson, Quixote, Digilog, Velo-Bind) to conduct research and development with respect to certain technology in a particular industry.

b. Pursuant to a license-option agreement, Diversified would grant to the research company options to joint venture the manufacturing and marketing of a product incorporating technology developed by Diversified, and to purchase technology developed by Diversified. In return, the research company would grant certain licenses to Diversified for the nonexclusive use of any existing technology owned by the research company related to the development of technology by Diversified.

c. In the event that the research company exercised its joint venture option, a joint venture agreement would govern the joint venture between the research company and Diversified concerning the manufacture and marketing of the product and would require Diversified to provide substantially all funds necessary for manufacturing and marketing operations.

d. In the event that the research company exercised its option to purchase technology developed by Diversified (which may be exercised only if the joint venture option is exercised), a technology purchase agreement would govern such purchase and provides for the payment of certain sums and royalties to Diversified.

e. In the event that the research company did not exercise the joint venture option or the purchase option and the joint venture terminated, or that technology developed by Diversified reverted to Diversified after default by the research company under the joint venture agreement or the technology purchase agreement, Diversified would endeavor to commercially exploit technology developed by it through the sale or license of such technology to others or through the direct manufacturing and marketing of the product incorporating technology developed by Diversified.

Diversified's objectives. Diversified operated with several well-defined objectives in selecting its research and development projects. It sought to show a return to the limited partners of at least 300 percent of their contributed capital (exclusive of tax benefits) over an eight-year period, although royalties could be received by Diversified over a longer period. A second objective was to generate current year tax deductions to limited partners in excess of 90 percent of their contributed capital. Finally, Diversified sought to generate royalty income from the sale of any of its successfully developed technologies, substantially all of which would be eligible for long-term capital gains treatment.

12.3.2 How to Raise the Return to the Limited Partners

Note that Diversified granted to the research company an option to manufacture and market the research and development products. This is also a fairly common arrangement for R&D partnerships. Rather than manufacturing and selling the developed product, the partnership sells the rights to the product to a third partner, often the research corporation, in exchange for royalties based on sales. The corporation will usually have the right, but not the obligation, to acquire the technology if the research is successful. There cannot be an obligation to purchase the technology because the partnership must bear the risk that the research will not be successful. The option agreement used by Diversified could not be exercised unless the research for the particular product was successful.

The sale of the manufacturing and marketing rights to the research company can substantially increase the return to the limited partner investors by allowing for the royalties[2] received by the investors to receive capital gains rather than ordinary income tax treatment.

---

[2] See discussion in 12.4.

CASE 12.2 CAMBRIDGE: AN R&D OFFERING WITH AN INTERESTING TWIST

An interesting modification to the standard R&D offering was utilized in 1982 by Cambridge Research and Development Group (CRDG). CRDG, a company in the business of commercializing technology, establishing a research and development limited partnership called Cambridge Research Partners.

A research agreement was executed between Cambridge Research Partners and CRDG as the research corporation, whereby Cambridge Research Partners was to pay CRDG a fee of $1.6 million per year for two years. Eighty percent of the gross revenues derived from CRDG's revenues under the research agreement was to be paid to Cambridge Research Partners.

The limited partner investors in Cambridge Research Partners were offered 110 units at $30,000 per unit for a total of $3,300,000 in limited partnership interests. The fee paid by Cambridge Research Partners to CRDG qualifies in the opinion of tax counsel, under Section 174 of the Internal Revenue Code as a deductible research and development expense. Because the limited partners in Cambridge Research Partners were allocated 99 percent of the partnership losses, the limited partner investors were able to deduct their entire investment in the partnership (i.e., $30,000 per unit) immediately at the time of their investment.

The twist. So far the structure described is a standard one for R&D Partnerships. CRDG then added the following novel element. CRDG indicated its intention to reorganize itself in the very near future into a corporation with the objective of having that corporation consummate a public offering. As part of the public offering, the limited partners' interests in the partnership were to automatically convert into registered stock of the corporate successor to CRDG in a tax-free transaction. Under Section 351 of the Internal Revenue Code, simultaneously with the conversion of CRDG into a corporation and the issuance of securities to the general public, Cambridge Research Partners would transfer all its assets, subject to all its liabilities, to the new Cambridge, Inc. in exchange for securities of the same class as would be offered to the public. Cambridge Research Partners would thereafter dissolve and distribute the new Cambridge public stock to the partners. The investors would receive publicly traded stock in CRDG equal in value, at the public offering price, to the full amount of their original investment. Capital gains tax treatment would be available to the limited partners upon the sale of the CRDG, Inc. stock one year after the investment in the original limited partnership.

Prior to the offering of the limited partnership units, CRDG had filed a Registration Statement in 1981 with the Securities and Exchange

Commission relating to its conversion to corporate form and to a public offering of $10 million of Common Stock at $10 per share. The Registration Statement relating to CRDG's reorganization to corporate form was declared effective in January 1982 by the SEC.

Because conditions in the stock market were not favorable for the proposed public offering, neither the reorganization nor the public offering was consummated. It was CRDG's hope and expectation to complete a public offering in 1983, subsequent to the offering of limited partnership units in Cambridge Research Partners, in essentially the same form as previously proposed. In the subsequent public offering, each purchaser of a $30,000 unit in Cambridge Research Partners would receive 3,000 shares of publicly tradable CRDG, Inc. stock.

How the limited partner investor benefits. Assuming, then, that the subsequent public offering could be effectuated, the expected return on investment for the limited partner investor would be calculated as follows. An initial investment of $30,000 would have a net cost of $15,000 after taxes, due to the immediate tax deduction of $30,000. The investor would then receive, on a tax-free basis, stock worth $30,000. If the investor had received the stock at least one year from the time of purchase of his limited partnership interest, or if the investor held the stock long enough so that a full year had elapsed, he would qualify for capital gains treatment upon sale of the stock. If, at the time of sale of the stock there had been no increase in the market value of the stock above its issue price of $30,000, the investor would receive $30,000 less capital gains tax of $6,000, leaving a net of $24,000 after taxes. Thus the net gain to the investor for the entire series of transactions would be calculated as follows:

Initial investment	(30,000)
Tax savings (50% of $30,000)	15,000
Stock sale proceeds	30,000
Capital gains tax	(6,000)
Net gain	9,000

The net gain of $9,000 on an initial net investment of $15,000 results in an after-tax return of 60 percent in one year. To the extent that the value of the stock rose above $30,000 prior to sale, the additional increment would only be taxed at the 20 percent capital gains rate.

How creating a limited partnership enhanced the chances of success of the public offering. It should be pointed out that the offering of limited partnership interests in Cambridge Research Partners actually improved the chances of success of the public offering of CRDG. Cambridge Research Partners increased CRDG earnings per share. Furthermore, the cash and notes received by CRDG from Cambridge Research Partners in payment of the research agreement were utilized by CRDG to reduce its interest binder. Also, the fee paid to CRDG was taken into revenues, for financial reporting purposes, at the rate of $1.6 million per year for two years. The impact of these factors was to contribute an estimated 97 cents before taxes per share after the issuance of shares both to the public and the investors in Cambridge Research Partners.

Protection for the limited partner investors. The limited partner investors were protected in the event that CRDG did not have a public offering. Under the terms of the Research Agreements, while the partnership remained in existence Cambridge Research Partners were to receive 80 percent of the gross receipts from the sale, licensing or other exploitation of any new products submitted to CRDG. These receipts were not limited to cash, and would include notes and other securities such as warrants, options, and stock obtained in new ventures if they went public.

For example, prior to the limited partnership offering, CRDG had sold a genetic testing research product to a venture called GENTEST. If the public offering of CRDG were not to occur, and if CRDG were to sell two new products on the same terms as the sale of GENTEST, Cambridge Research Partners would receive nearly $2 million in cash, $10 million in notes, and options to purchase 20 percent of the equity in the new ventures. For each partnership unit (with an initial after-tax cost of $15,000 for a 50 percent tax payer), these receipts would represent roughly $9,000 in cash, $98,000 in notes, and an equity option of $\frac{1}{8}$ percent in each new venture.

The unusual nature of CRDG's business. Another unusual feature of the Cambridge offering was the nature of the business in which the sponsor, CRDG, was engaged. Unlike the other R&D partnerships that have been discussed, where the sponsoring entity was in one or several specific and established lines of business, CRDG was engaged principally in the generic business of identifying inventions (processes, inventories, models, products, formulae, etc.), conducting research and technical activities to develop inventions for future commercialization, and placing suitable inventions in a position for future commercialization, principally by selling them to companies organized to acquire and then commercialize the inventions.

Prior to the offering of limited partnership units, CRDG had established six separate companies to acquire and commercialize the following products: (1) an electronic system for speeding or slowing the playback of recorded speech without a change in pitch, (2) a water-powered entry and fire extinguishing tool for use by fire fighters, (3) an accessory for a conventional chest x-ray machine that allows, during a routine chest x-ray, the excursion of the heart wall to be engaged and displayed on a single film to aid in the deduction of heart abnormalities, (4) a chambered acoustic device worn in conjunction with hearing aids to reduce background noise and improve speech discrimination, (5) a tablet dispenser designed to help the user follow a medication regimen, (6) and small, hand-held mechanical calculating devices that provide an individual schedule for family planning. At the time of the offering, a seventh company was in the process of raising funds to commercialize a human cell genetic toxicity test designed to measure gene mutations caused by chemicals.

It was anticipated that upon consummation of the limited partnership offering and for the two-year period thereafter, CRDG would continue such activities on behalf of Cambridge Research Partners pursuant to the research agreement. Cambridge Research Partners would consider development of inventions in any scientific, technical, or industrial field, and would not direct its activities to any specific field.

Specifically, CRDG would encourage and solicit the submission of inventions for the benefit of Cambridge Research Partners, screening inventions for technical merit and practicability for future commercialization, conducting technical research for commercially promising inventions, and performing other investigations and tests needed to place inventions in suitable form for future commercialization.

Once a particular invention was considered commercially viable, it was contemplated that Cambridge Research Partners could acquire rights to the invention and then sell or license such rights to a new independent venture formed to acquire and commercialize the invention. CRDG's prior experience had indicated that more than 95 percent of the submissions that it received were unsuitable for development, and that it generally required between one and two years to identify a suitable invention and place it in a satisfactory form for commercialization. Approximately 600 formal, unsolicited new product submissions were received by Cambridge in 1982. Under the terms of the research agreement, all 1982 submissions were deemed to have been received on behalf of Cambridge Research Partners.

12.3.3 Separate Venture Companies for Funding Commercialization of New Products

After an invention has been selected and developed by CRDG, and a determination has been made to place such an invention in a position for future commercialization, a new venture company format would typically be utilized. Under that format, the rights to the invention would be acquired from the invention's owners under a profit-sharing formula whereby the owner and Cambridge Research Partners share in the net proceeds, after related expenses, from the partnership's resale or license of the invention. An executive entrepreneur would then be recruited to head the new venture.

The new venture would then be funded through private financing sources, and all rights to the invention would be acquired at a previously negotiated purchase price from Cambridge Research Partners. The purchase would consist of a down payment plus a promissory note of the new venture company, which would be collateralized by a security interest in all of the venture company's assets. The note would have a mandatory prepayment provision requiring that a certain percentage of the new company's profits or sales be applied to prepayment of the note. Cambridge Research Partners would typically share both the cash down payment and any payments received on the promissory note equally with the prior owner of the new product.

Aside from the new venture company approach to funding the commercialization of a new product, alternative methods of commercializing inventions that CRDG might utilize could include licensing, particularly where an invention represents an improvement to technology already being commercialized by an established business.

12.4 TAX CONSIDERATIONS FOR R&D PARTNERSHIPS

A primary consideration in the formation of an R&D partnership is to assure that the limited partner investors are not precluded from receiving the maximum tax benefit.

12.4.1 How to Ensure That Limited Partners Receive the Maximum Tax Benefit

The limited partner should be able to deduct his pro-rata portion of qualifying research expenditures of the partnership. R&D expenditures made in connection with a new partnership's trade or business will be deductible under Section 174 of the Internal Revenue Code. If the expenditures do not qualify as Section 174 expenses, the partnership may have to capitalize those expenses as part of the ultimate product cost. (Section 174 is less restrictive than the usual trade or business requirement of Section 162, which does not consider an entity carrying on a trade or business until it has actually offered a product for sale or has been recognized in one.)

Of equal importance to the allowability of deductions for tax purposes is the timing of these deductions. Qualifying expenditures under Section 174 are deductible when paid or incurred. Thus they can be deducted in full (or prepaid) to the research corporation even though the work may not be completed for a significant period of time.

12.4.2 Types of Expenditures That Qualify as Deductions—and How to Treat Them

A taxpayer may elect under Section 174 to treat research or experimental expenditures that are paid or incurred by it during the taxable year in connection with its trade or business as expenses that are not capitalized. A partnership can elect to expense such costs for tax purposes if the trade or business requirement is met. More will be said about this requirement in the next section.

Which expenditures qualify? Qualifying expenditures include costs in the experimental or laboratory sense incident to the development of an experimental or pilot model, a product, an invention or improvement of existing property. Expenditures for the ordinary testing or inspection of materials or products for quality control or efficiency surveys are excluded.

If the partnership acquires land or depreciable equipment, even though necessary to the research and development activities of the partnership, the cost of such property does not qualify as an expenditure under Section 174. The cost of depreciable property or land will be excluded from the Section 174 allowable expense provision only if the partnership obtains rights of ownership to the property. If the partnership does not obtain ownership (i.e., ownership is retained by the research corporation or contractor), and such property is necessary to complete the research and development agreement, the acquisition costs of the property can be passed on the partnership and will be allowable Section 174 expenditures. Depreciation on the equipment, however, will qualify as an expense. Despite the fact that the end result of the research and development activity is a piece of equipment (which is depreciable property) that is used in the partnership's trade or business, the deduction will be limited to the amount expended on research and experimentation. The direct cost of the materials and labor of the depreciable property must be capitalized.

Be aware of these problem areas. Problems have arisen in a number of R&D partnerships regarding the question of whether the contracted research resulted in qualifying or nonqualifying expenditures. In one instance a prototype was used in the partnership's marketing effort. In another case, costly tooling was developed that had substantial value in the actual manufacture of the commercial model.

In both these situations, attempts were made to include the start-up and marketing costs, and the manufacturing start-up costs within the research contract. Neither of these items were allowable Section

174 expenditures. The Partnership's Section 174 deductions were reduced upon audit by the excess of the marketing or manufacturing expenditures over the contractor's normal profit margin on the R&D contract. Note that the propriety of Section 174 deductions is subject to greater scrutiny when the contracting parties (the sponsor/inventor, R&D partnership, and research corporation) are related.

In the case of the aforementioned prototype, the deductibility of direct costs associated with it were disallowed because it had considerable value as a marketing tool. More thought could have been given to the use and ownership of the prototype. It would have been to the partnership's advantage to have the research corporation retain ownership of the prototype, with the partnership having the right to use the prototype under a licensing agreement for marketing or to apply for patents. Such an arrangement would have avoided the depreciable property question.

A key factor: Who bears the risk? A factor that is weighted heavily in determining the allowability of the deduction is who bears the economic risk of the research. If there is a turn-key contract where the contractor guarantees to deliver a finished and operating piece of depreciable equipment that is to be used in the partnership's trade or business, the entire cost of the R&D contract with the research corporation would have to be capitalized by the partnership as a cost of obtaining the resulting asset. When, however, the partnership is at risk for the actual research and development costs, the partnership can deduct the expenditures involved, less the direct costs of producing the equipment. The direct costs of labor and materials would be capitalized, and the normal depreciation expense on this capitalized equipment would qualify as a Section 174 expenditure.

12.4.3 The Trade or Business Requirement

The trade or business issue regarding R&D partnerships is whether the deductions claimed by the partnership under Section 174 were paid or incurred in connection with the partnership's trade or business. Traditionally, a company engaged in a new venture had been considered by the courts to be engaged in a trade or business if a sale or offering of a product had taken place prior to or within the year of the expenditure in question. Clearly, this approach would have severely limited the use of R&D partnerships where newly developed products would not be offered for sale until several years in the future.

The courts have taken a more liberal approach to R&D partnerships, applying a much less restrictive trade or business requirement. The deduction is allowed for expenditures by R&D partnerships despite the fact that the partnership did not offer the product for sale in the year of the expenditure. The partnership must simply be actively engaged in the research and development of a product under a profit motivation.

Another question then arises regarding the trade or business requirement because most R&D partnerships subcontract the research and development under a research agreement with a separate research corporation, granting an option to this corporation to purchase all rights to the technology once the research is completed successfully. Under such circumstances, are the limited activities of the R&D partnership sufficient for its deductible expenditures to have been made in connection with a trade or business?

The answer to this question turns on whether the partnership truly bears the risks and obtains the rewards of being in a business for profit. Several factors are determinative of the question of risk. First, the entire investment by the limited partners can be lost if the product under development is not commercially viable. Second, the amount paid by the partnership to the research corporation may be insufficient to complete the research and develop the product. Third, even if successfully developed, there may not be sufficient funds to manufacture and market the new product. Obviously, the research corporation cannot guarantee successful completion of the research contract. Thus the contracting out of the research does not reduce the risks for the investors in the R&D partnership, and therefore the partnership should qualify for the trade and business requirement under Section 174.

Furthermore, the proposed purchasers of the completed research receive an option rather than enter into a sales agreement. There can be no prearranged sales agreement that would require the purchaser to make fixed minimum payments sufficient to eliminate the marketability risk to the limited partner investors. Despite the business and economic advantages that might accrue to the corporation if it exercises its option, there is always the chance that the product might become obsolete and prove more costly than anticipated. Under these circumstances the holder of the option would let it lapse, and the partnership would incur significant risk.

Regarding the question of "rewards," the partnership must stand in a position to benefit from the technology if it is developed successfully. This requirement is not undermined by the fact that the partnership has negotiated a predetermined sales price in the option agreement. However, this requirement might not be met in a situation where the partnership is developing or refining an existing technology that is controlled by another corporation. If the corporation controlling the base technology does grant a license to the R&D partnership for a reasonable period of time after completion of the research, then the partnership research—even if successful—would be useless, and the partnership would not have the requisite profit potential.

12.4.4 How Deduction of Paid or Incurred Expenses Enhances the Tax Shelter Aspects of R&D Partnerships

R&D expenses under section 174 may be deducted when "paid or incurred." This is true even though the expense would ordinarily have to be capitalized. The ability to prepay the research contract and obtain a current deduction for this expenditure greatly enhances the tax shelter aspects for the limited partner investors.

For example, in the Cambridge offering discussed earlier, Cambridge was to pay a fee of $1.6 million per year for two years to the research corporation. However, as an accrual basis partnership, the entire contract liability of $3.2 million was accrued at execution of the contract, creating a deduction for the entire $3.2 million.

A key element supporting the accrual in the case of Cambridge was the fact that the partnership had a firm obligation to pay a fixed amount. Cambridge Research Partner was not entitled to forego or recover either of its payments to the research corporation if the research corporation performed properly under the terms of the research agreement.

12.4.5 Structuring the Sale of Products So That Investors Can Realize a Long-Term Capital Gain

A major potential benefit for investors in an R&D tax shelter is capital gains treatment of amounts received on the exploitation of successful research. If the research company exercises its purchase option and purchases the new product or technology (as in the case of Diversified) or if the partnership eventually sells all its rights to the product to an unrelated third party, it is desirable to structure the transaction in such a way that the partnership (and the limited partner investors) will realize a gain that is eligible to be treated as long-term capital gain.

In order for the gain to be treated as long-term capital gain, it must qualify as either gain from the sale or exchange of assets qualifying under the general capital gain provisions, or, to the extent a patent is sold, the sale could qualify under the special code provisions (Section 1235) relating to the transfer of patents.

13.6.1 Equity Investment

If the financing is by a means of a direct equity investment, the cost of the stock will be determined by negotiations between the SBIC and the company, and will be based upon book value or a multiple of earnings, a discounted cash-flow analysis, or a combination of these.

Advantage. The advantage of this form of financing is that the company will not be burdened with debt service requirements.

Disadvantage. The disadvantage of equity financing as compared to debt financing is that the company pays a premium, in the form of an ownership position in its future, in order to compensate the SBIC for an investment that may have little or no current return. The stock may be common stock or dividend-paying preferred stock.

13.6.2 Debt

If the financing takes the form of a loan, it will probably require security as evidenced by a lien on the company's assets and/or personal guarantees of the principals. The interest rate, which is also determined by negotiation, may be a fixed rate or a floating rate.

13.6.3 Debt and Equity Combined

More frequently, an SBIC will provide financing using a combination of debt and equity. If this takes the form of common stock and a loan, the company would issue "units" of stock and debt. Alternatively, the loan may be made in conjunction with warrants or it may take the form of a convertible note or debenture. If the loan is combined with warrants, the exercise price of the warrant for a share of common stock in the company is typically more than the conversion of the convertible note. This occurs because the amount of the note that can be converted is reduced as the principal of the loan is repaid while the exercise period of warrants usually extends for the entire life of the loan.

The attractiveness to the SBIC of an investment involving a combination of debt plus warrants is due to the fact that the debt may be completely repaid while the SBIC has a period of time to decide whether to exercise the warrants. The appeal of the convertible note approach is that it ultimately provides the SBIC with a larger ownership position in the company than would the exercise of warrants.

CASE 13.3 HOW GSK INDUSTRIES USED SBIC FUNDING TO GENERATE WORKING CAPITAL DURING RAPID EXPANSION

GSK Industries, Inc., is a California based company founded by Messr. GS&K with expertise in the field of high pressure fluids, sought

TABLE 13.6 ABC Corp. Projected Income, Cash Flow ($000)

Year	1984	1985	1986	1987	1988	1989	1990	1991
Sales	36,400	39,494	42,851	46,493	50,445	54,733	59,385	64,432
CGS	23,390	28,633	31,066	33,707	36,572	39,681	43,054	46,713
Gross Profit	10,010	10,861	11,783	12,785	13,872	15,051	14,931	17,719
Operating Expense	3,458	3,752	4,070	4,417	4,792	5,199	2,141	6,121
Adjustment for Bonus Pool	1,000	781	841	907	977	1,054	1,038	1,229
INCOME BEFORE TAXES AND FINANCING EFFECTS	5,782	6,328	6,871	7,462	8,101	8,796	9,550	10,368
Add: Interest on Excess Cash	37	48	61	70	95	145	218	291
Less: Short Term Debt Interest	—	—	—	—	—	—	—	—
Acquisition Debt Interest	1,848	1,701	1,491	1,281	1,071	861	686	441
Subordinated Debt Interest	686	686	686	661	600	514	404	171
Seller's Note Interest	420	378	336	304	241	178	115	42
Organization Amortization	140	140	140	140	140	—	—	—
INCOME BEFORE TAX AND AFTER FINANCING EFFECTS	2,725	3,471	4,280	5,145	6,144	7,388	8,598	10,005
Federal Taxes	1,172	1,492	1,840	2,212	2,642	3,177	3,697	4,302
State and Local Tax	191	242	299	429	429	517	602	700
Investment Tax Credit	13	13	13	13	13	13	13	13
NET INCOME AFTER TAX	1,376	1,748	2,153	3,085	3,085	3,707	4,312	5,014
Goodwill Amortization	427	427	427	427	427	427	427	427
ADJUSTED NET INCOME	948	1,320	1,725	2,158	2,657	3,279	3,884	4,587

Cash Flow Analysis	1984	1985	1986	1987	1988	1989	1990	1991
CASH FLOW								
Add: Depreciation (Tax)	105	105	105	105	105	105	105	105
Organization Amortization	140	140	140	140	140	140	0	0
Goodwill	427	427	427	427	427	427	427	427
FUNDS FROM OPERATIONS	1,698	2,422	2,826	3,259	3,758	4,240	4,845	5,548

	1984	1985	1986	1987	1988	1989	1990	1991
Less: Capital Expenditure	140	140	140	140	140	140	140	140
Working Capital (Dec.)	87	309	336	364	395	429	465	504
Seller Note Repayment	700	0	525	525	525	525	700	0
Aquis Debt Repay	700	1,750	1,750	1,750	1,750	1,750	1,750	1,750
EXCESS CASH	421	222	75	129	423	696	914	703
CUMULATIVE EXCESS CASH	421	644	719	849	1,272	1,969	2,884	3,587

ABC Corp. Balance Sheet

	1983	1984	1985	1986	1987	1988	1989	1990	1991
ASSETS:									
Excess Cash	449	617	644	718	849	1,272	1,969	2,884	3,587
Net Working Capital	3,061	3,127	3,458	3,794	4,158	4,552	4,981	5,447	5,952
Fixed Assets	4,200	4,200	4,340	4,305	4,340	4,375	4,473	4,445	4,489
Organization Expense	700	560	420	280	140	0	0	0	0
Goodwill	14,353	13,994	13,636	13,276	12,918	12,559	12,200	11,841	11,404
LIABILITIES									
Bank Term Loan	15,750	15,050	13,300	11,550	9,800	8,050	6,300	4,550	2,800
Subordinated Note	4,900	4,900	4,900	4,900	4,550	4,025	3,325	2,450	0
Seller's Note	3,500	2,800	2,800	2,275	1,750	1,225	700	0	0
TOTAL	24,150	22,750	21,000	18,725	16,100	13,300	10,325	7,000	2,800
ABC Equity	700	1,648	2,969	4,694	6,853	9,510	12,790	16,674	21,262
TOTAL EQUITY	700	1,648	2,969	4,694	6,853	9,510	12,790	16,674	21,262
DEBT AND EQUITY	24,850	24,398	23,969	23,419	22,953	22,810	23,115	23,674	24,062

funds from an SBIC for working capital purposes during a period of rapid expansion. GSK had exhausted its ability to borrow additional funds from its bank, and also wished to remove the personal guarantee of Messrs. GS&K from the existing bank loan. GSK projected its immediate funding requirements at approximately $1.0 million and approached a west coast SBIC as a source of funds.

How It Worked. After some negotiations, it became apparent that both parties favored a financing combining equity and debt in the form of units of common stock and subordinated debt.

As a trade-off to reduce the amount of equity given up by GSK, the company agreed to a higher rate of interest on the loan in exchange for a reduction in the amount of equity required by the SBIC. In place of the SBIC's initial bargaining position that it have the right to buy 35 percent of GSK at a price of $100,000 with a loan at one percent over prime, management of GSK offered the SBIC the right to buy 20 percent of the stock at a price of $20,000, with the interest rate on the $1.0 million loan at a fixed rate of 4 percent above the existing prime rate. Ten units were offered by GSK, each comprised of 2 percent of the common stock (at $1000 per 1 percent) and a $100,000 note (issued at par of $100,000), for a total of $102,000 per unit.

A complication arose because of a regulatory restriction on the size of the permissible investment by the SBIC on the West Coast. It could not provide the entire amount because the $1,020,000 exceeded its limitation of investments to no more than 20 percent of paid-in capital in any one company. The West Coast SBIC therefore offered one half of the units to another SBIC, whose paid-in capital exceeded $2.5 million, and was not prevented by the 20 percent capital limitation from taking the five units totalling $510,000.

As result of the additional infusion of capital, GSK's bank permitted the removal of Messrs GS&K's personal guarantees from the existing bank loan.

Reducing the Stock Dilution. During the course of further negotiations, the management of GSK was able to obtain the SBIC's approval to further reduce the stock dilution incurred by GSK by giving GSK and/or its management the right to repurchase each year for five years 1 percent of the total outstanding stock (5 percent of the 20 percent being bought by the SBICs) on a pro-rata basis at a predetermined price of eight times the after-tax earnings per share of GSK. The multiple of eight was substantially more than the multiple of five or six times after-tax earnings traditionally applied to companies in the same or similar industries as GSK. Under this structure, GSK and/or its management had the opportunity to defer stock repurchases until the most opportune moment.

GSK, which had a net worth of $250,000 and was earning $150,000 after taxes at the time of the transaction, was expected by management to earn $400,000 within four years. Valuing GSK at six times its after-tax earnings, it was then worth $900,000 and was expected to be worth $2.4 million in four years. GSK's management ownership at the end of the four-year period under the 20-percent approach would be worth $1.92 million and the SBIC's ownership would be worth $480,000. This is in contrast to the 35-percent approach under which GSK'S management ownership would be worth $1.56 million and the SBIC's ownership worth $840,000.

By reducing the SBIC's investment in GSK by $80,000, management was able to retain $360,000 of ownership. As GSK's earnings continued to grow, the benefit of this strategy to management became evident.

Index

A

B

273

C

D